STEAMPUNK ORIGINALS

PRESENTS

JOHN HENRY

THE STEAM AGE©

CREATED BY:
DWAYNE HARRIS

-THIS ONE'S FOR MOM. WE DIDN'T HAVE A LOT OF MONEY GROWING UP, BUT SHE ALWAYS MANAGED TO FIND A LITTLE EXTRA CHANGE WHENEVER I WANTED A COMIC. EVEN THOUGH HER OWN TASTE IN COMICS RAN MORE TOWARD "ARCHIE", STILL, I THINK SHE WOULD HAVE LIKE THIS ONE.

ARCANA
www.arcana.com

CHAPTER ONE

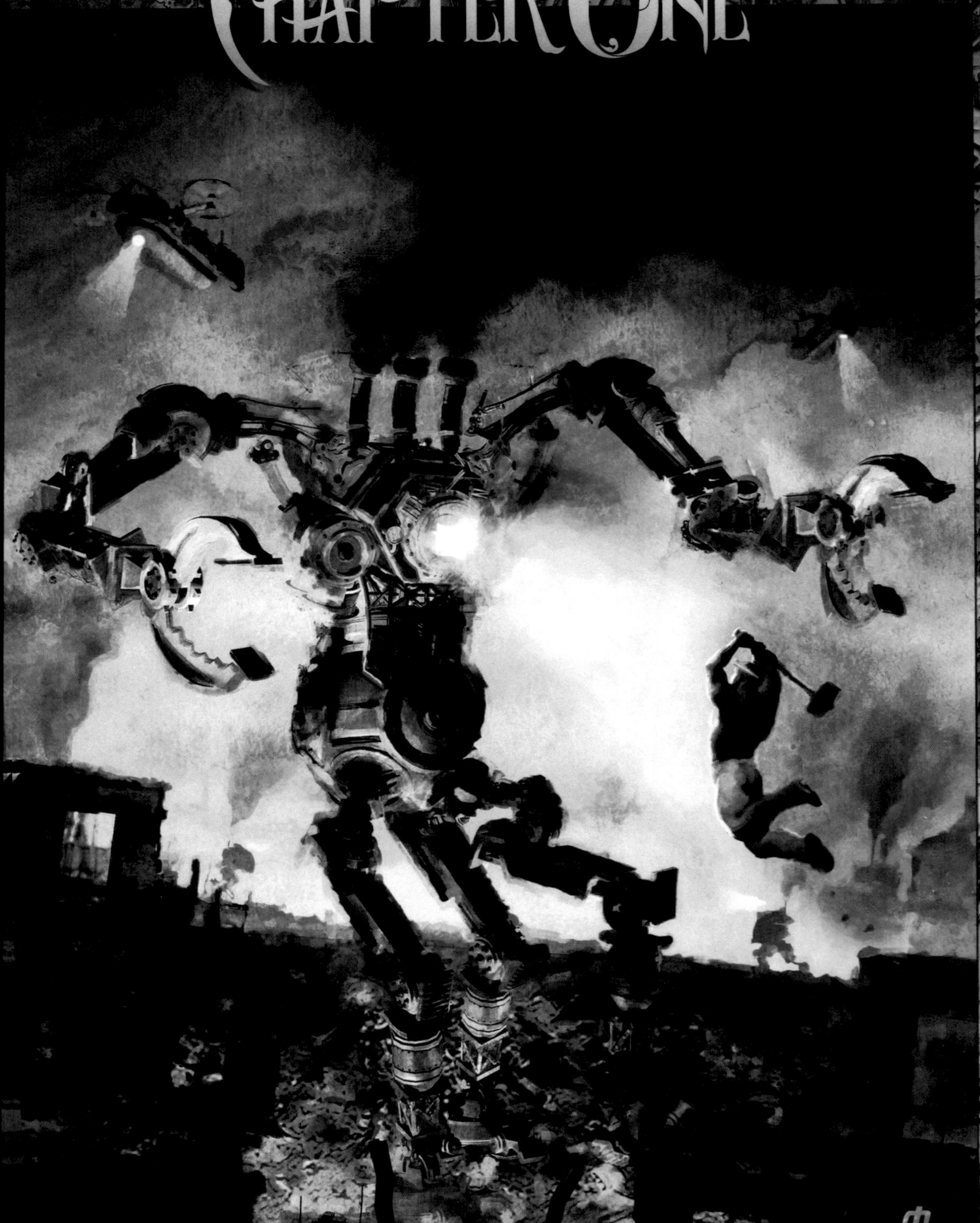

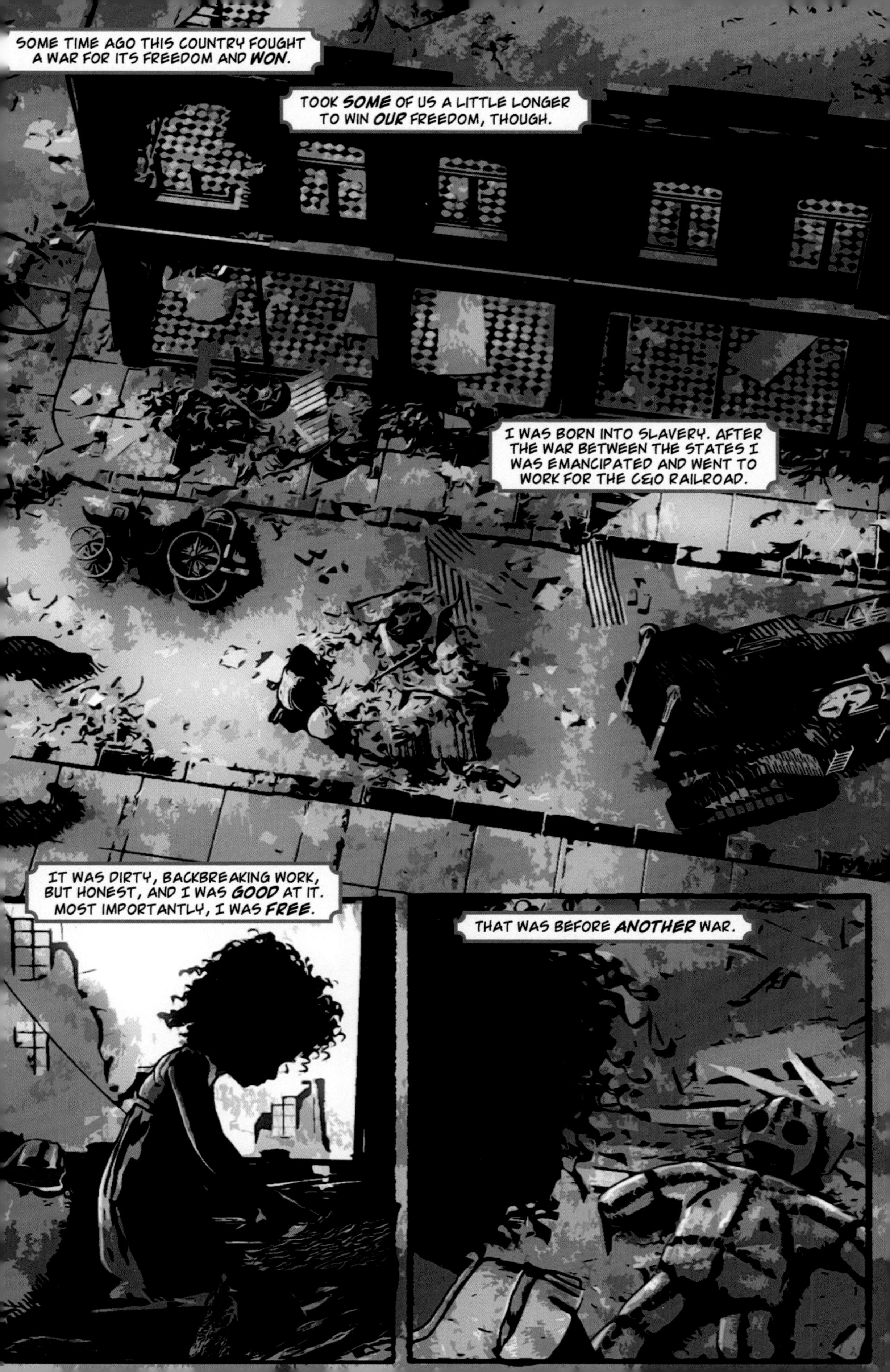
SOME TIME AGO THIS COUNTRY FOUGHT A WAR FOR ITS FREEDOM AND WON.
TOOK SOME OF US A LITTLE LONGER TO WIN OUR FREEDOM, THOUGH.
I WAS BORN INTO SLAVERY. AFTER THE WAR BETWEEN THE STATES I WAS EMANCIPATED AND WENT TO WORK FOR THE C&O RAILROAD.
IT WAS DIRTY, BACKBREAKING WORK, BUT HONEST, AND I WAS GOOD AT IT. MOST IMPORTANTLY, I WAS FREE.
THAT WAS BEFORE ANOTHER WAR.

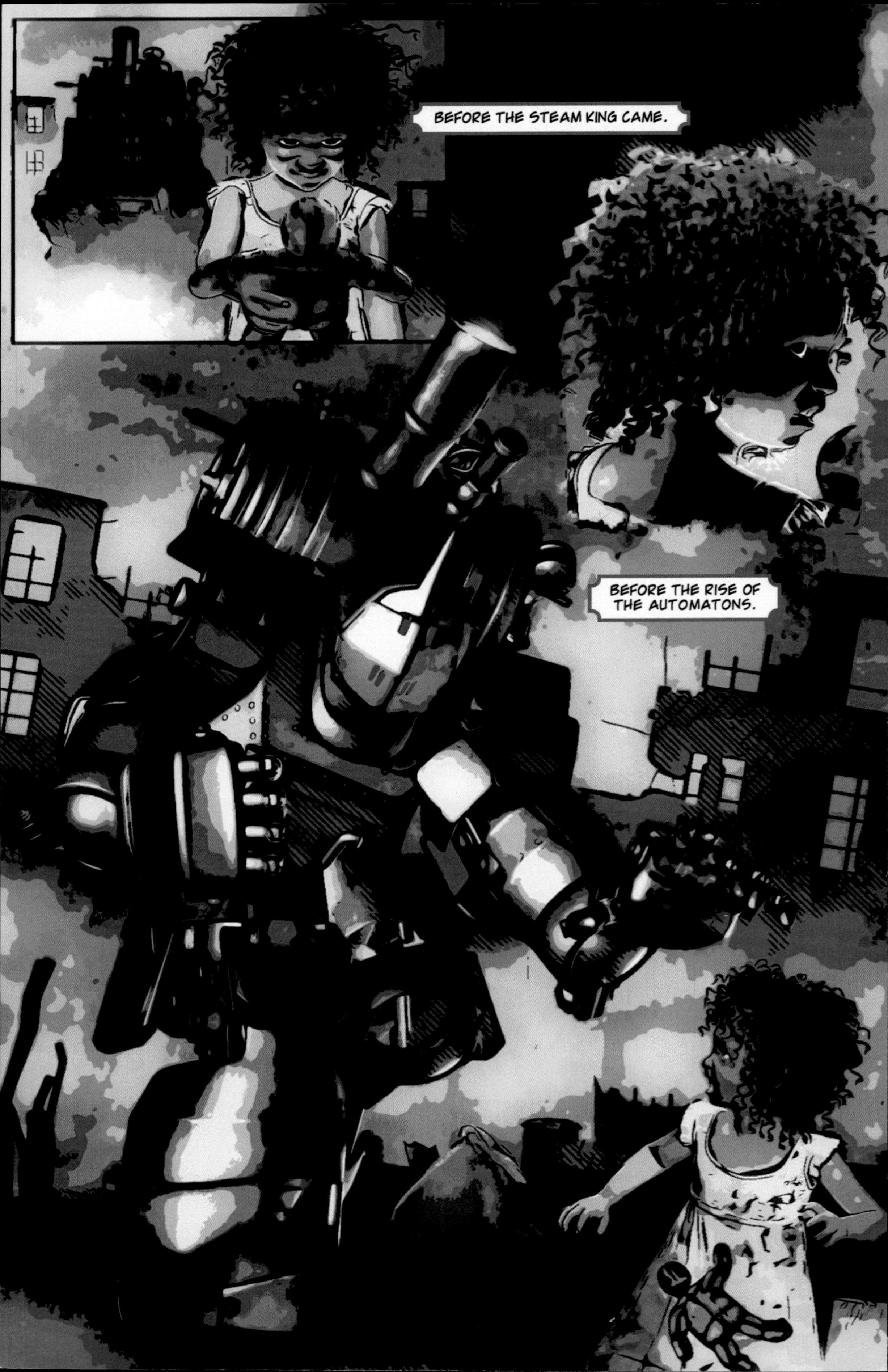
BEFORE THE STEAM KING CAME.
BEFORE THE RISE OF THE AUTOMATONS.

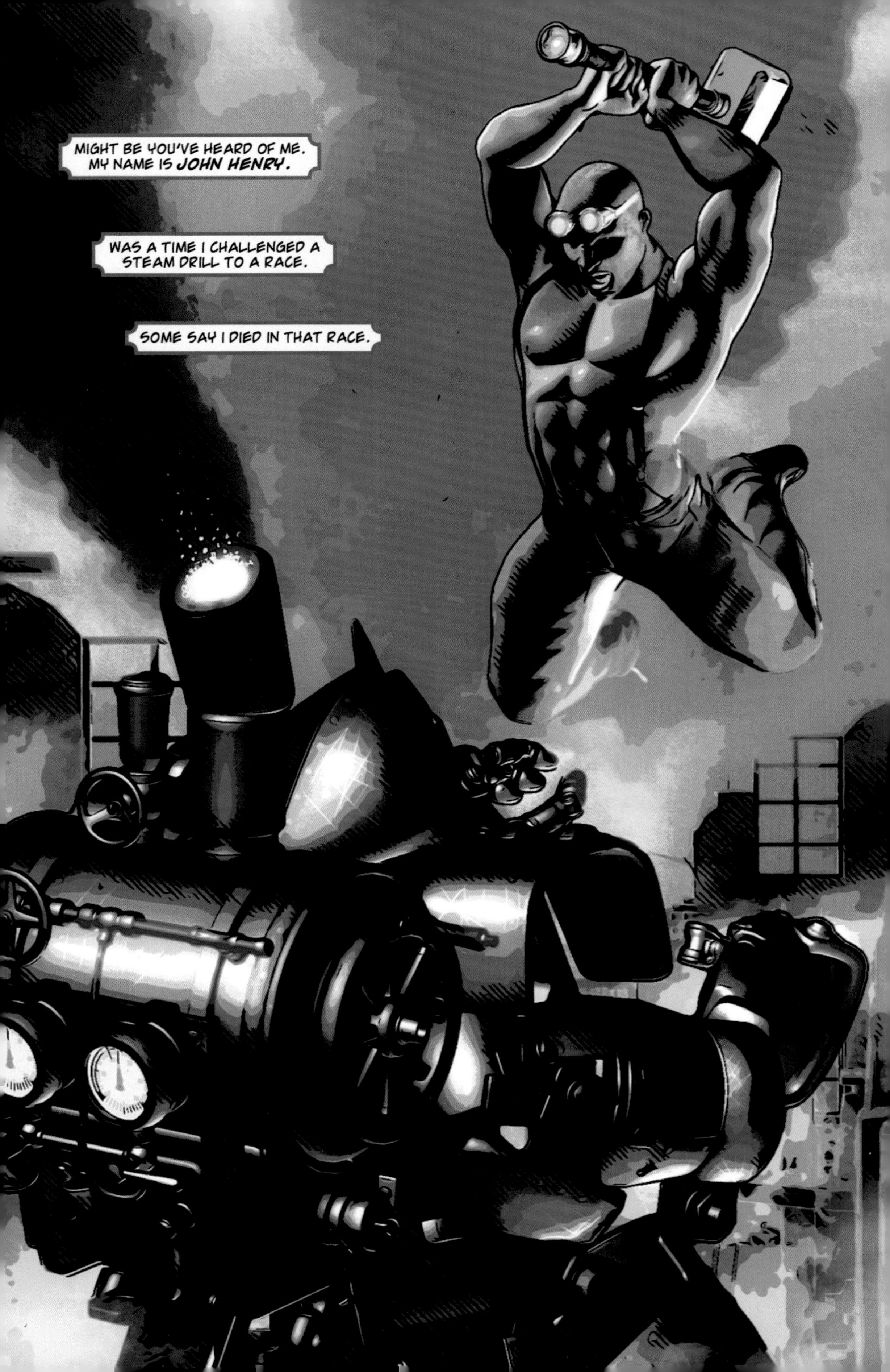
MIGHT BE YOU'VE HEARD OF ME. MY NAME IS JOHN HENRY.
WAS A TIME I CHALLENGED A STEAM DRILL TO A RACE.
SOME SAY I DIED IN THAT RACE.

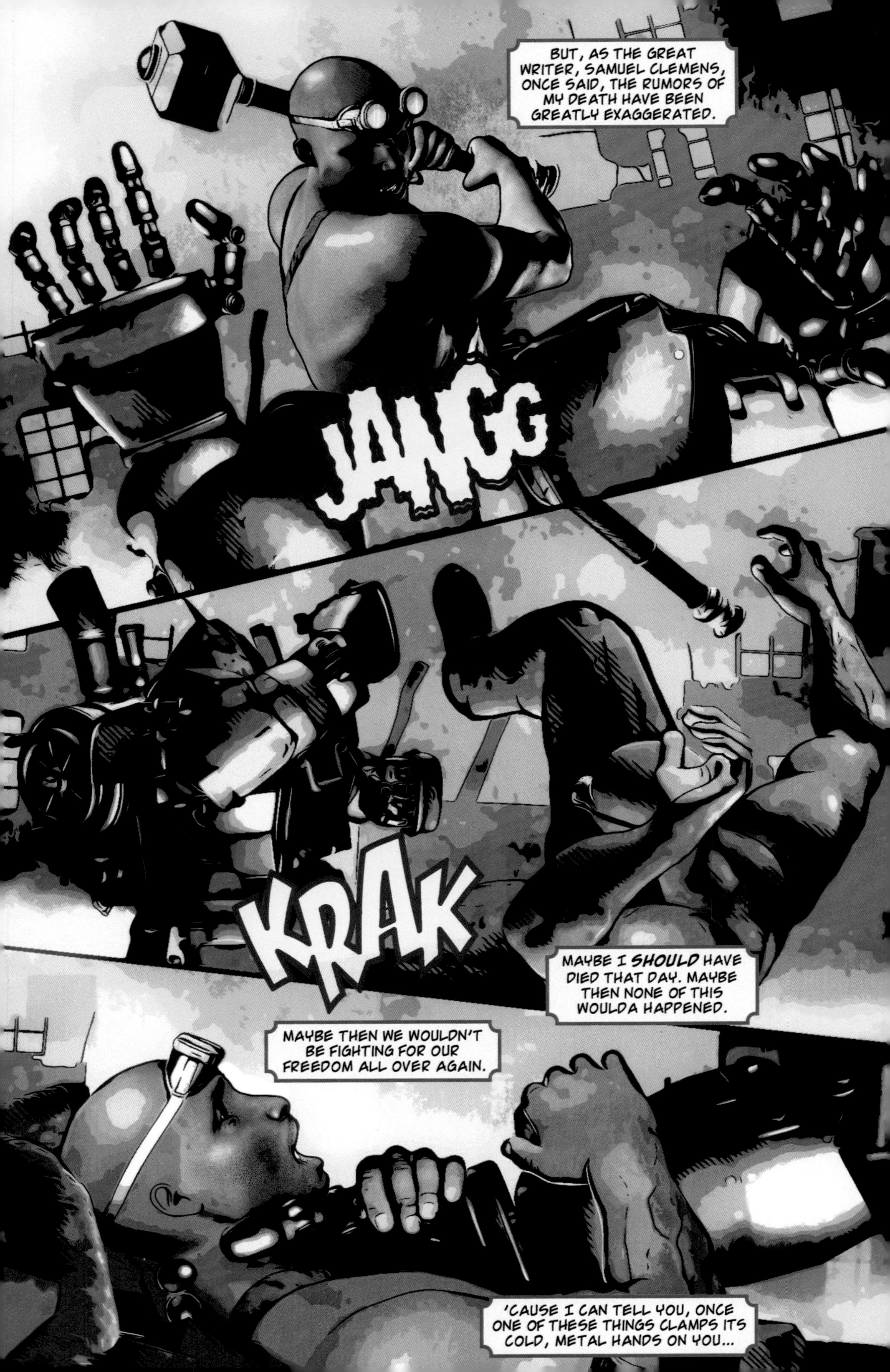
BUT, AS THE GREAT WRITER, SAMUEL CLEMENS, ONCE SAID, THE RUMORS OF MY DEATH HAVE BEEN GREATLY EXAGGERATED.
JANGG
KRAK
MAYBE I SHOULD HAVE DIED THAT DAY. MAYBE THEN NONE OF THIS WOULDA HAPPENED.
MAYBE THEN WE WOULDN'T BE FIGHTING FOR OUR FREEDOM ALL OVER AGAIN.
'CAUSE I CAN TELL YOU, ONCE ONE OF THESE THINGS CLAMPS ITS COLD, METAL HANDS ON YOU...

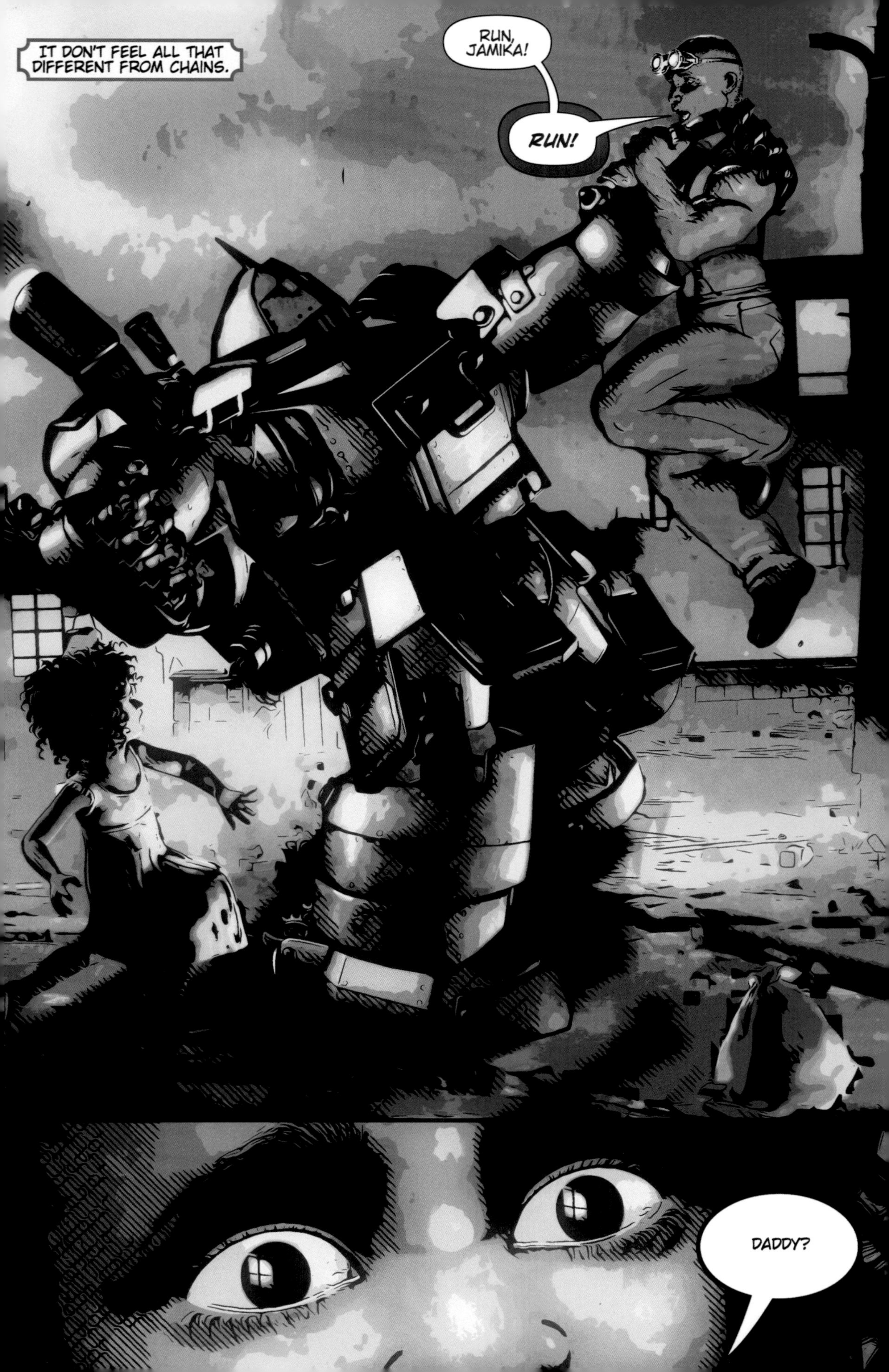
IT DON'T FEEL ALL THAT DIFFERENT FROM CHAINS.
RUN, JAMIKA!
RUN!
DADDY?

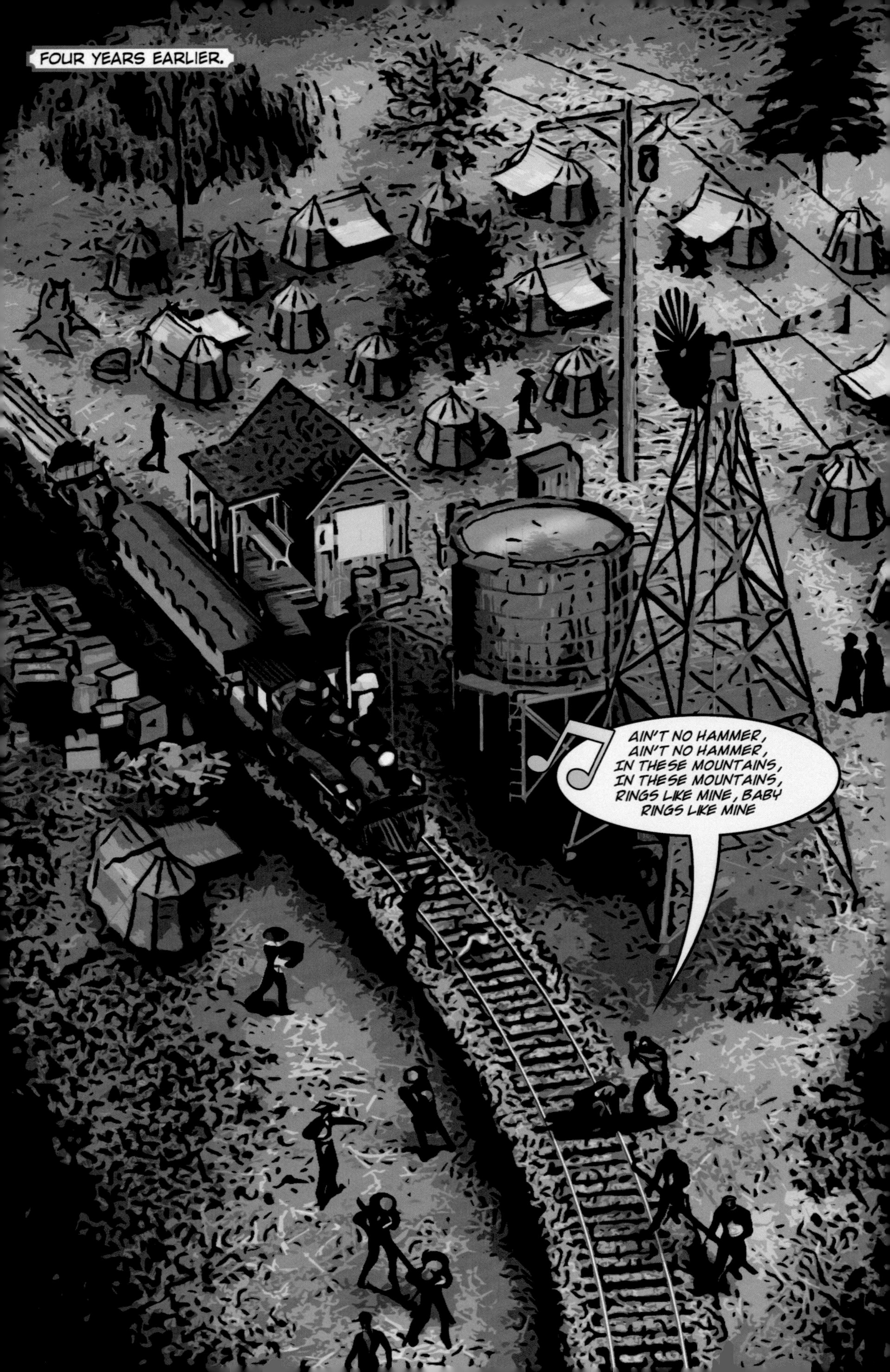
FOUR YEARS EARLIER.
AIN'T NO HAMMER, AIN'T NO HAMMER, IN THESE MOUNTAINS, IN THESE MOUNTAINS, RINGS LIKE MINE, BABY RINGS LIKE MINE

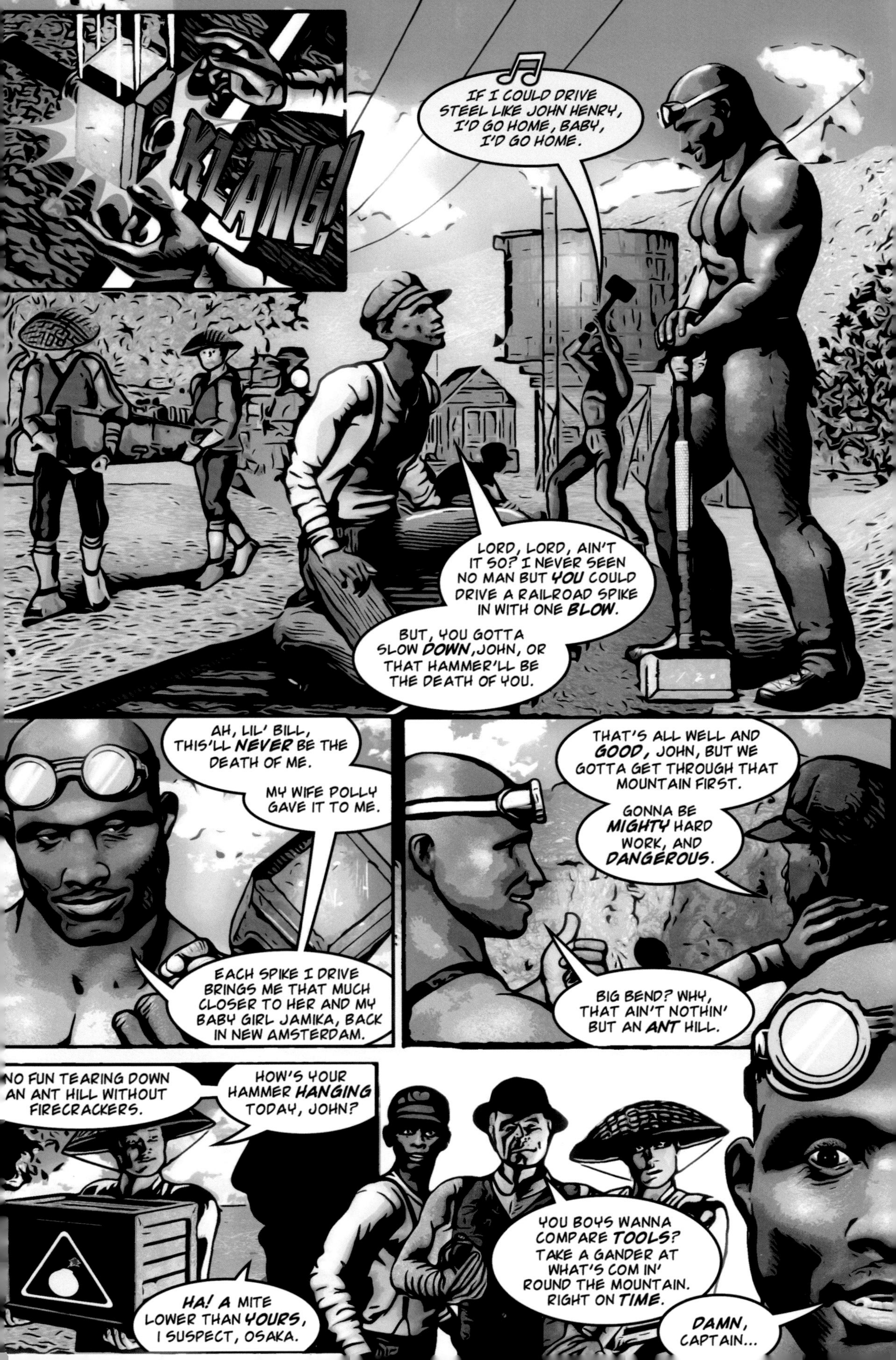
KLANG!
IF I COULD DRIVE STEEL LIKE JOHN HENRY, I'D GO HOME, BABY, I'D GO HOME.
LORD, LORD, AIN'T IT SO? I NEVER SEEN NO MAN BUT YOU COULD DRIVE A RAILROAD SPIKE IN WITH ONE BLOW.
BUT, YOU GOTTA SLOW DOWN, JOHN, OR THAT HAMMER'LL BE THE DEATH OF YOU.
AH, LIL' BILL, THIS'LL NEVER BE THE DEATH OF ME.
MY WIFE POLLY GAVE IT TO ME.
EACH SPIKE I DRIVE BRINGS ME THAT MUCH CLOSER TO HER AND MY BABY GIRL JAMIKA, BACK IN NEW AMSTERDAM.
THAT'S ALL WELL AND GOOD, JOHN, BUT WE GOTTA GET THROUGH THAT MOUNTAIN FIRST.
GONNA BE MIGHTY HARD WORK, AND DANGEROUS.
BIG BEND? WHY, THAT AIN'T NOTHIN' BUT AN ANT HILL.
NO FUN TEARING DOWN AN ANT HILL WITHOUT FIRECRACKERS.
HOW'S YOUR HAMMER HANGING TODAY, JOHN?
HA! A MITE LOWER THAN YOURS, I SUSPECT, OSAKA.
YOU BOYS WANNA COMPARE TOOLS? TAKE A GANDER AT WHAT'S COM IN' ROUND THE MOUNTAIN. RIGHT ON TIME.
DAMN, CAPTAIN...

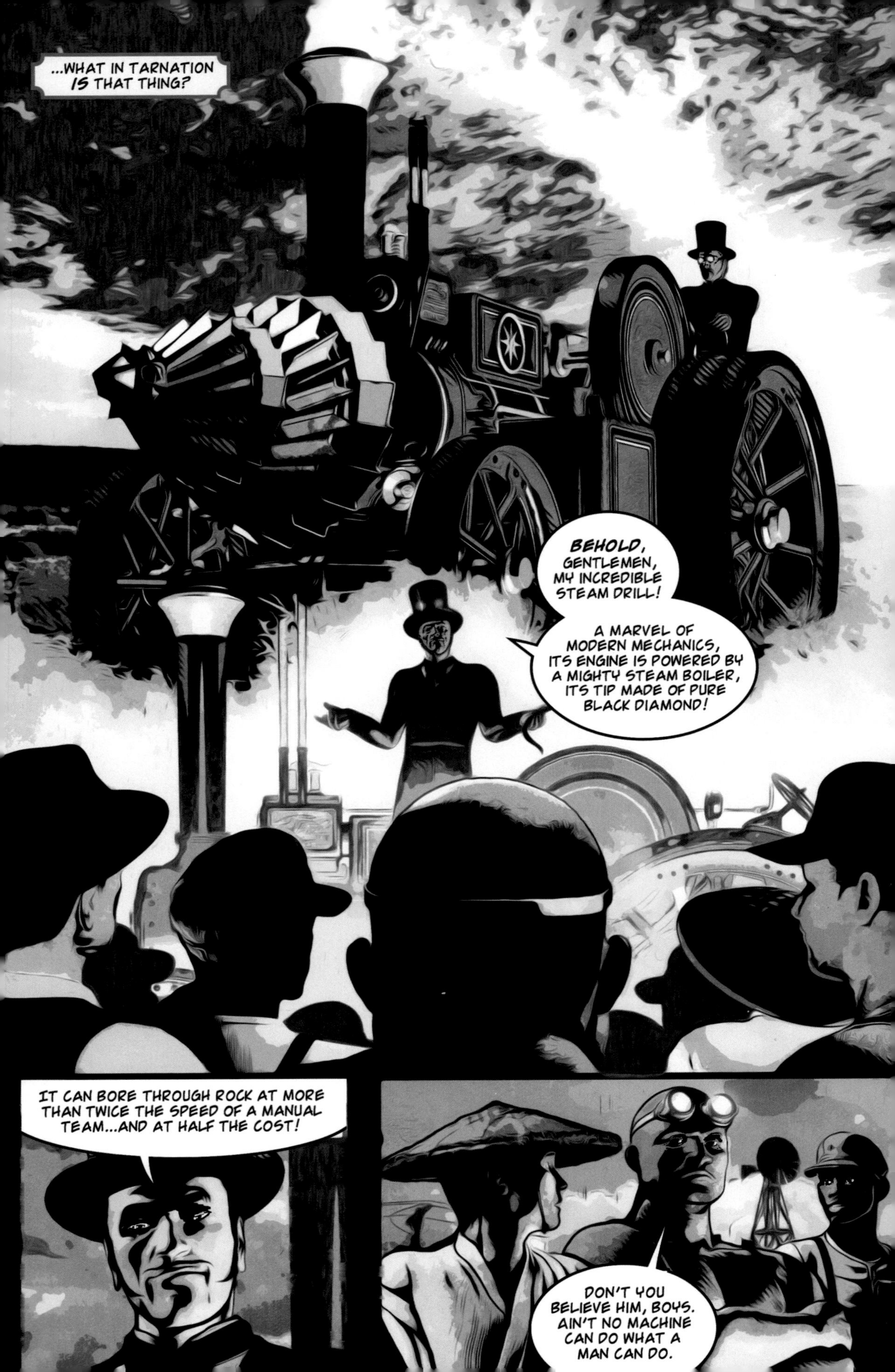
...WHAT IN TARNATION IS THAT THING?
BEHOLD, GENTLEMEN, MY INCREDIBLE STEAM DRILL!
A MARVEL OF MODERN MECHANICS, ITS ENGINE IS POWERED BY A MIGHTY STEAM BOILER, ITS TIP MADE OF PURE BLACK DIAMOND!
IT CAN BORE THROUGH ROCK AT MORE THAN TWICE THE SPEED OF A MANUAL TEAM...AND AT HALF THE COST!
DON'T YOU BELIEVE HIM, BOYS. AIN'T NO MACHINE CAN DO WHAT A MAN CAN DO.

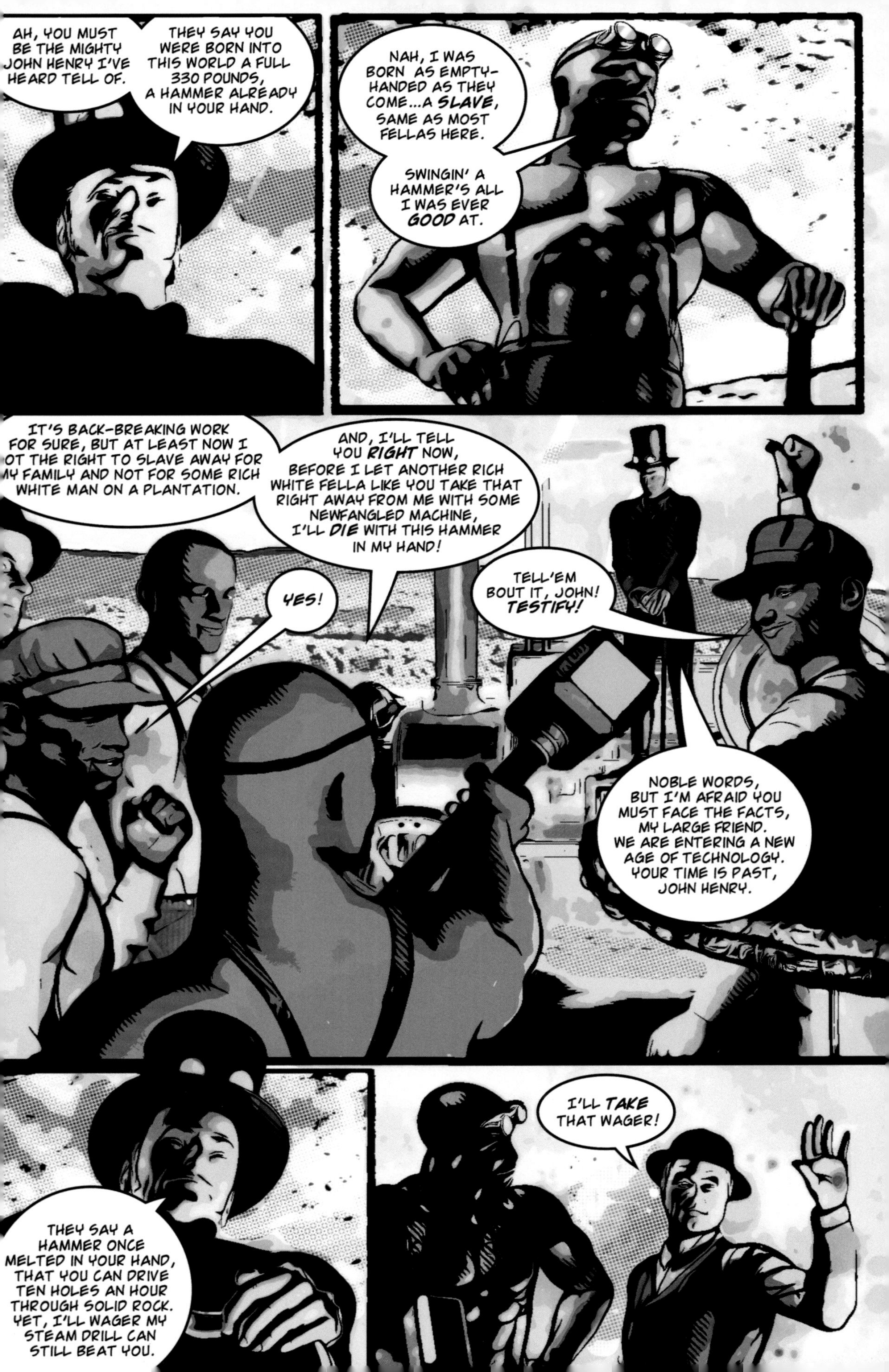
AH, YOU MUST BE THE MIGHTY JOHN HENRY I'VE HEARD TELL OF.
THEY SAY YOU WERE BORN INTO THIS WORLD A FULL 330 POUNDS, A HAMMER ALREADY IN YOUR HAND.
NAH, I WAS BORN AS EMPTY-HANDED AS THEY COME...A SLAVE, SAME AS MOST FELLAS HERE.
SWINGIN' A HAMMER'S ALL I WAS EVER GOOD AT.
IT'S BACK-BREAKING WORK FOR SURE, BUT AT LEAST NOW I OT THE RIGHT TO SLAVE AWAY FOR MY FAMILY AND NOT FOR SOME RICH WHITE MAN ON A PLANTATION.
AND, I'LL TELL YOU RIGHT NOW, BEFORE I LET ANOTHER RICH WHITE FELLA LIKE YOU TAKE THAT RIGHT AWAY FROM ME WITH SOME NEWFANGLED MACHINE, I'LL DIE WITH THIS HAMMER IN MY HAND!
YES!
TELL'EM BOUT IT, JOHN! TESTIFY!
NOBLE WORDS, BUT I'M AFRAID YOU MUST FACE THE FACTS, MY LARGE FRIEND. WE ARE ENTERING A NEW AGE OF TECHNOLOGY. YOUR TIME IS PAST, JOHN HENRY.
THEY SAY A HAMMER ONCE MELTED IN YOUR HAND, THAT YOU CAN DRIVE TEN HOLES AN HOUR THROUGH SOLID ROCK. YET, I'LL WAGER MY STEAM DRILL CAN STILL BEAT YOU.
I'LL TAKE THAT WAGER!

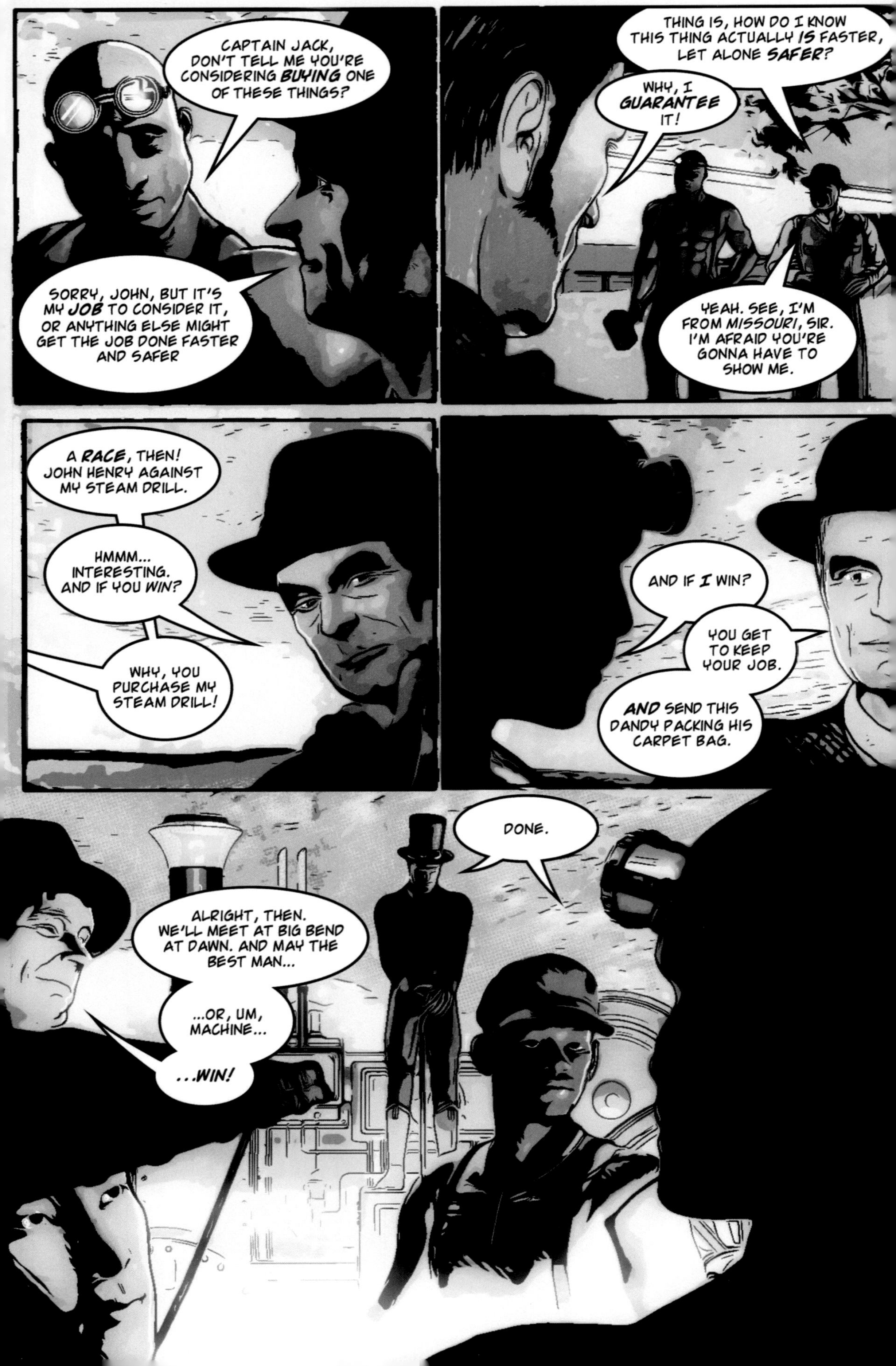
CAPTAIN JACK, DON'T TELL ME YOU'RE CONSIDERING BUYING ONE OF THESE THINGS?
SORRY, JOHN, BUT IT'S MY JOB TO CONSIDER IT, OR ANYTHING ELSE MIGHT GET THE JOB DONE FASTER AND SAFER
THING IS, HOW DO I KNOW THIS THING ACTUALLY IS FASTER, LET ALONE SAFER?
WHY, I GUARANTEE IT!
YEAH. SEE, I'M FROM MISSOURI, SIR. I'M AFRAID YOU'RE GONNA HAVE TO SHOW ME.
A RACE, THEN! JOHN HENRY AGAINST MY STEAM DRILL.
HMMM... INTERESTING. AND IF YOU WIN?
WHY, YOU PURCHASE MY STEAM DRILL!
AND IF I WIN?
YOU GET TO KEEP YOUR JOB.
AND SEND THIS DANDY PACKING HIS CARPET BAG.
ALRIGHT, THEN. WE'LL MEET AT BIG BEND AT DAWN. AND MAY THE BEST MAN...
...OR, UM, MACHINE...
...WIN!
DONE.

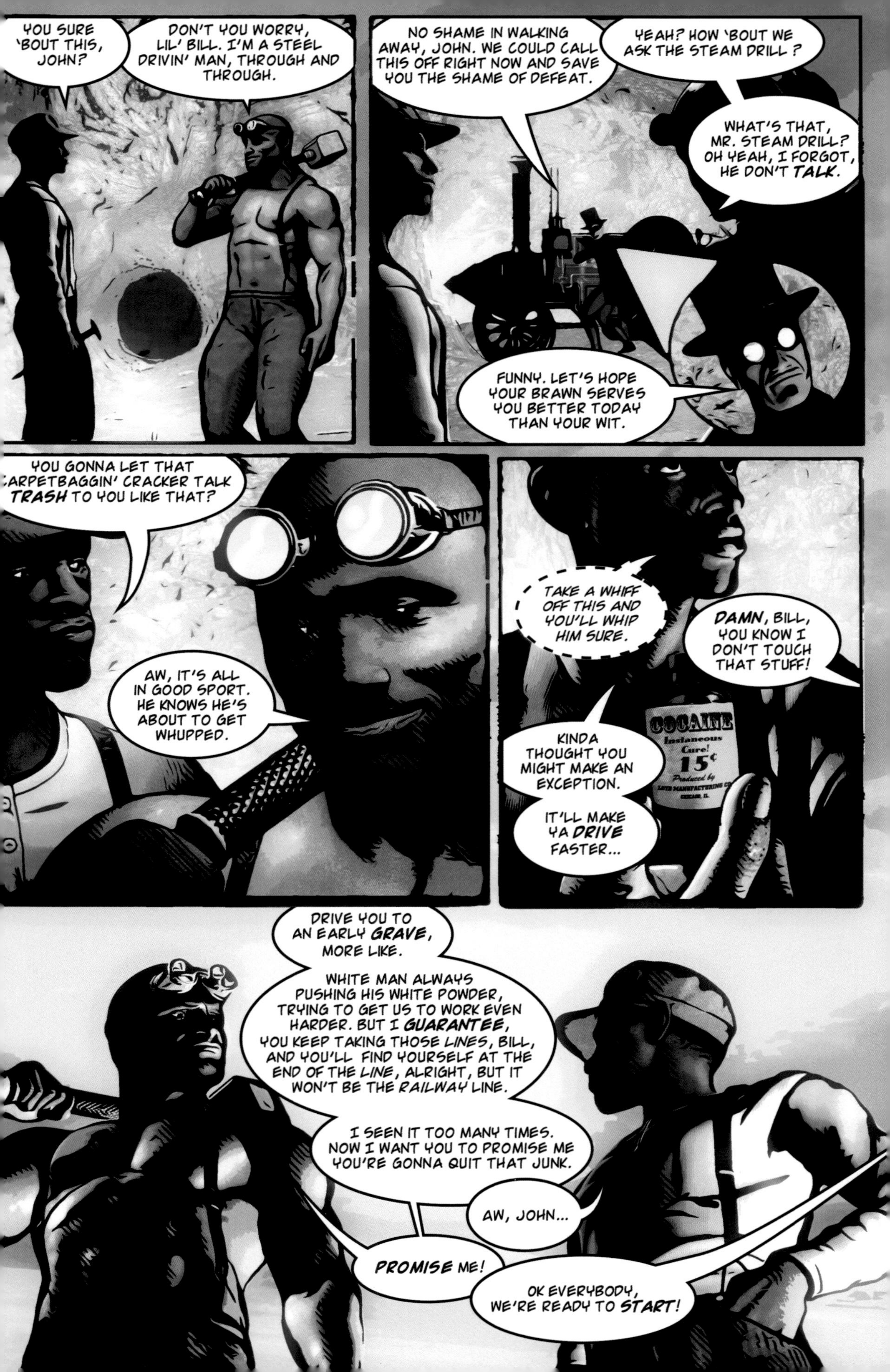

YOU SURE 'BOUT THIS, JOHN?
DON'T YOU WORRY, LIL' BILL. I'M A STEEL DRIVIN' MAN, THROUGH AND THROUGH.
NO SHAME IN WALKING AWAY, JOHN. WE COULD CALL THIS OFF RIGHT NOW AND SAVE YOU THE SHAME OF DEFEAT.
YEAH? HOW 'BOUT WE ASK THE STEAM DRILL ?
WHAT'S THAT, MR. STEAM DRILL? OH YEAH, I FORGOT, HE DON'T *TALK*.
FUNNY. LET'S HOPE YOUR BRAWN SERVES YOU BETTER TODAY THAN YOUR WIT.
YOU GONNA LET THAT CARPETBAGGIN' CRACKER TALK *TRASH* TO YOU LIKE THAT?
AW, IT'S ALL IN GOOD SPORT. HE KNOWS HE'S ABOUT TO GET WHUPPED.
TAKE A WHIFF OFF THIS AND YOU'LL WHIP HIM SURE.
DAMN, BILL, YOU KNOW I DON'T TOUCH THAT STUFF!
KINDA THOUGHT YOU MIGHT MAKE AN EXCEPTION.
IT'LL MAKE YA *DRIVE* FASTER...
COCAINE Instaneous Cure! 15¢
DRIVE YOU TO AN EARLY *GRAVE*, MORE LIKE.
WHITE MAN ALWAYS PUSHING HIS WHITE POWDER, TRYING TO GET US TO WORK EVEN HARDER. BUT I *GUARANTEE*, YOU KEEP TAKING THOSE *LINES*, BILL, AND YOU'LL FIND YOURSELF AT THE END OF THE *LINE*, ALRIGHT, BUT IT WON'T BE THE *RAILWAY* LINE.
I SEEN IT TOO MANY TIMES. NOW I WANT YOU TO PROMISE ME YOU'RE GONNA QUIT THAT JUNK.
AW, JOHN...
PROMISE ME!
OK EVERYBODY, WE'RE READY TO *START*!

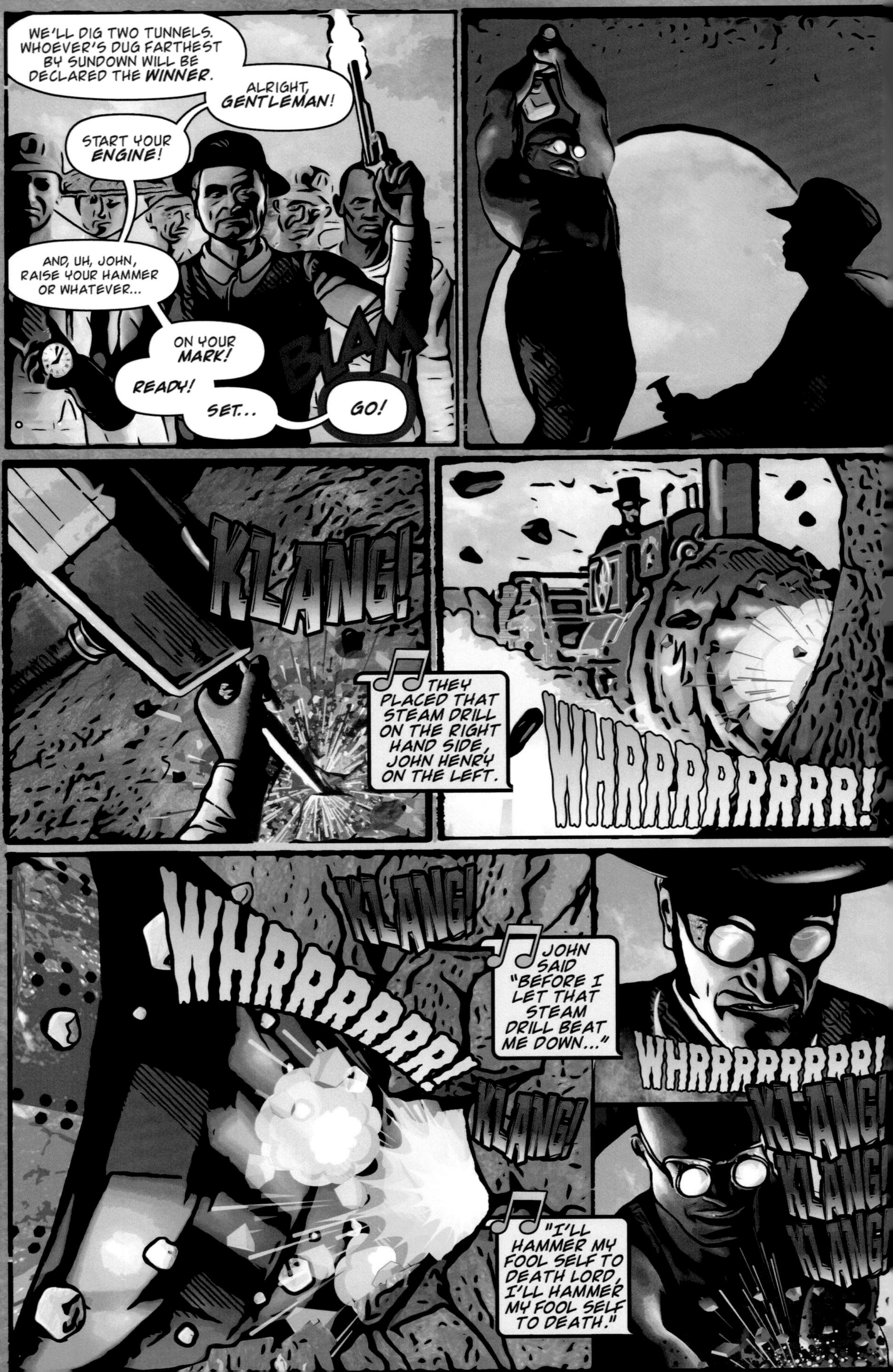
WE'LL DIG TWO TUNNELS. WHOEVER'S DUG FARTHEST BY SUNDOWN WILL BE DECLARED THE WINNER.
ALRIGHT, GENTLEMAN!
START YOUR ENGINE!
AND, UH, JOHN, RAISE YOUR HAMMER OR WHATEVER...
ON YOUR MARK!
READY!
SET...
GO!
BLAM
KLANG!
THEY PLACED THAT STEAM DRILL ON THE RIGHT HAND SIDE, JOHN HENRY ON THE LEFT.
WHRRRRRRRRR!
WHRRRRRRR!
KLANG!
JOHN SAID "BEFORE I LET THAT STEAM DRILL BEAT ME DOWN..."
KLANG!
WHRRRRRRRR!
KLANG! KLANG! KLANG!
"I'LL HAMMER MY FOOL SELF TO DEATH LORD, I'LL HAMMER MY FOOL SELF TO DEATH."

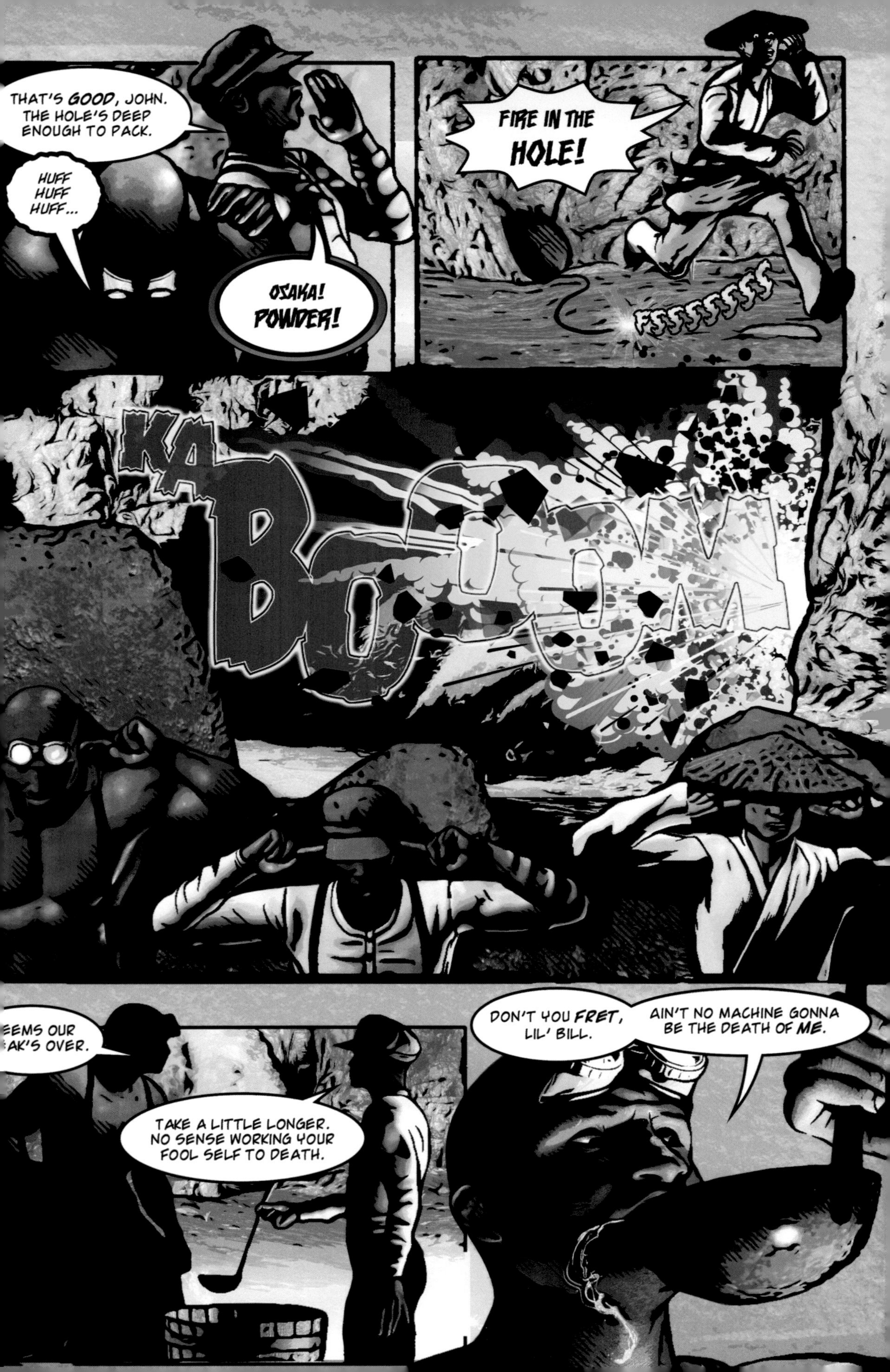
THAT'S GOOD, JOHN. THE HOLE'S DEEP ENOUGH TO PACK.
HUFF HUFF HUFF...
OSAKA! POWDER!
FIRE IN THE HOLE!
FSSSSSSSS
KA BOOOM!
EEMS OUR AK'S OVER.
TAKE A LITTLE LONGER. NO SENSE WORKING YOUR FOOL SELF TO DEATH.
DON'T YOU FRET, LIL' BILL.
AIN'T NO MACHINE GONNA BE THE DEATH OF ME.

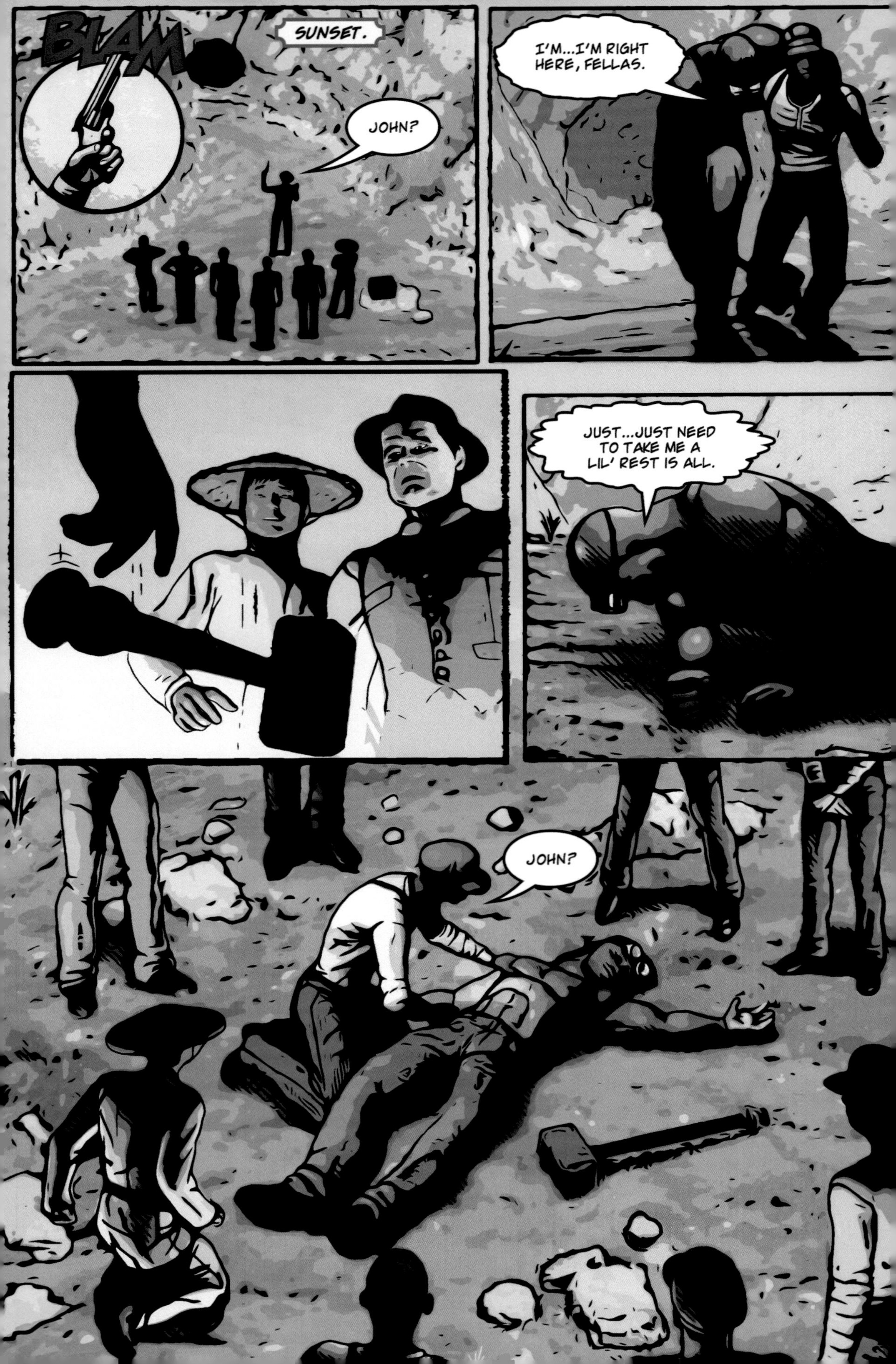
BLAM
SUNSET.
JOHN?
I'M...I'M RIGHT HERE, FELLAS.
JUST...JUST NEED TO TAKE ME A LIL' REST IS ALL.
JOHN?

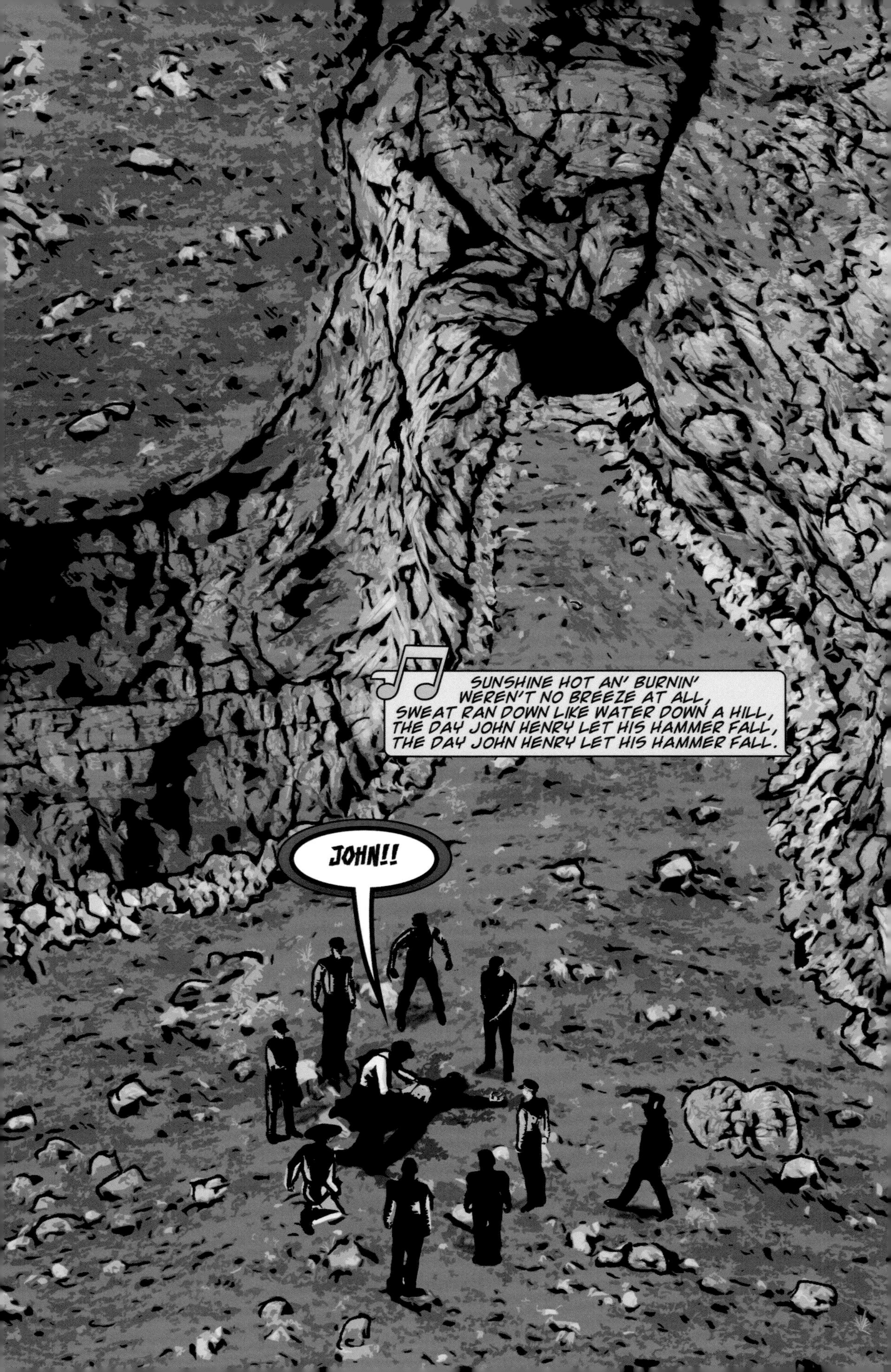
SUNSHINE HOT AN' BURNIN'
WEREN'T NO BREEZE AT ALL,
SWEAT RAN DOWN LIKE WATER DOWN A HILL,
THE DAY JOHN HENRY LET HIS HAMMER FALL,
THE DAY JOHN HENRY LET HIS HAMMER FALL.
JOHN!!

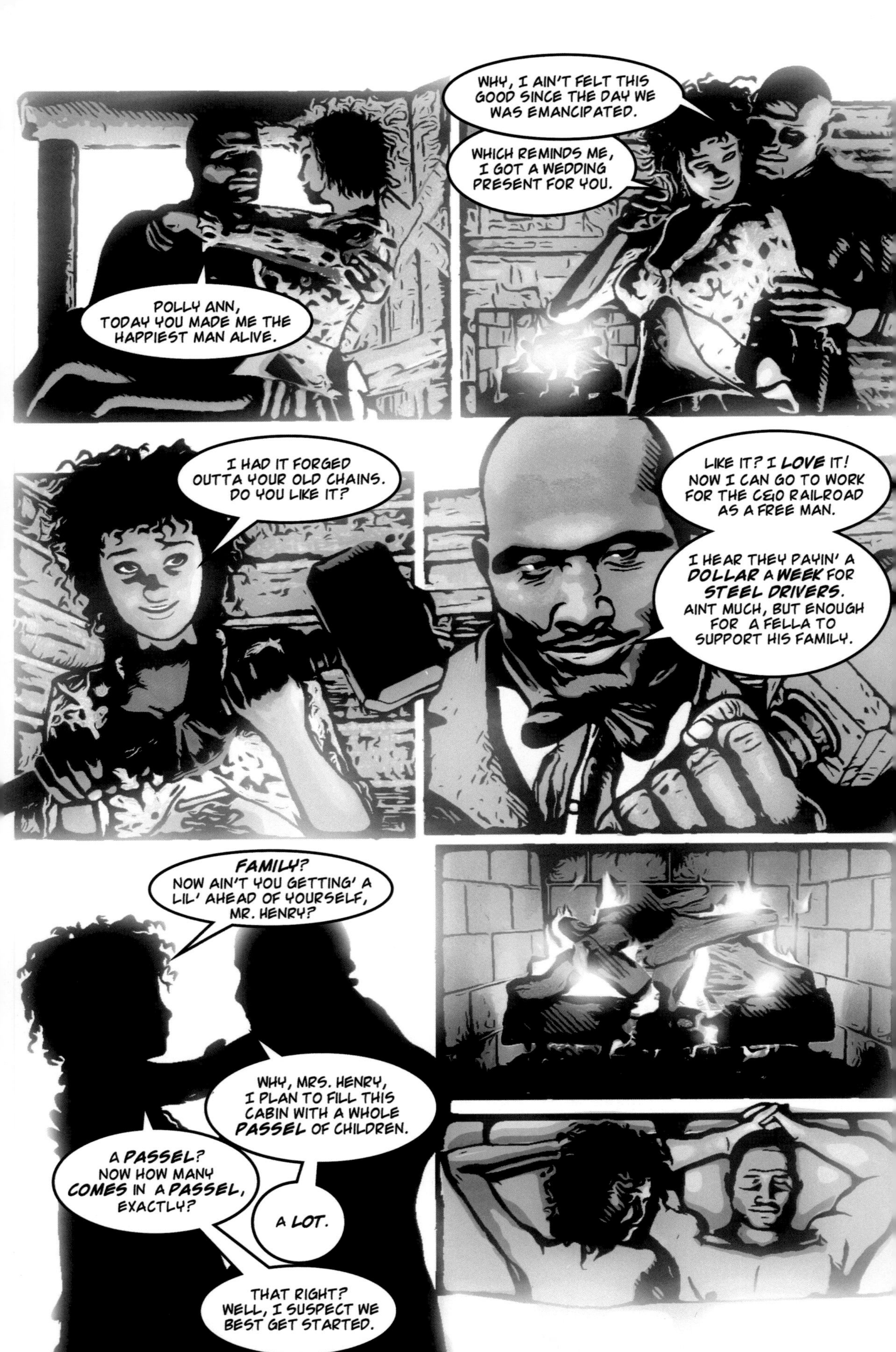
POLLY ANN, TODAY YOU MADE ME THE HAPPIEST MAN ALIVE.
WHY, I AIN'T FELT THIS GOOD SINCE THE DAY WE WAS EMANCIPATED.
WHICH REMINDS ME, I GOT A WEDDING PRESENT FOR YOU.
I HAD IT FORGED OUTTA YOUR OLD CHAINS. DO YOU LIKE IT?
LIKE IT? I LOVE IT! NOW I CAN GO TO WORK FOR THE C&O RAILROAD AS A FREE MAN.
I HEAR THEY PAYIN' A DOLLAR A WEEK FOR STEEL DRIVERS. AINT MUCH, BUT ENOUGH FOR A FELLA TO SUPPORT HIS FAMILY.
FAMILY? NOW AIN'T YOU GETTING' A LIL' AHEAD OF YOURSELF, MR. HENRY?
WHY, MRS. HENRY, I PLAN TO FILL THIS CABIN WITH A WHOLE PASSEL OF CHILDREN.
A PASSEL? NOW HOW MANY COMES IN A PASSEL, EXACTLY?
A LOT.
THAT RIGHT? WELL, I SUSPECT WE BEST GET STARTED.

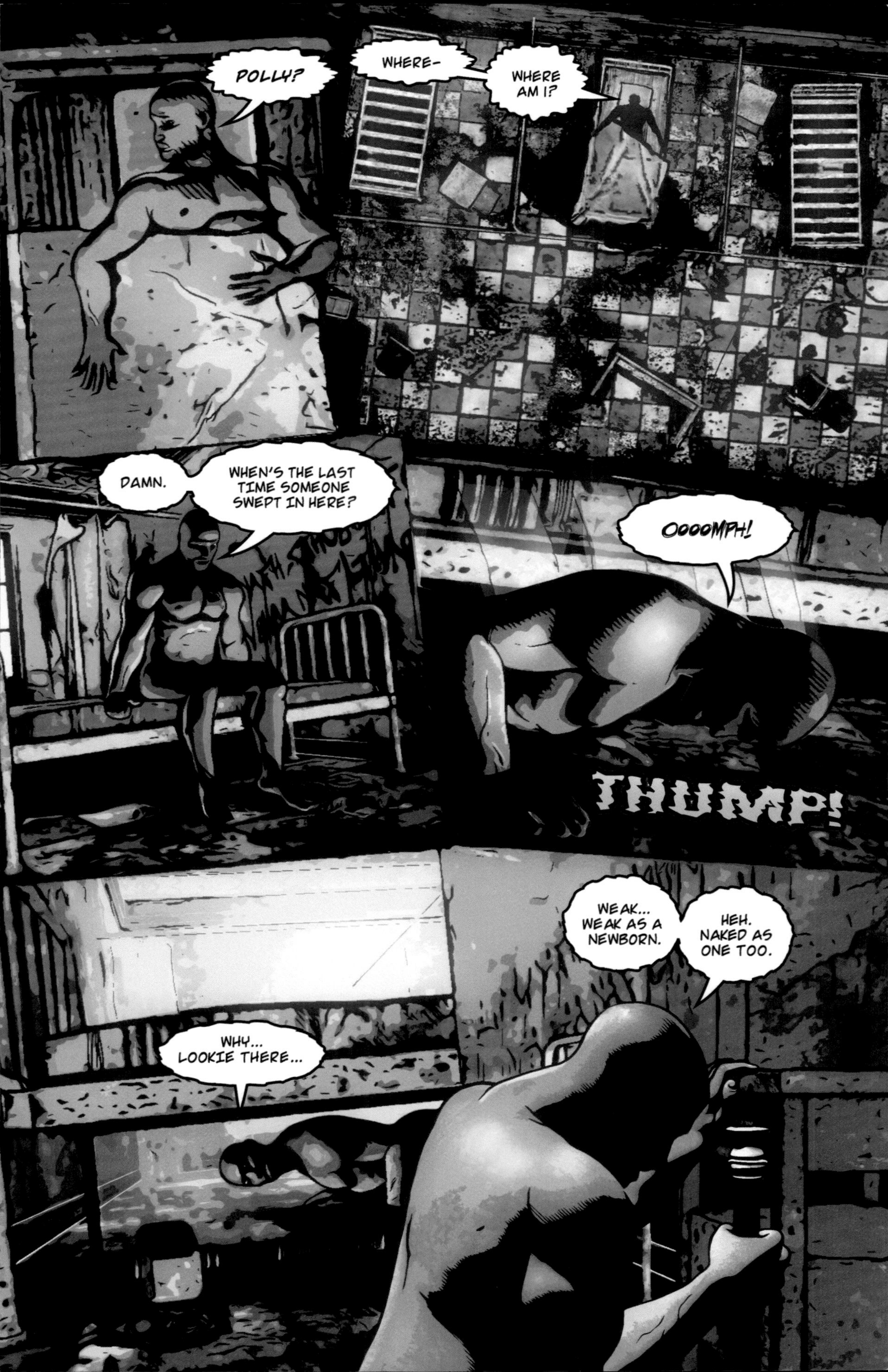
POLLY?
WHERE-
WHERE AM I?
DAMN.
WHEN'S THE LAST TIME SOMEONE SWEPT IN HERE?
OOOOMPH!
THUMP!
WEAK... WEAK AS A NEWBORN.
HEH. NAKED AS ONE TOO.
WHY... LOOKIE THERE...

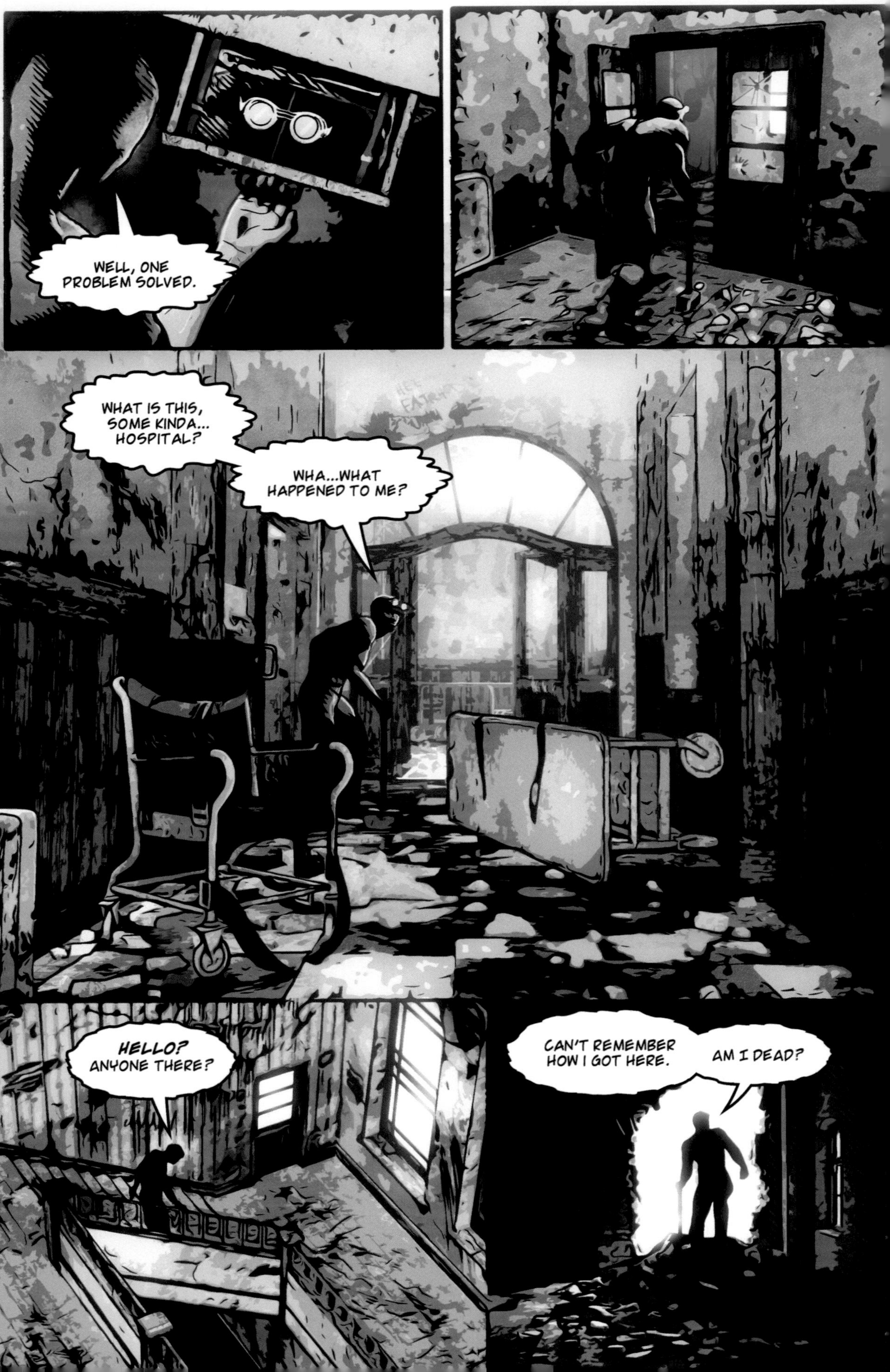
WELL, ONE PROBLEM SOLVED.
WHAT IS THIS, SOME KINDA... HOSPITAL?
WHA...WHAT HAPPENED TO ME?
HELLO? ANYONE THERE?
CAN'T REMEMBER HOW I GOT HERE.
AM I DEAD?

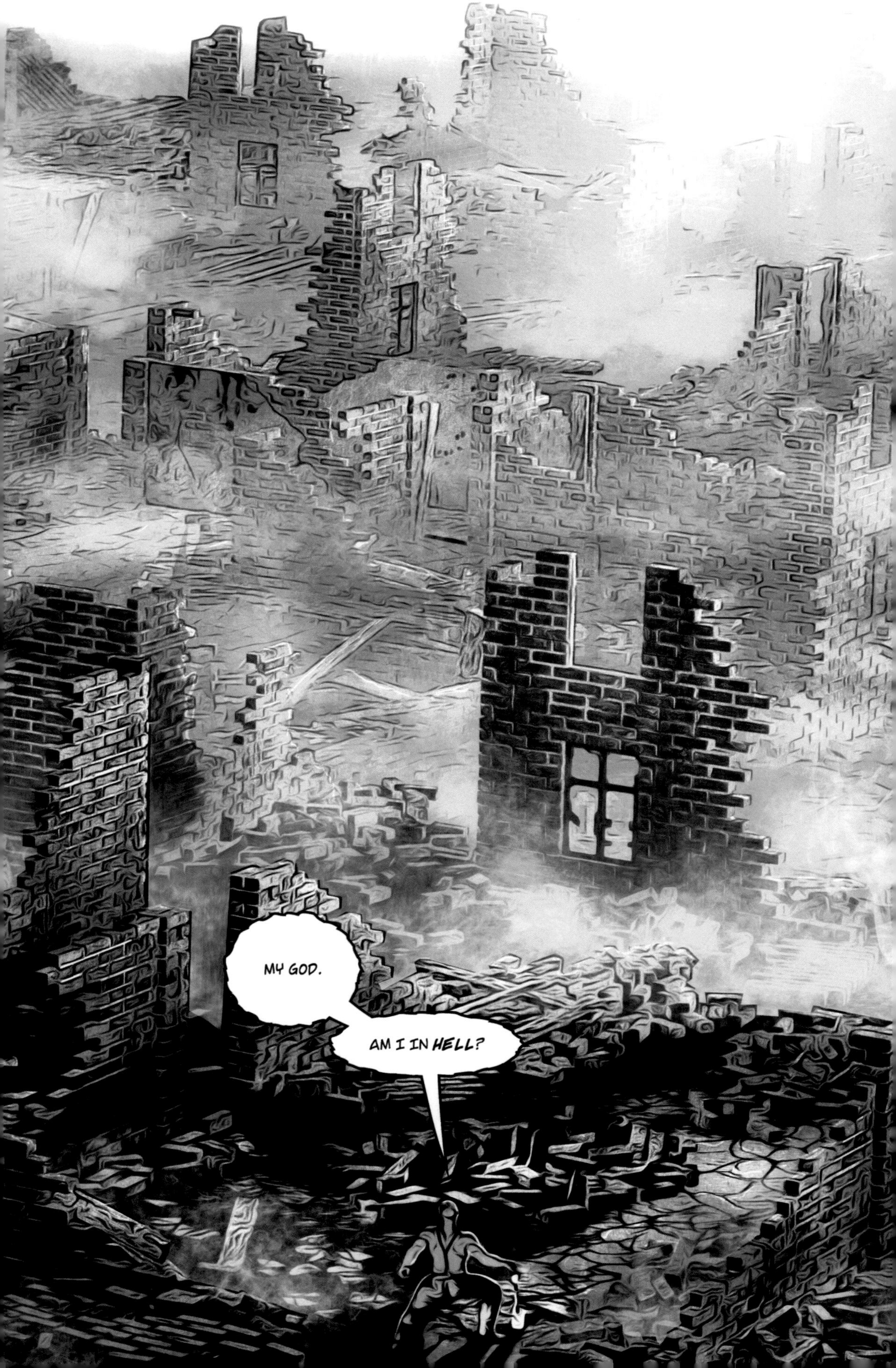
MY GOD.
AM I IN HELL?

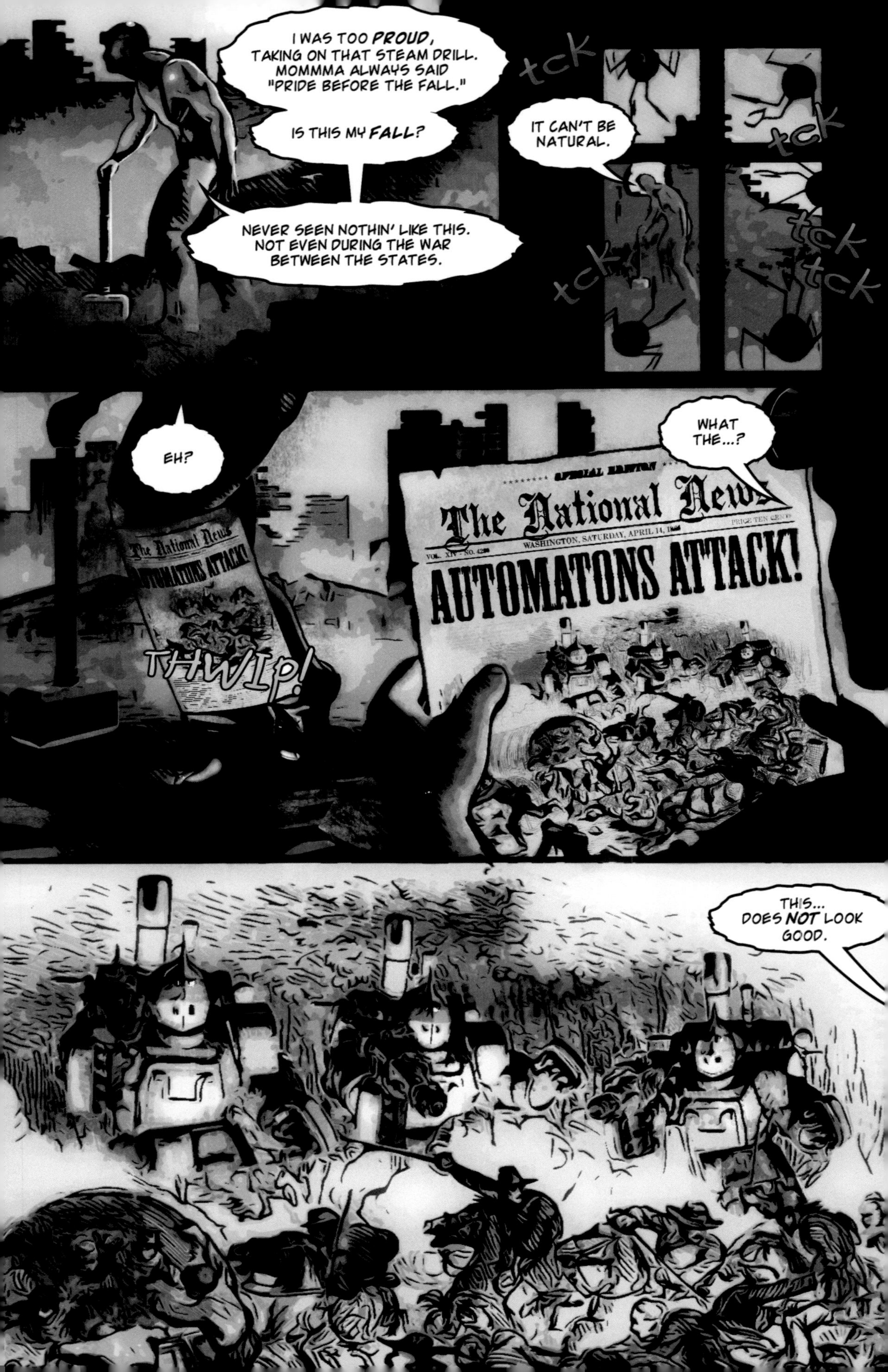
I WAS TOO PROUD, TAKING ON THAT STEAM DRILL. MOMMMA ALWAYS SAID "PRIDE BEFORE THE FALL."
IS THIS MY FALL?
NEVER SEEN NOTHIN' LIKE THIS. NOT EVEN DURING THE WAR BETWEEN THE STATES.
tck
IT CAN'T BE NATURAL.
tck
tck
tck
tck
EH?
WHAT THE...?
The National News
WASHINGTON, SATURDAY, APRIL 14,
PRICE TEN CENTS
AUTOMATONS ATTACK!
THWIP!
THIS... DOES NOT LOOK GOOD.

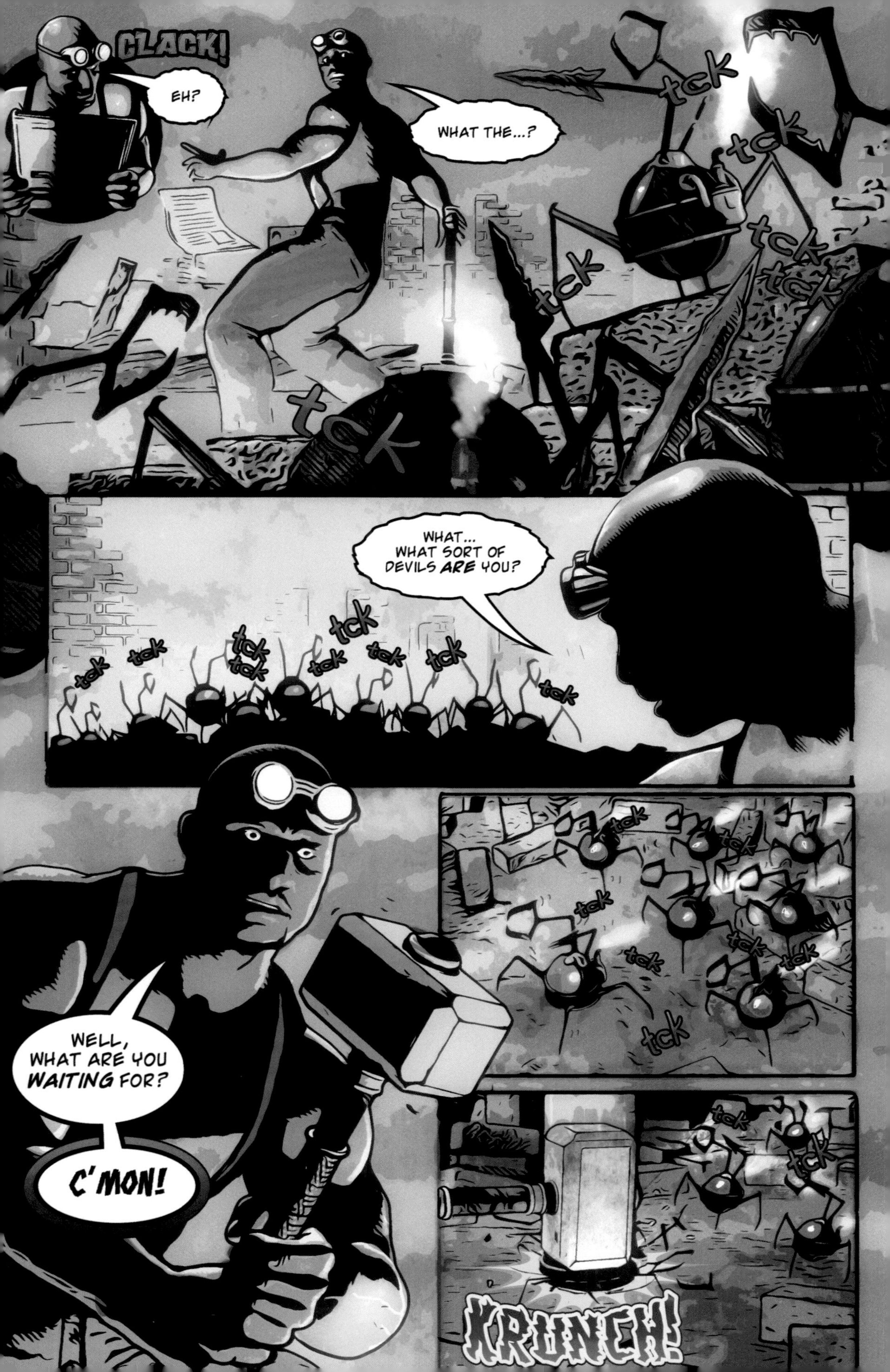
CLACK!
EH?
WHAT THE...?
tck
tck
tck
tck
tck
tck
WHAT... WHAT SORT OF DEVILS ARE YOU?
tck
tck
tck
tck
tck
tck
tck
tck
WELL, WHAT ARE YOU WAITING FOR?
C'MON!
tck
tck
tck
tck
tck
tck
tck
tck
KRUNCH!

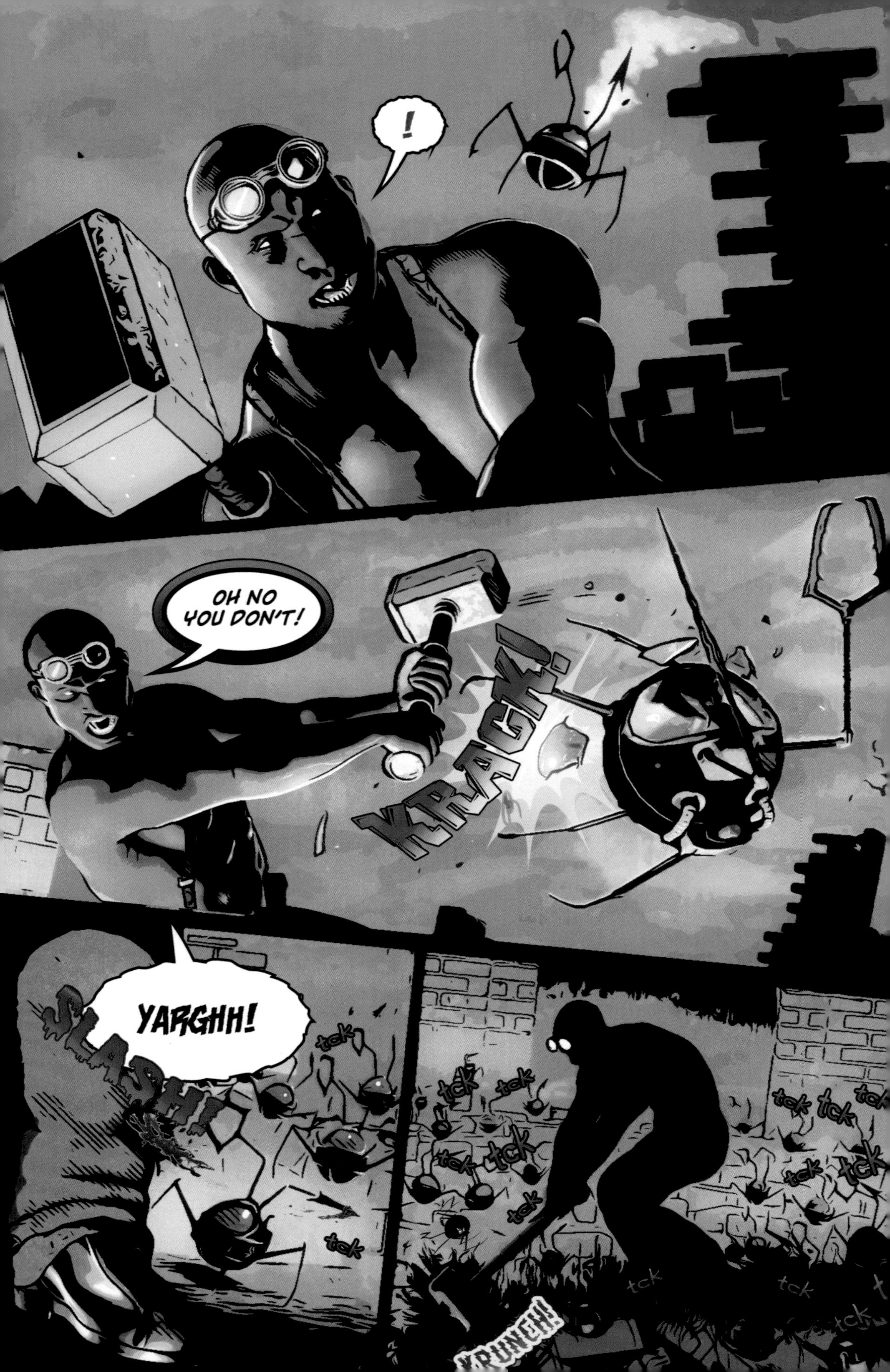
!
OH NO YOU DON'T!
KRACK!
YARGHH!
SLASH!
tck
tck
tck tck
tck tck
tck tck
tck
tck
tck
tck
tck
tck
KRUNCH!

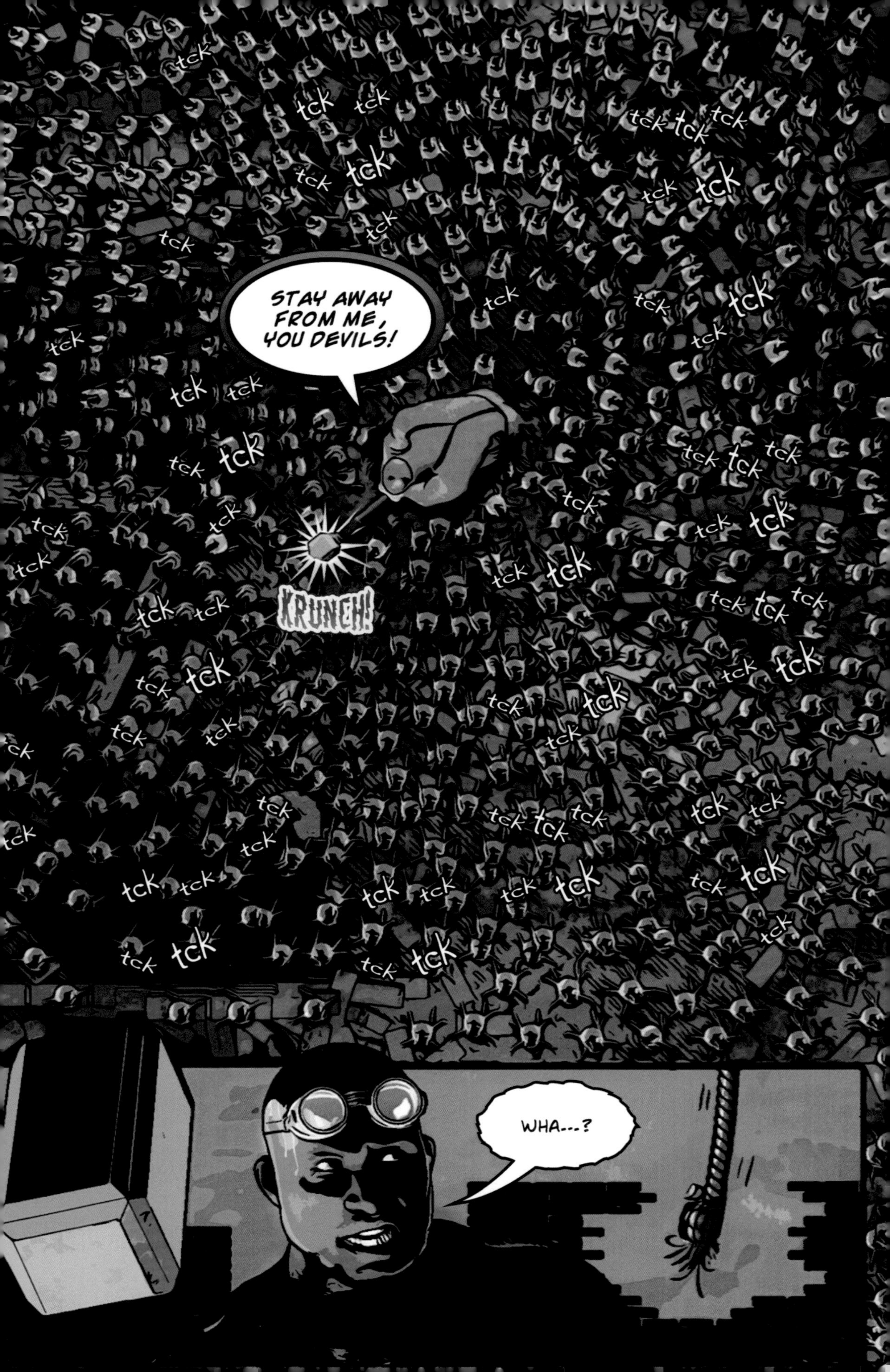
tck tck tck
STAY AWAY FROM ME, YOU DEVILS!
KRUNCH!
WHA...?

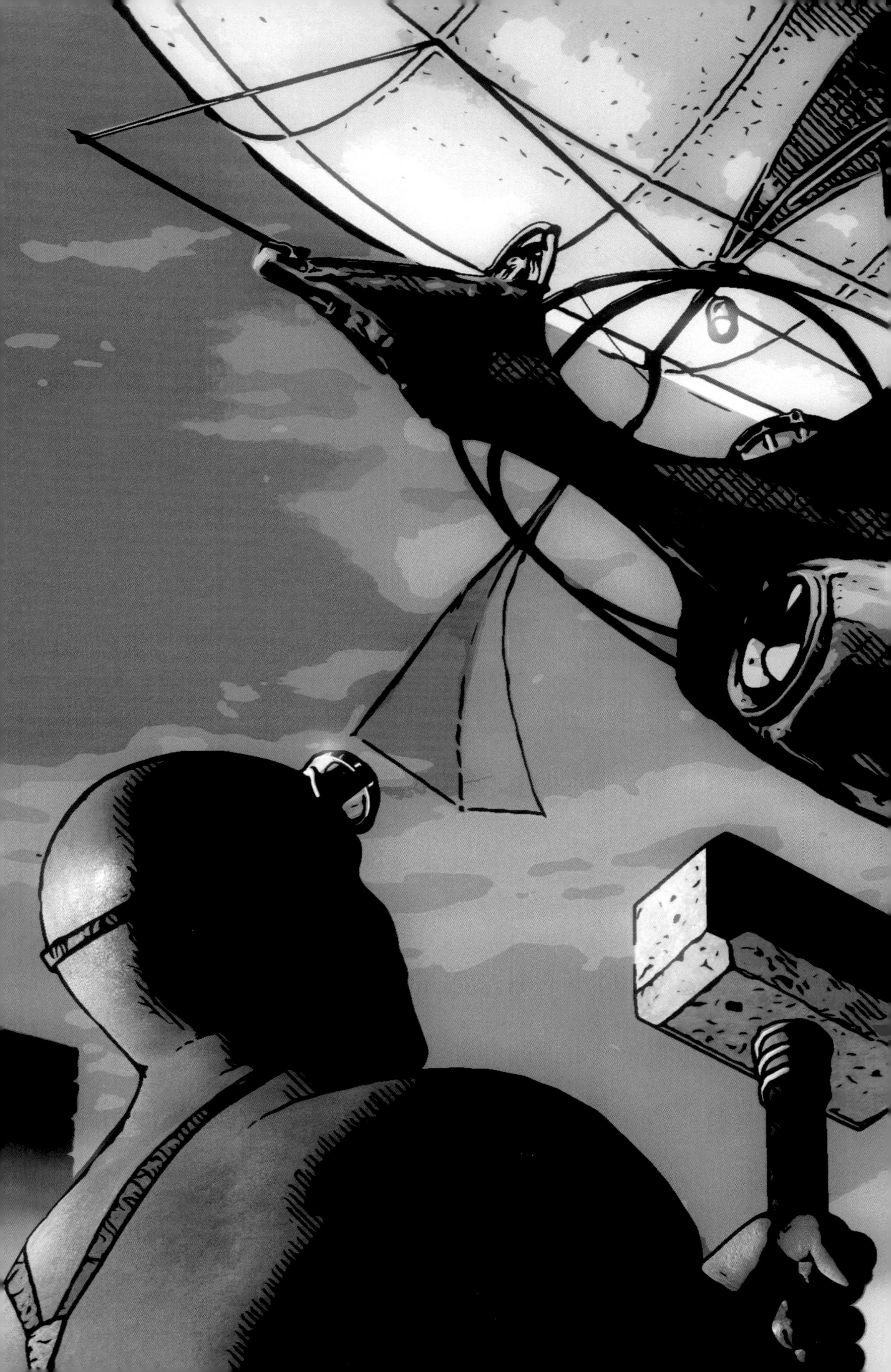

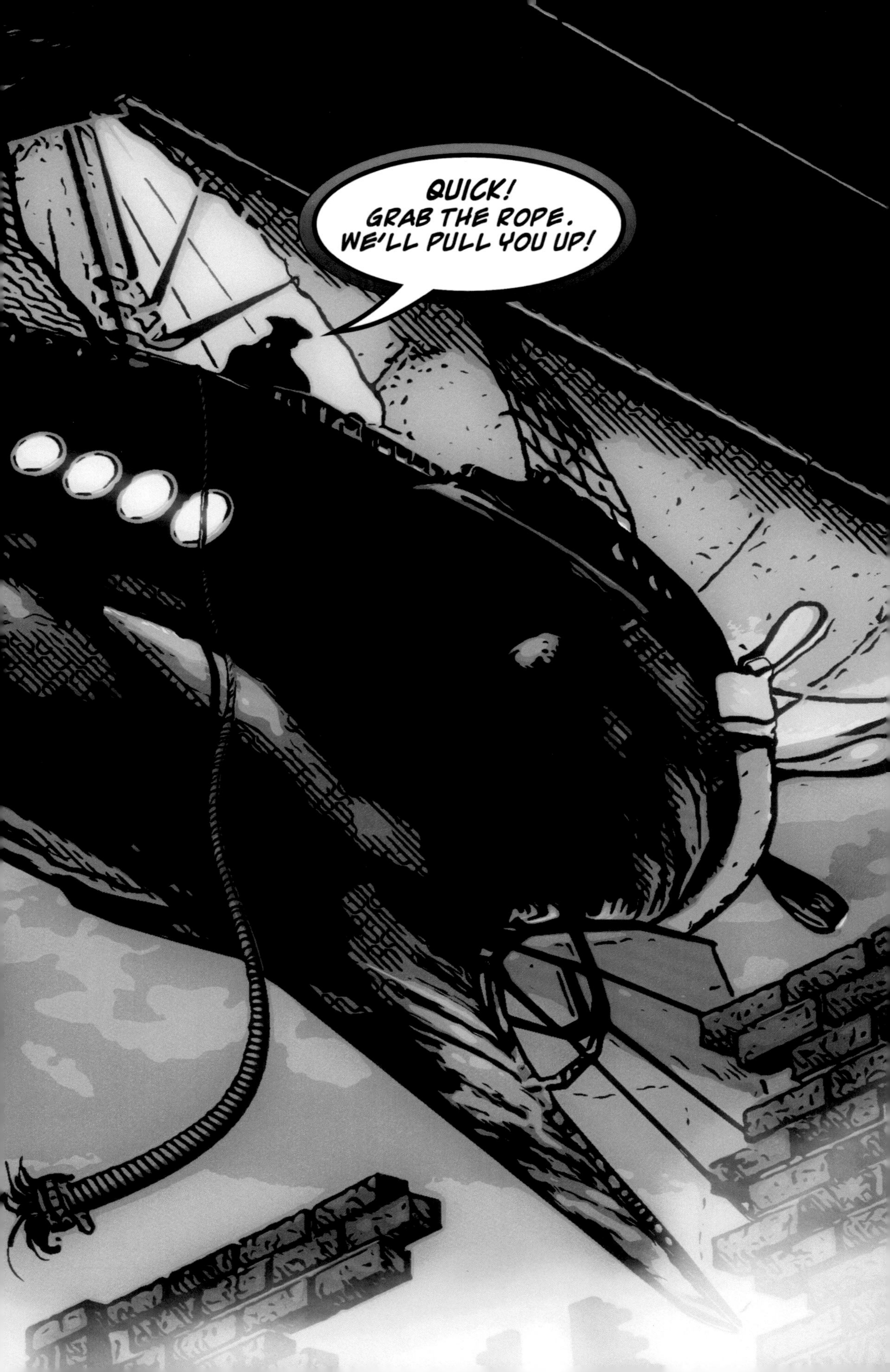
QUICK! GRAB THE ROPE. WE'LL PULL YOU UP!

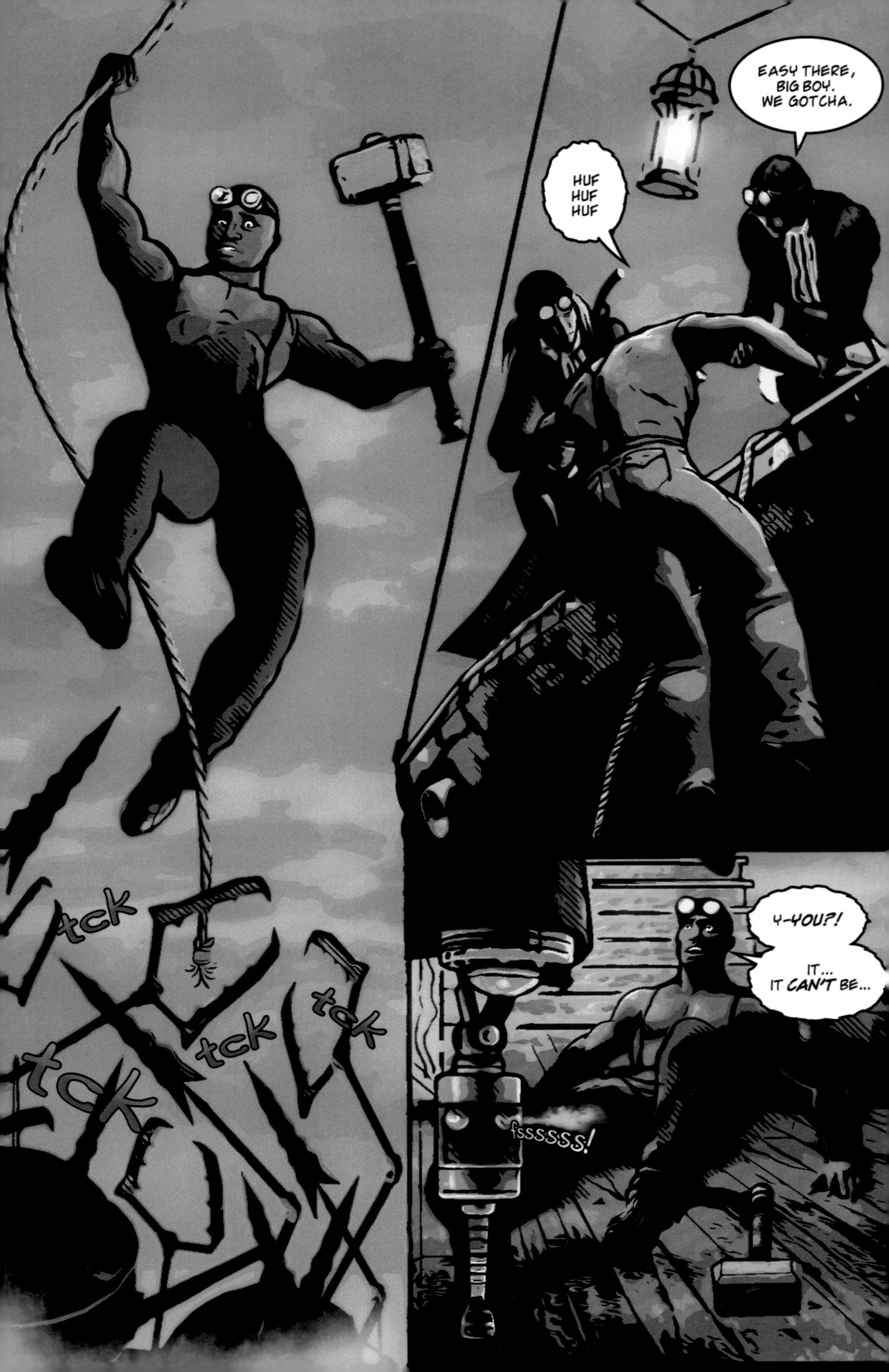
tck
tck
tck
tck
EASY THERE, BIG BOY. WE GOTCHA.
HUF HUF HUF
Y-YOU?!
IT... IT CAN'T BE...
fsssSSS!

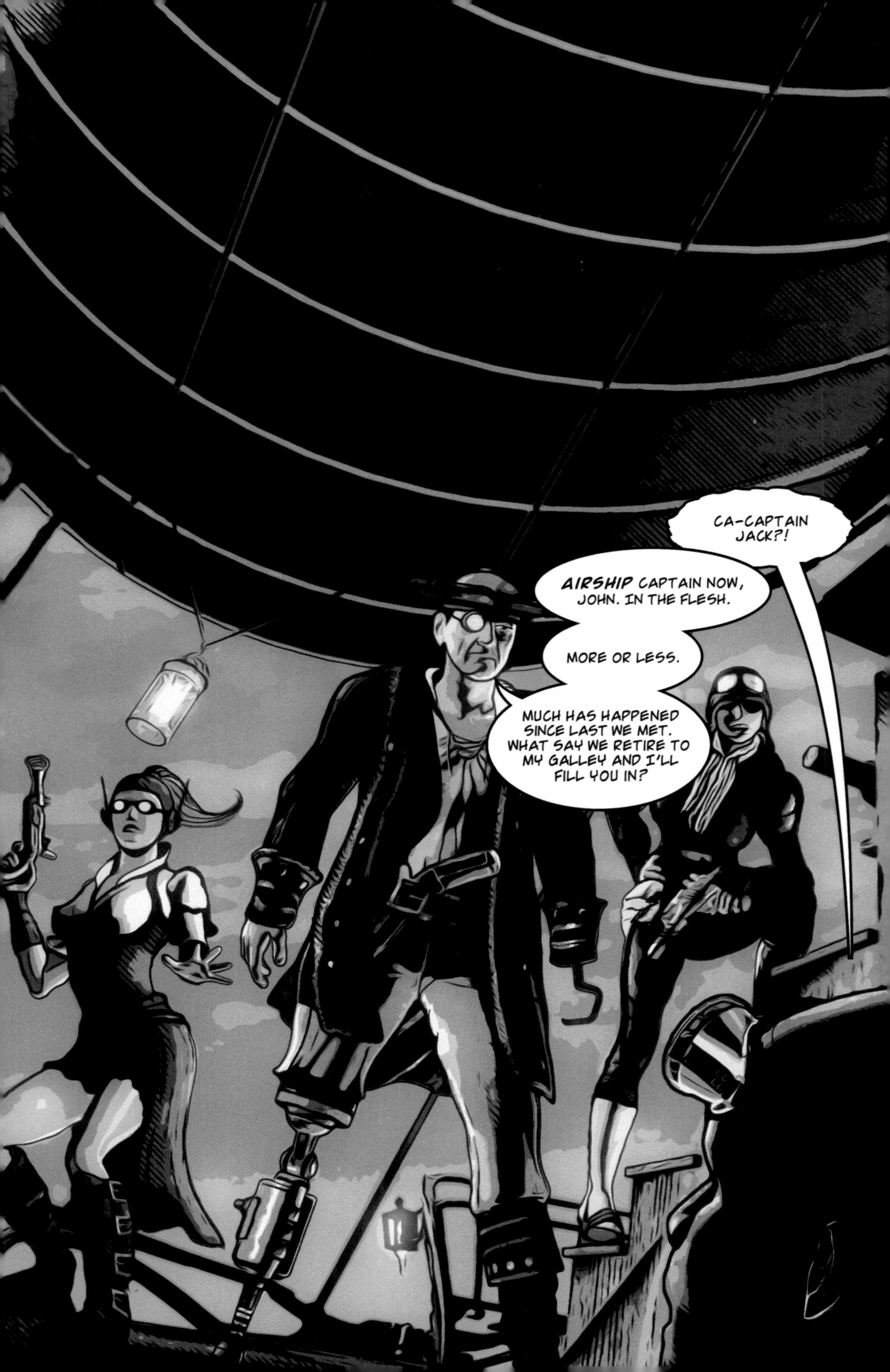
CA-CAPTAIN JACK?!
AIRSHIP CAPTAIN NOW, JOHN. IN THE FLESH.
MORE OR LESS.
MUCH HAS HAPPENED SINCE LAST WE MET. WHAT SAY WE RETIRE TO MY GALLEY AND I'LL FILL YOU IN?

Chapter Two

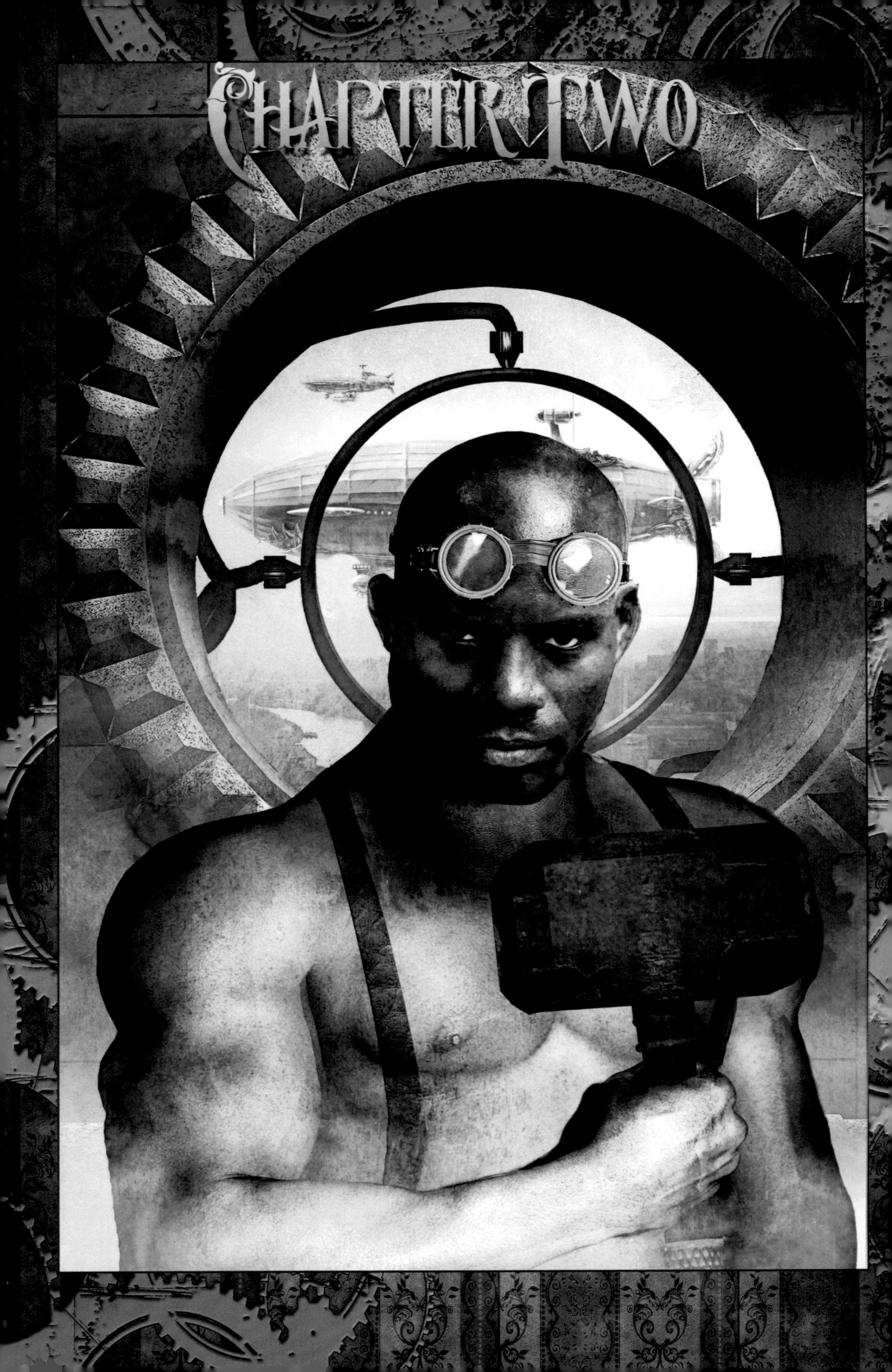

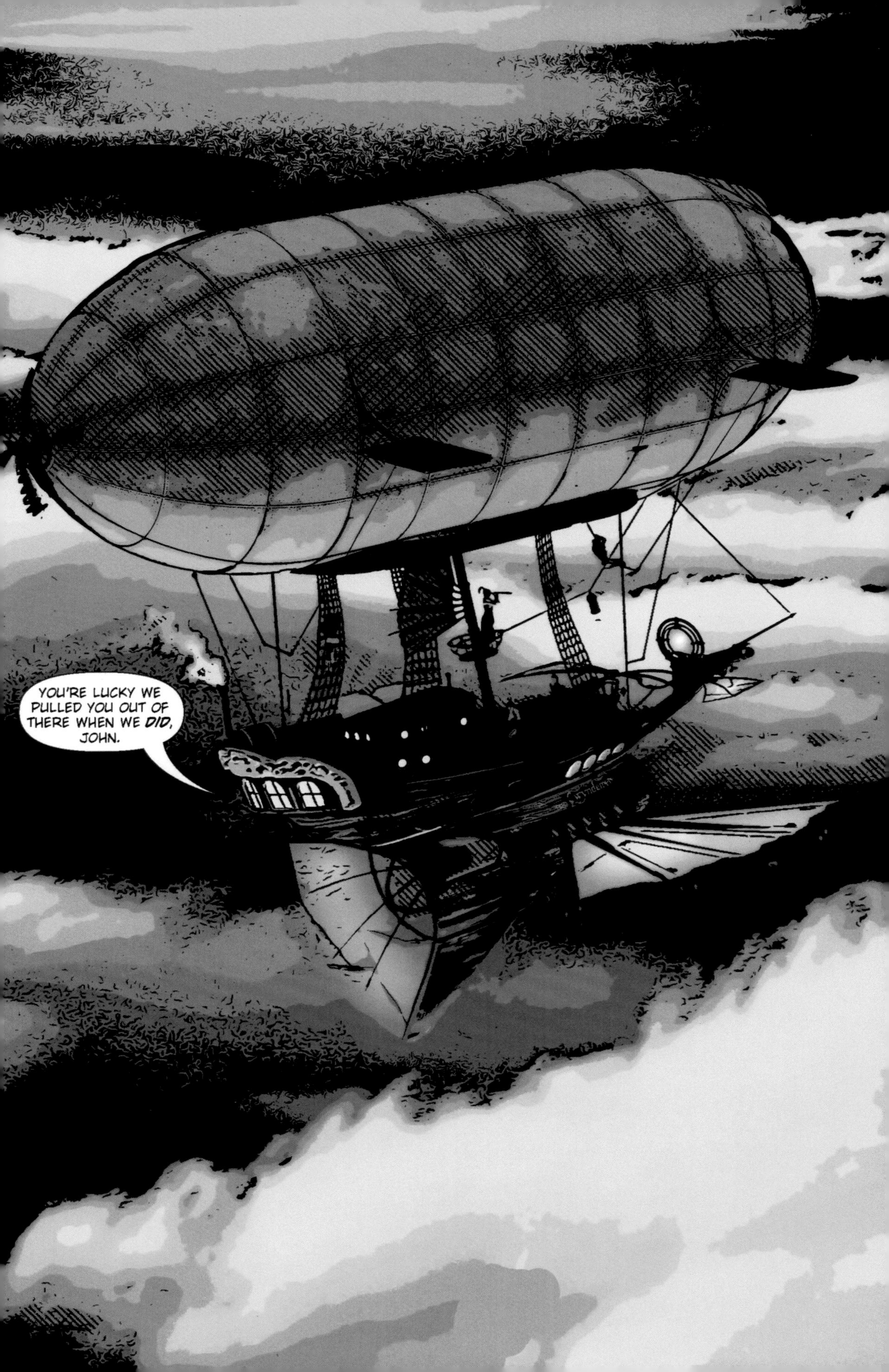
YOU'RE LUCKY WE PULLED YOU OUT OF THERE WHEN WE *DID*, JOHN.

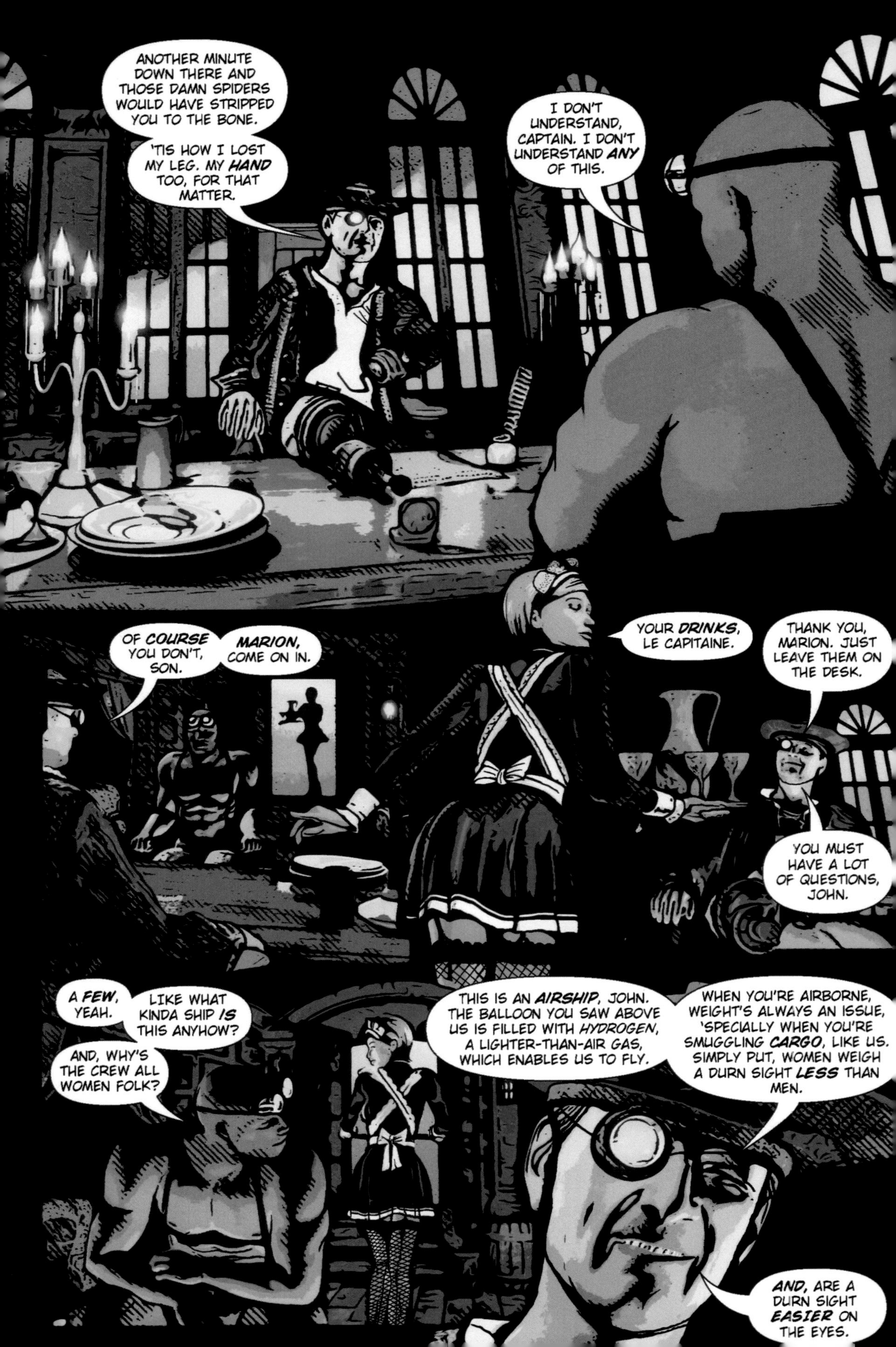

ANOTHER MINUTE DOWN THERE AND THOSE DAMN SPIDERS WOULD HAVE STRIPPED YOU TO THE BONE.
'TIS HOW I LOST MY LEG. MY *HAND* TOO, FOR THAT MATTER.
I DON'T UNDERSTAND, CAPTAIN. I DON'T UNDERSTAND *ANY* OF THIS.
OF *COURSE* YOU DON'T, SON.
MARION, COME ON IN.
YOUR *DRINKS,* LE CAPITAINE.
THANK YOU, MARION. JUST LEAVE THEM ON THE DESK.
YOU MUST HAVE A LOT OF QUESTIONS, JOHN.
A *FEW,* YEAH.
LIKE WHAT KINDA SHIP *IS* THIS ANYHOW?
AND, WHY'S THE CREW ALL WOMEN FOLK?
THIS IS AN *AIRSHIP*, JOHN. THE BALLOON YOU SAW ABOVE US IS FILLED WITH *HYDROGEN*, A LIGHTER-THAN-AIR GAS, WHICH ENABLES US TO FLY.
WHEN YOU'RE AIRBORNE, WEIGHT'S ALWAYS AN ISSUE, 'SPECIALLY WHEN YOU'RE SMUGGLING *CARGO*, LIKE US. SIMPLY PUT, WOMEN WEIGH A DURN SIGHT *LESS* THAN MEN.
AND, ARE A DURN SIGHT *EASIER* ON THE EYES.

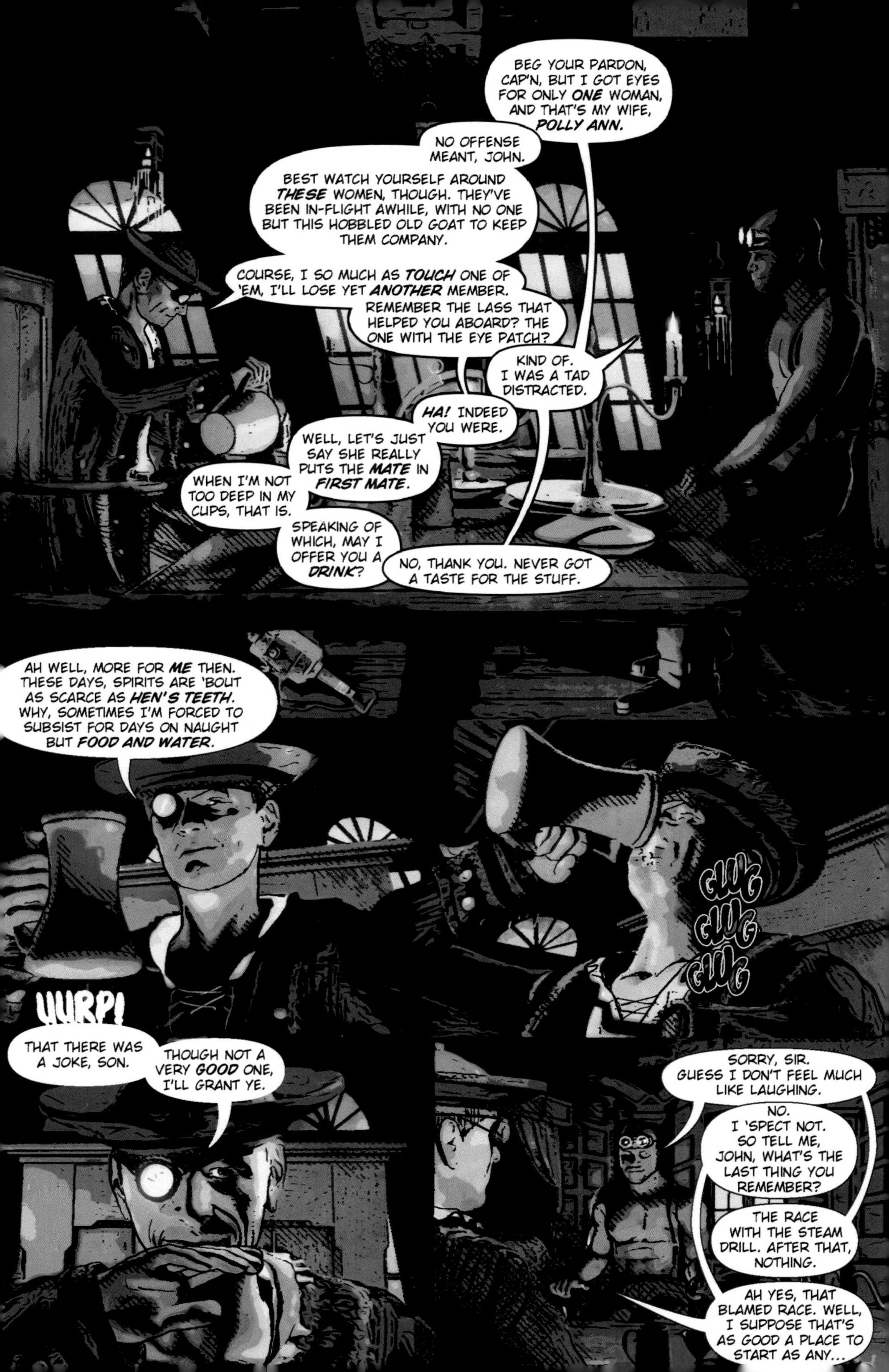
BEG YOUR PARDON, CAP'N, BUT I GOT EYES FOR ONLY ONE WOMAN, AND THAT'S MY WIFE, POLLY ANN.
NO OFFENSE MEANT, JOHN.
BEST WATCH YOURSELF AROUND THESE WOMEN, THOUGH. THEY'VE BEEN IN-FLIGHT AWHILE, WITH NO ONE BUT THIS HOBBLED OLD GOAT TO KEEP THEM COMPANY.
COURSE, I SO MUCH AS TOUCH ONE OF 'EM, I'LL LOSE YET ANOTHER MEMBER.
REMEMBER THE LASS THAT HELPED YOU ABOARD? THE ONE WITH THE EYE PATCH?
KIND OF. I WAS A TAD DISTRACTED.
HA! INDEED YOU WERE.
WELL, LET'S JUST SAY SHE REALLY PUTS THE MATE IN FIRST MATE.
WHEN I'M NOT TOO DEEP IN MY CUPS, THAT IS.
SPEAKING OF WHICH, MAY I OFFER YOU A DRINK?
NO, THANK YOU. NEVER GOT A TASTE FOR THE STUFF.
AH WELL, MORE FOR ME THEN. THESE DAYS, SPIRITS ARE 'BOUT AS SCARCE AS HEN'S TEETH. WHY, SOMETIMES I'M FORCED TO SUBSIST FOR DAYS ON NAUGHT BUT FOOD AND WATER.
GLUG GLUG GLUG
UURP!
THAT THERE WAS A JOKE, SON.
THOUGH NOT A VERY GOOD ONE, I'LL GRANT YE.
SORRY, SIR. GUESS I DON'T FEEL MUCH LIKE LAUGHING.
NO. I 'SPECT NOT. SO TELL ME, JOHN, WHAT'S THE LAST THING YOU REMEMBER?
THE RACE WITH THE STEAM DRILL. AFTER THAT, NOTHING.
AH YES, THAT BLAMED RACE. WELL, I SUPPOSE THAT'S AS GOOD A PLACE TO START AS ANY...

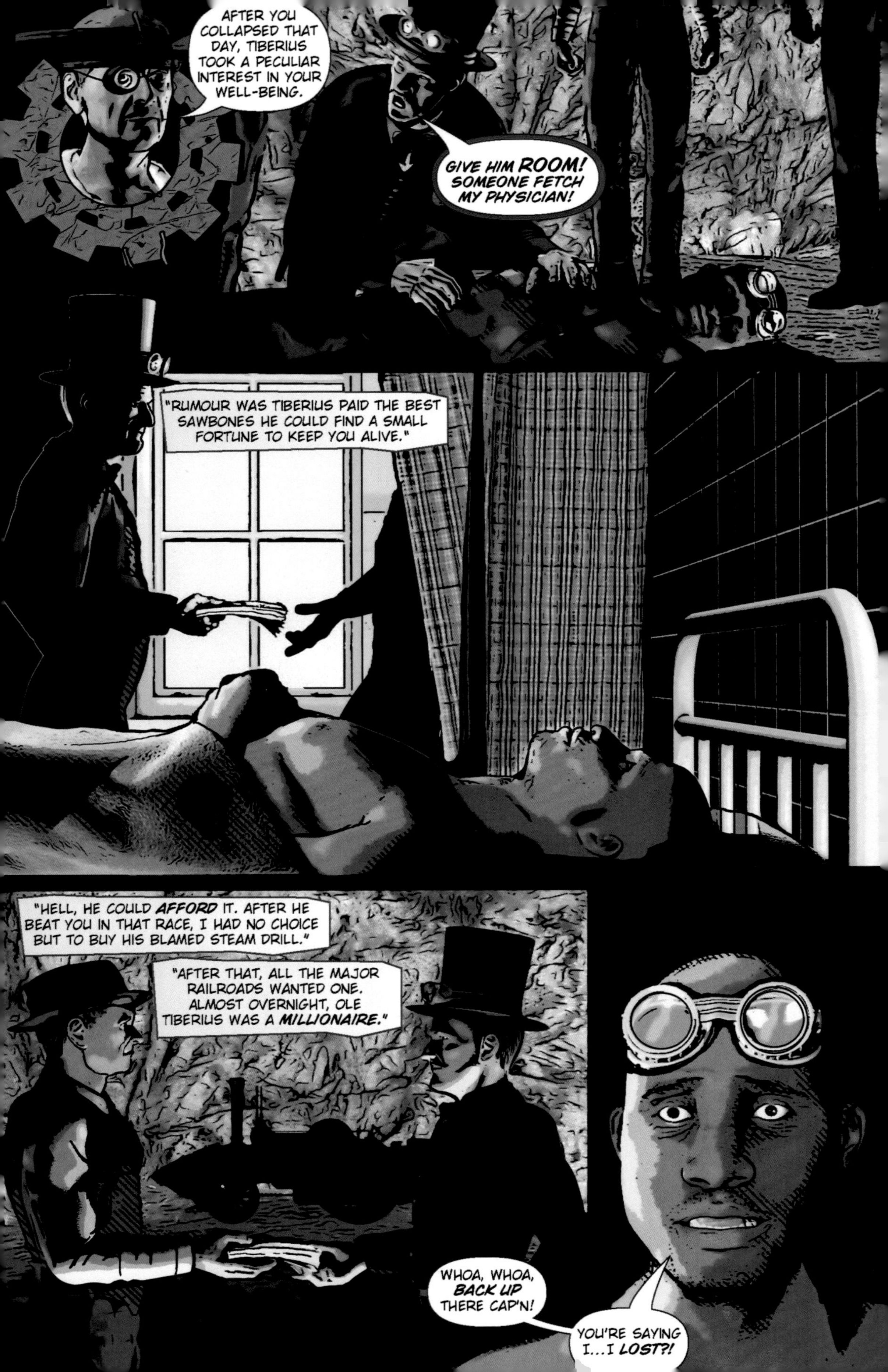
AFTER YOU COLLAPSED THAT DAY, TIBERIUS TOOK A PECULIAR INTEREST IN YOUR WELL-BEING.
GIVE HIM ROOM! SOMEONE FETCH MY PHYSICIAN!
"RUMOUR WAS TIBERIUS PAID THE BEST SAWBONES HE COULD FIND A SMALL FORTUNE TO KEEP YOU ALIVE."
"HELL, HE COULD AFFORD IT. AFTER HE BEAT YOU IN THAT RACE, I HAD NO CHOICE BUT TO BUY HIS BLAMED STEAM DRILL."
"AFTER THAT, ALL THE MAJOR RAILROADS WANTED ONE. ALMOST OVERNIGHT, OLE TIBERIUS WAS A MILLIONAIRE."
WHOA, WHOA, BACK UP THERE CAP'N!
YOU'RE SAYING I...I LOST?!

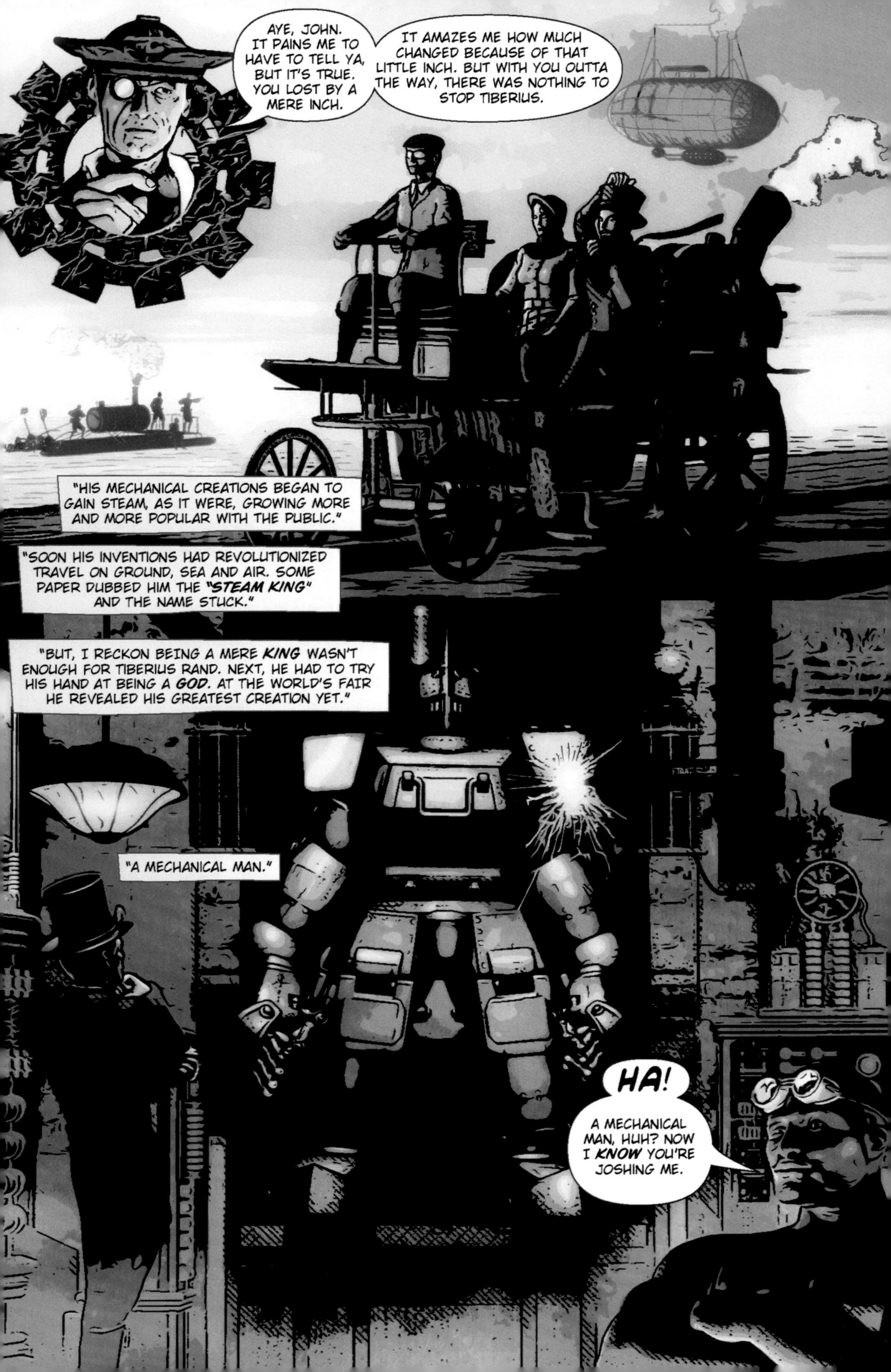
AYE, JOHN. IT PAINS ME TO HAVE TO TELL YA, BUT IT'S TRUE. YOU LOST BY A MERE INCH.
IT AMAZES ME HOW MUCH CHANGED BECAUSE OF THAT LITTLE INCH. BUT WITH YOU OUTTA THE WAY, THERE WAS NOTHING TO STOP TIBERIUS.
"HIS MECHANICAL CREATIONS BEGAN TO GAIN STEAM, AS IT WERE, GROWING MORE AND MORE POPULAR WITH THE PUBLIC."
"SOON HIS INVENTIONS HAD REVOLUTIONIZED TRAVEL ON GROUND, SEA AND AIR. SOME PAPER DUBBED HIM THE ***"STEAM KING"*** AND THE NAME STUCK."
"BUT, I RECKON BEING A MERE ***KING*** WASN'T ENOUGH FOR TIBERIUS RAND. NEXT, HE HAD TO TRY HIS HAND AT BEING A ***GOD***. AT THE WORLD'S FAIR HE REVEALED HIS GREATEST CREATION YET."
"A MECHANICAL MAN."
HA!
A MECHANICAL MAN, HUH? NOW I ***KNOW*** YOU'RE JOSHING ME.

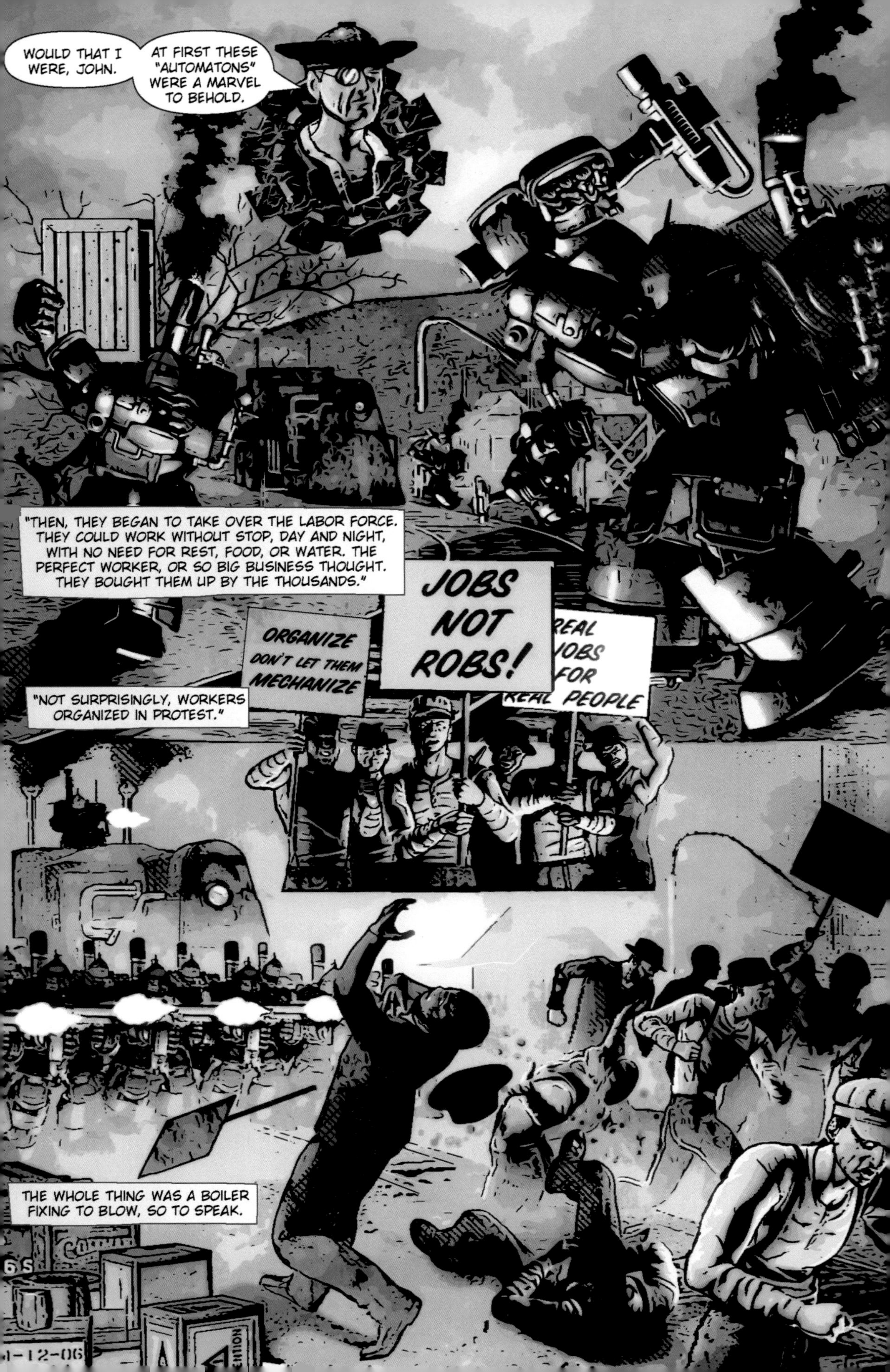
WOULD THAT I WERE, JOHN.
AT FIRST THESE "AUTOMATONS" WERE A MARVEL TO BEHOLD.
"THEN, THEY BEGAN TO TAKE OVER THE LABOR FORCE. THEY COULD WORK WITHOUT STOP, DAY AND NIGHT, WITH NO NEED FOR REST, FOOD, OR WATER. THE PERFECT WORKER, OR SO BIG BUSINESS THOUGHT. THEY BOUGHT THEM UP BY THE THOUSANDS."
JOBS NOT ROBS!
ORGANIZE DON'T LET THEM MECHANIZE
REAL JOBS FOR REAL PEOPLE
"NOT SURPRISINGLY, WORKERS ORGANIZED IN PROTEST."
THE WHOLE THING WAS A BOILER FIXING TO BLOW, SO TO SPEAK.

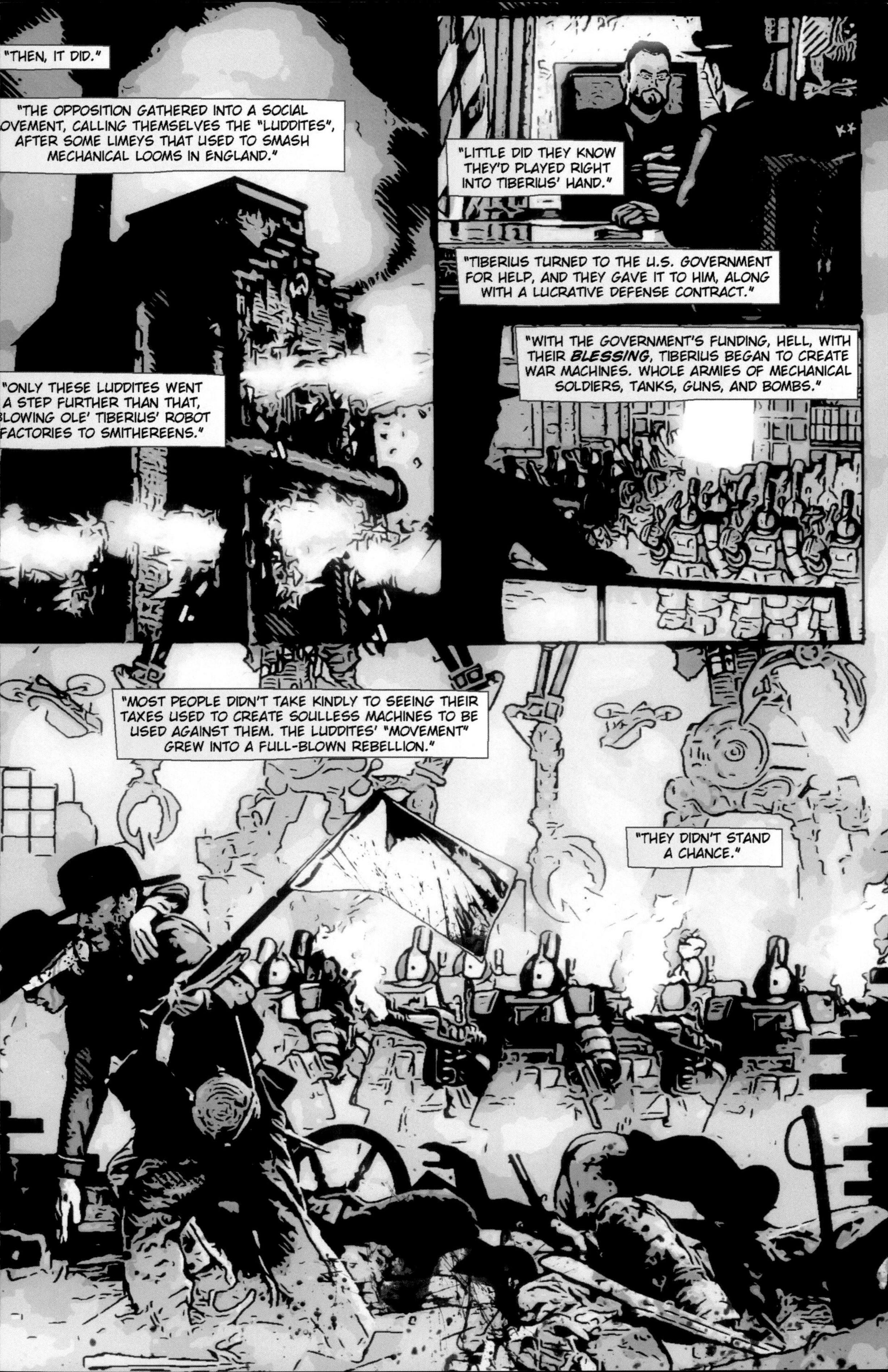
"THEN, IT DID."
"THE OPPOSITION GATHERED INTO A SOCIAL OVEMENT, CALLING THEMSELVES THE "LUDDITES", AFTER SOME LIMEYS THAT USED TO SMASH MECHANICAL LOOMS IN ENGLAND."
"ONLY THESE LUDDITES WENT A STEP FURTHER THAN THAT, LOWING OLE' TIBERIUS' ROBOT FACTORIES TO SMITHEREENS."
"LITTLE DID THEY KNOW THEY'D PLAYED RIGHT INTO TIBERIUS' HAND."
"TIBERIUS TURNED TO THE U.S. GOVERNMENT FOR HELP, AND THEY GAVE IT TO HIM, ALONG WITH A LUCRATIVE DEFENSE CONTRACT."
"WITH THE GOVERNMENT'S FUNDING, HELL, WITH THEIR *BLESSING*, TIBERIUS BEGAN TO CREATE WAR MACHINES. WHOLE ARMIES OF MECHANICAL SOLDIERS, TANKS, GUNS, AND BOMBS."
"MOST PEOPLE DIDN'T TAKE KINDLY TO SEEING THEIR TAXES USED TO CREATE SOULLESS MACHINES TO BE USED AGAINST THEM. THE LUDDITES' "MOVEMENT" GREW INTO A FULL-BLOWN REBELLION."
"THEY DIDN'T STAND A CHANCE."

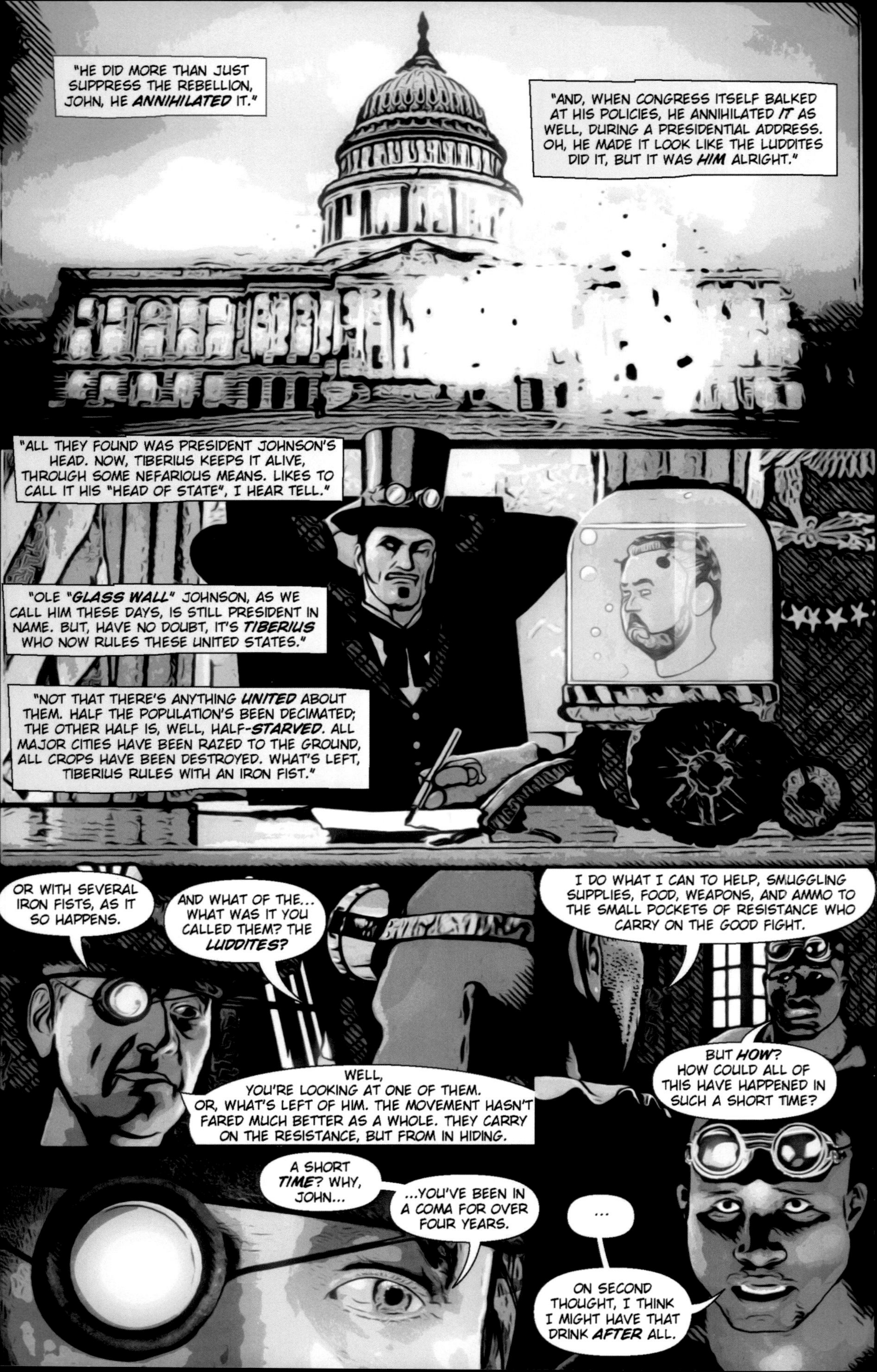
"HE DID MORE THAN JUST SUPPRESS THE REBELLION, JOHN, HE ANNIHILATED IT."
"AND, WHEN CONGRESS ITSELF BALKED AT HIS POLICIES, HE ANNIHILATED IT AS WELL, DURING A PRESIDENTIAL ADDRESS. OH, HE MADE IT LOOK LIKE THE LUDDITES DID IT, BUT IT WAS HIM ALRIGHT."
"ALL THEY FOUND WAS PRESIDENT JOHNSON'S HEAD. NOW, TIBERIUS KEEPS IT ALIVE, THROUGH SOME NEFARIOUS MEANS. LIKES TO CALL IT HIS "HEAD OF STATE", I HEAR TELL."
"OLE "GLASS WALL" JOHNSON, AS WE CALL HIM THESE DAYS, IS STILL PRESIDENT IN NAME. BUT, HAVE NO DOUBT, IT'S TIBERIUS WHO NOW RULES THESE UNITED STATES."
"NOT THAT THERE'S ANYTHING UNITED ABOUT THEM. HALF THE POPULATION'S BEEN DECIMATED; THE OTHER HALF IS, WELL, HALF-STARVED. ALL MAJOR CITIES HAVE BEEN RAZED TO THE GROUND, ALL CROPS HAVE BEEN DESTROYED. WHAT'S LEFT, TIBERIUS RULES WITH AN IRON FIST."
OR WITH SEVERAL IRON FISTS, AS IT SO HAPPENS.
AND WHAT OF THE... WHAT WAS IT YOU CALLED THEM? THE LUDDITES?
WELL, YOU'RE LOOKING AT ONE OF THEM. OR, WHAT'S LEFT OF HIM. THE MOVEMENT HASN'T FARED MUCH BETTER AS A WHOLE. THEY CARRY ON THE RESISTANCE, BUT FROM IN HIDING.
I DO WHAT I CAN TO HELP, SMUGGLING SUPPLIES, FOOD, WEAPONS, AND AMMO TO THE SMALL POCKETS OF RESISTANCE WHO CARRY ON THE GOOD FIGHT.
BUT HOW? HOW COULD ALL OF THIS HAVE HAPPENED IN SUCH A SHORT TIME?
A SHORT TIME? WHY, JOHN...
...YOU'VE BEEN IN A COMA FOR OVER FOUR YEARS.
...
ON SECOND THOUGHT, I THINK I MIGHT HAVE THAT DRINK AFTER ALL.

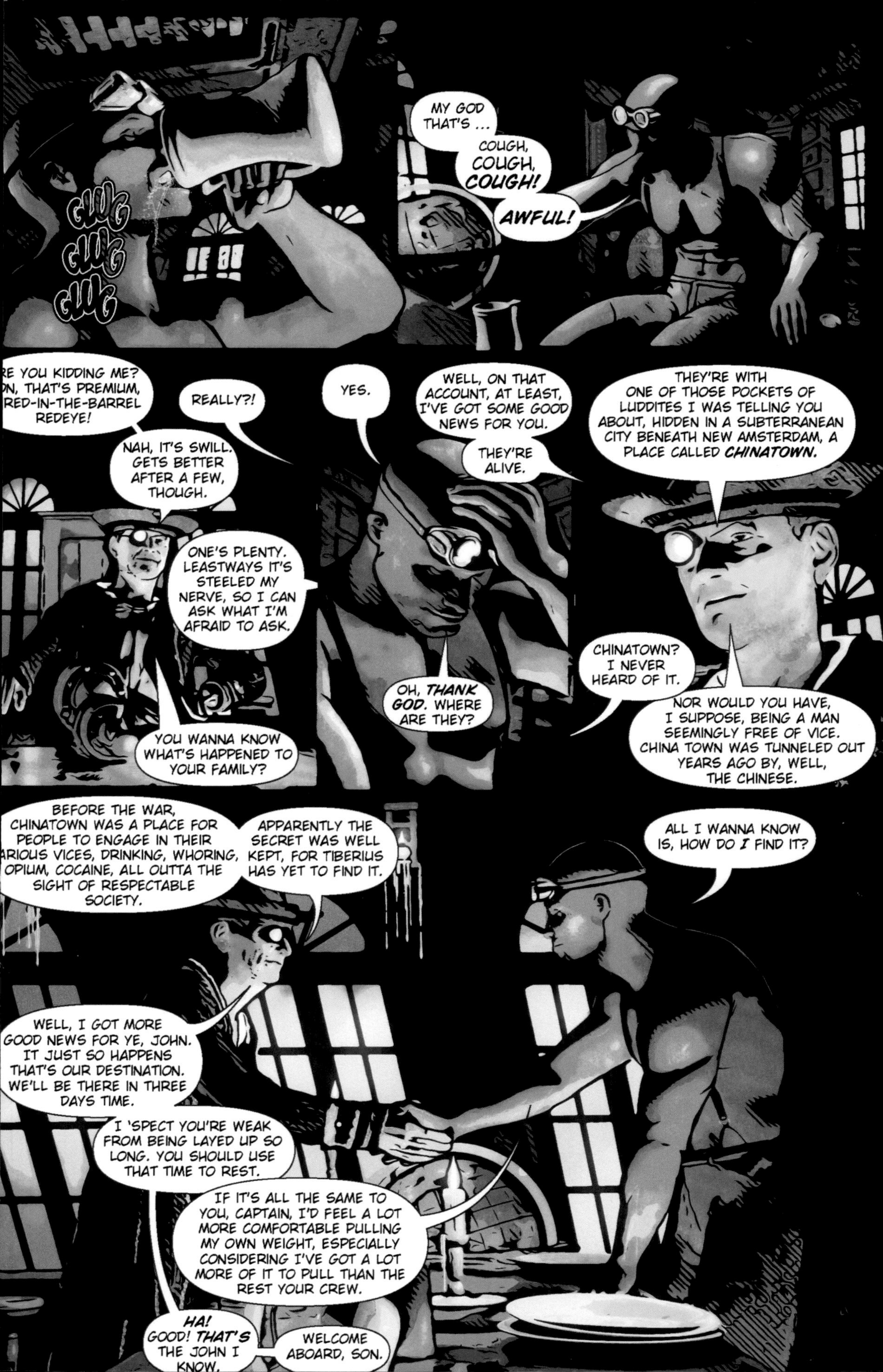
GLUG
GLUG
GLUG
MY GOD THAT'S ...
COUGH, COUGH, COUGH!
AWFUL!
RE YOU KIDDING ME? ON, THAT'S PREMIUM, RED-IN-THE-BARREL REDEYE!
REALLY?!
NAH, IT'S SWILL. GETS BETTER AFTER A FEW, THOUGH.
ONE'S PLENTY. LEASTWAYS IT'S STEELED MY NERVE, SO I CAN ASK WHAT I'M AFRAID TO ASK.
YOU WANNA KNOW WHAT'S HAPPENED TO YOUR FAMILY?
YES.
WELL, ON THAT ACCOUNT, AT LEAST, I'VE GOT SOME GOOD NEWS FOR YOU.
THEY'RE ALIVE.
OH, THANK GOD. WHERE ARE THEY?
THEY'RE WITH ONE OF THOSE POCKETS OF LUDDITES I WAS TELLING YOU ABOUT, HIDDEN IN A SUBTERRANEAN CITY BENEATH NEW AMSTERDAM, A PLACE CALLED CHINATOWN.
CHINATOWN? I NEVER HEARD OF IT.
NOR WOULD YOU HAVE, I SUPPOSE, BEING A MAN SEEMINGLY FREE OF VICE. CHINA TOWN WAS TUNNELED OUT YEARS AGO BY, WELL, THE CHINESE.
BEFORE THE WAR, CHINATOWN WAS A PLACE FOR PEOPLE TO ENGAGE IN THEIR ARIOUS VICES, DRINKING, WHORING, OPIUM, COCAINE, ALL OUTTA THE SIGHT OF RESPECTABLE SOCIETY.
APPARENTLY THE SECRET WAS WELL KEPT, FOR TIBERIUS HAS YET TO FIND IT.
ALL I WANNA KNOW IS, HOW DO I FIND IT?
WELL, I GOT MORE GOOD NEWS FOR YE, JOHN. IT JUST SO HAPPENS THAT'S OUR DESTINATION. WE'LL BE THERE IN THREE DAYS TIME.
I 'SPECT YOU'RE WEAK FROM BEING LAYED UP SO LONG. YOU SHOULD USE THAT TIME TO REST.
IF IT'S ALL THE SAME TO YOU, CAPTAIN, I'D FEEL A LOT MORE COMFORTABLE PULLING MY OWN WEIGHT, ESPECIALLY CONSIDERING I'VE GOT A LOT MORE OF IT TO PULL THAN THE REST YOUR CREW.
HA! GOOD! THAT'S THE JOHN I KNOW.
WELCOME ABOARD, SON.

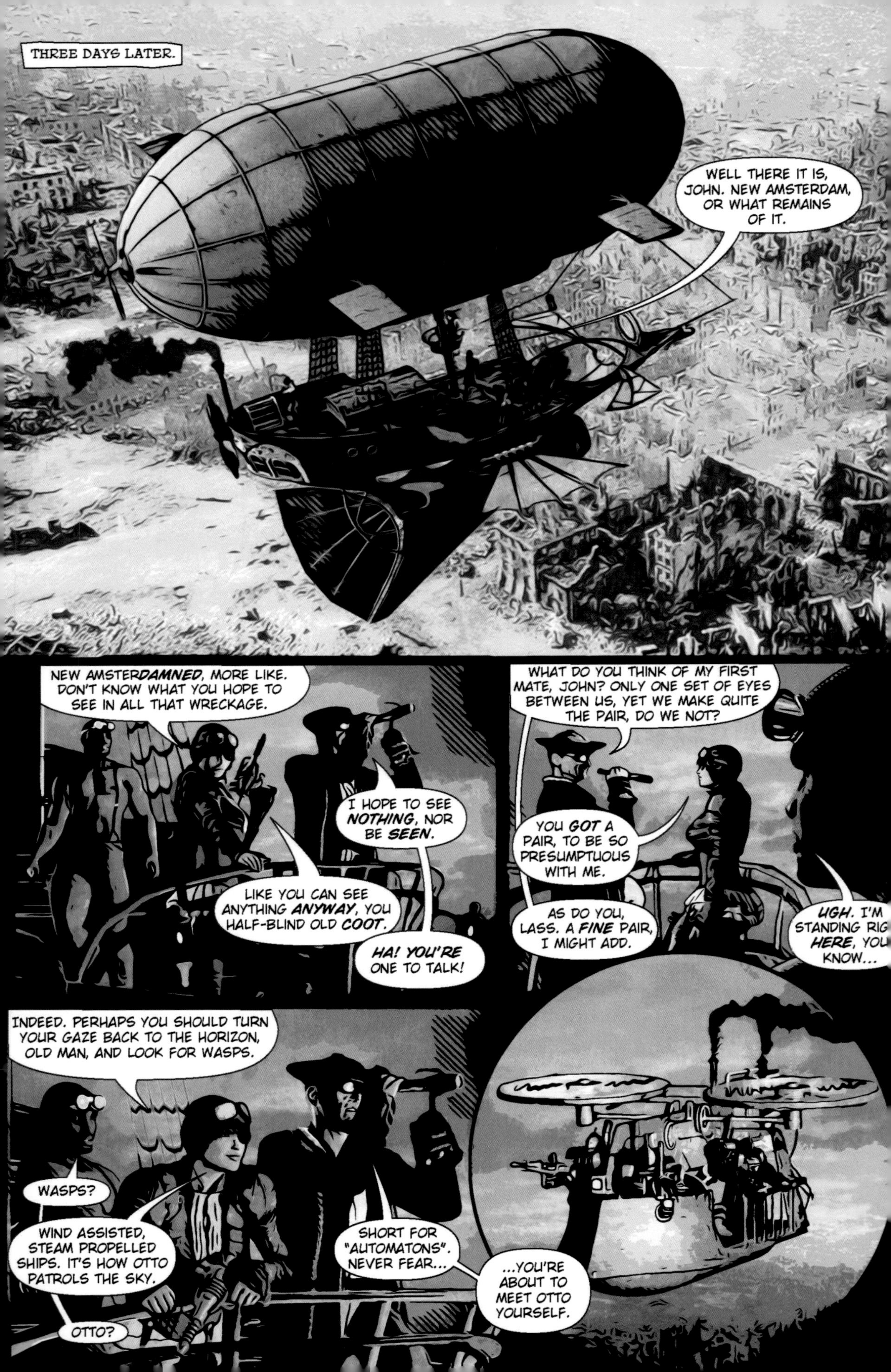
THREE DAYS LATER.
WELL THERE IT IS, JOHN. NEW AMSTERDAM, OR WHAT REMAINS OF IT.
NEW AMSTERDAMNED, MORE LIKE. DON'T KNOW WHAT YOU HOPE TO SEE IN ALL THAT WRECKAGE.
I HOPE TO SEE NOTHING, NOR BE SEEN.
LIKE YOU CAN SEE ANYTHING ANYWAY, YOU HALF-BLIND OLD COOT.
HA! YOU'RE ONE TO TALK!
WHAT DO YOU THINK OF MY FIRST MATE, JOHN? ONLY ONE SET OF EYES BETWEEN US, YET WE MAKE QUITE THE PAIR, DO WE NOT?
YOU GOT A PAIR, TO BE SO PRESUMPTUOUS WITH ME.
AS DO YOU, LASS. A FINE PAIR, I MIGHT ADD.
UGH. I'M STANDING RIG HERE, YOU KNOW...
INDEED. PERHAPS YOU SHOULD TURN YOUR GAZE BACK TO THE HORIZON, OLD MAN, AND LOOK FOR WASPS.
WASPS?
WIND ASSISTED, STEAM PROPELLED SHIPS. IT'S HOW OTTO PATROLS THE SKY.
OTTO?
SHORT FOR "AUTOMATONS". NEVER FEAR...
...YOU'RE ABOUT TO MEET OTTO YOURSELF.

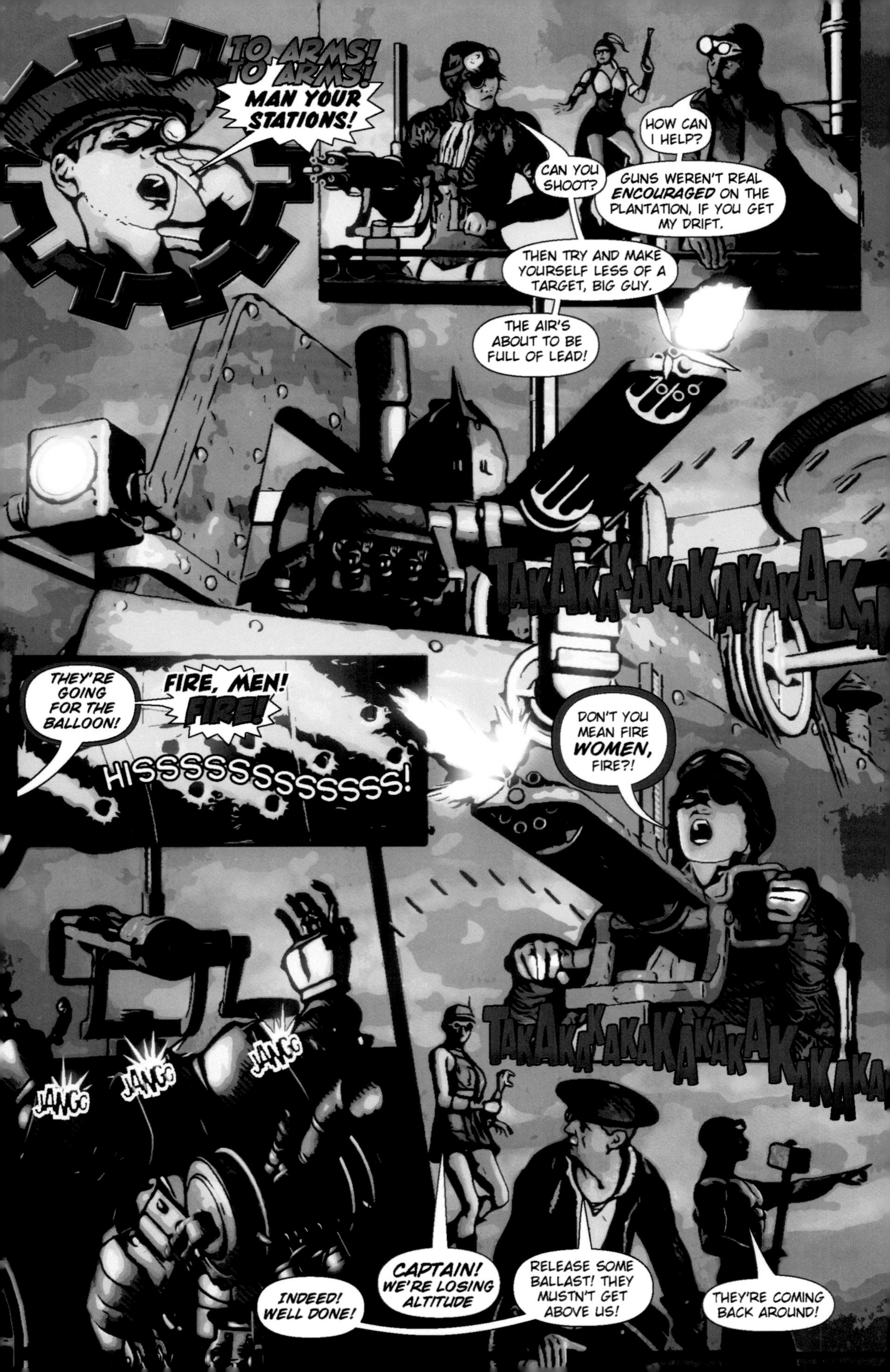

TO ARMS! TO ARMS!
MAN YOUR STATIONS!
HOW CAN I HELP?
CAN YOU SHOOT?
GUNS WEREN'T REAL ENCOURAGED ON THE PLANTATION, IF YOU GET MY DRIFT.
THEN TRY AND MAKE YOURSELF LESS OF A TARGET, BIG GUY.
THE AIR'S ABOUT TO BE FULL OF LEAD!
TAKAKAKAKAKAKAKAKAKAKA
THEY'RE GOING FOR THE BALLOON!
FIRE, MEN! FIRE!
HISSSSSSSSSSSSS!
DON'T YOU MEAN FIRE WOMEN, FIRE?!
TAKAKAKAKAKAKAKAKAKAKA
JANGG
JANGG
JANGG
INDEED! WELL DONE!
CAPTAIN! WE'RE LOSING ALTITUDE
RELEASE SOME BALLAST! THEY MUSTN'T GET ABOVE US!
THEY'RE COMING BACK AROUND!

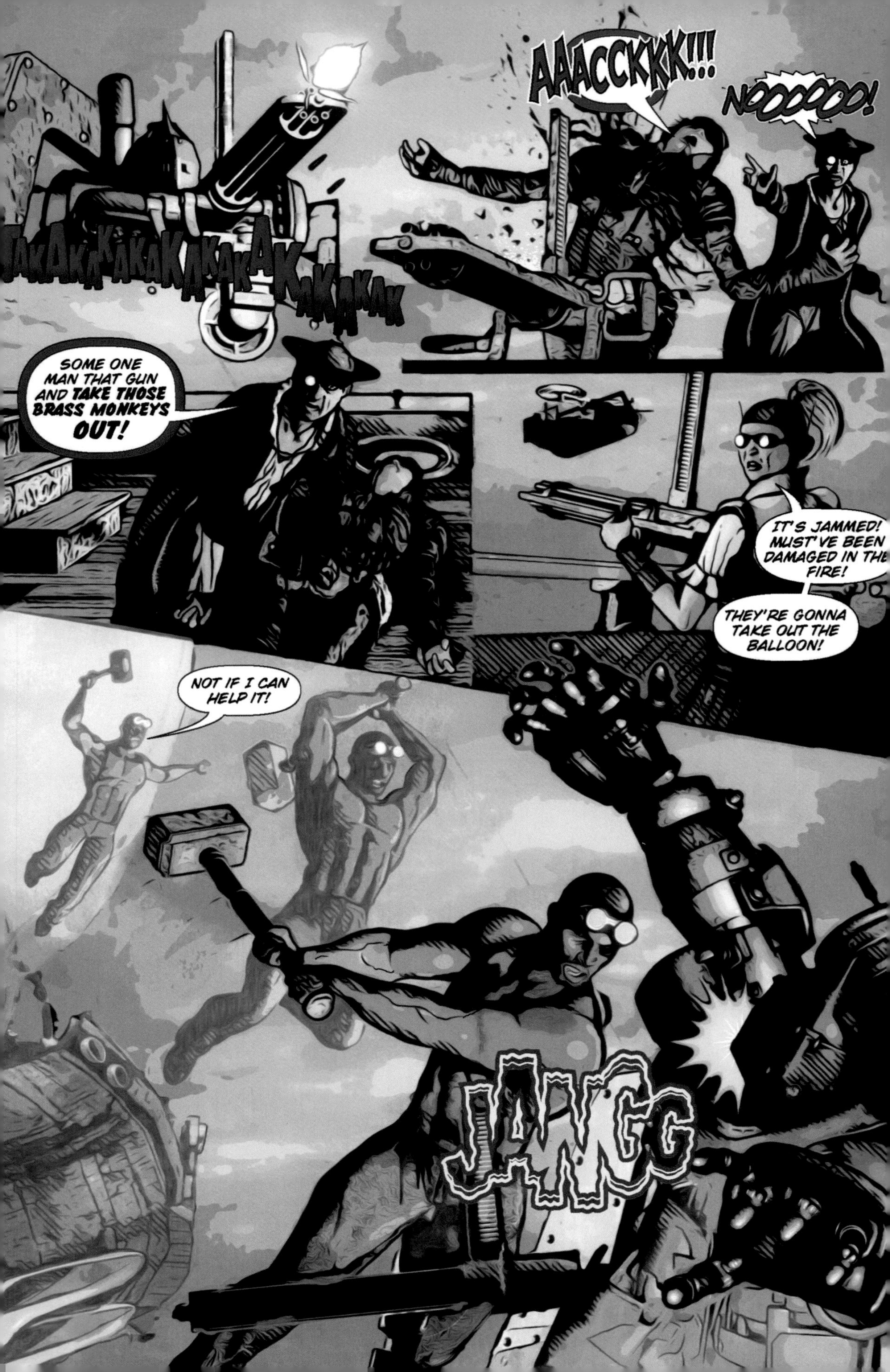
TAKAKAKAKAKAKAKAKAKAKAKAKAK
AAACCKKK!!!
NOOOOOO!
SOME ONE MAN THAT GUN AND TAKE THOSE BRASS MONKEYS OUT!
IT'S JAMMED! MUST'VE BEEN DAMAGED IN THE FIRE!
THEY'RE GONNA TAKE OUT THE BALLOON!
NOT IF I CAN HELP IT!
JANGG

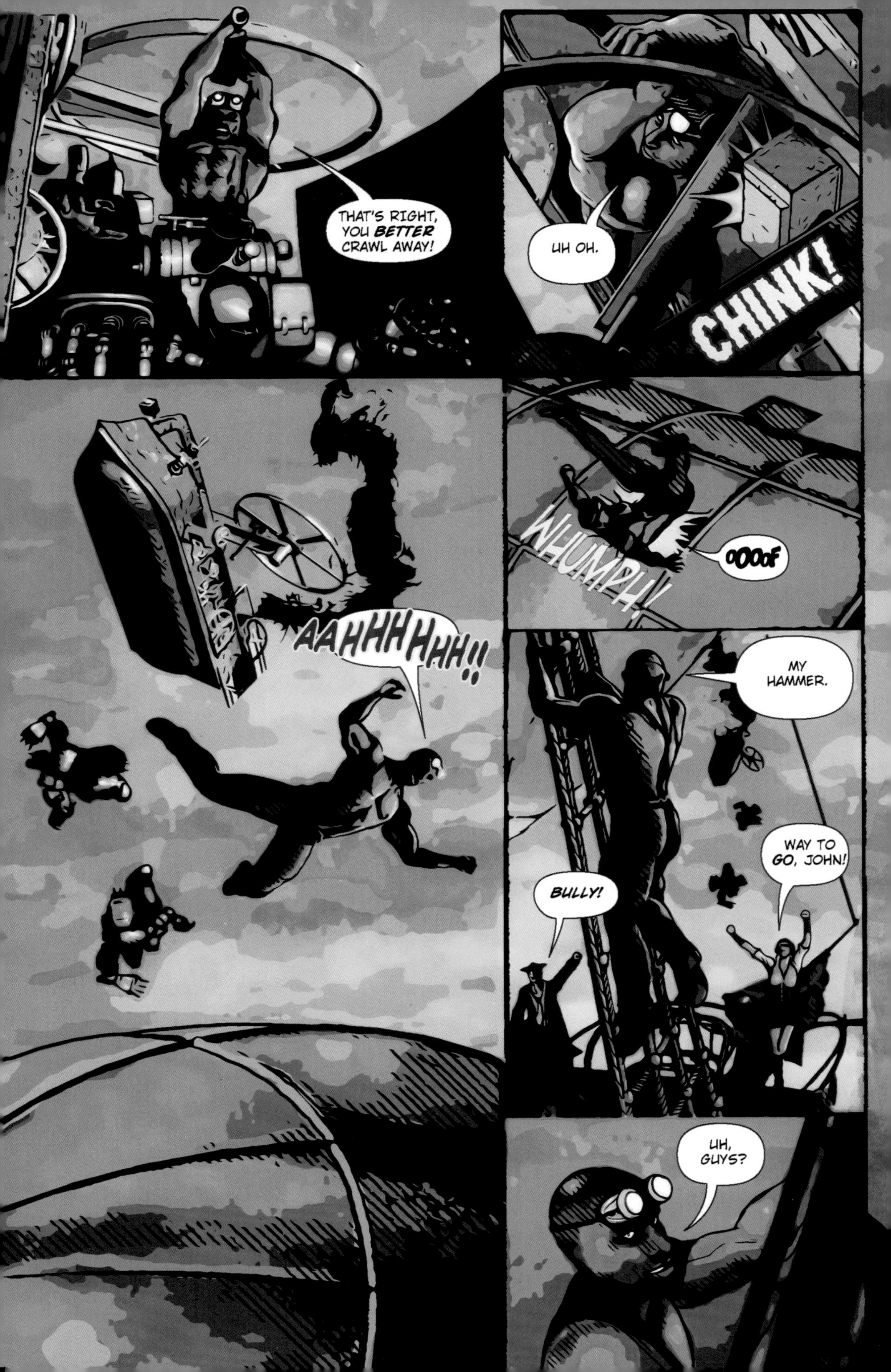
THAT'S RIGHT, YOU BETTER CRAWL AWAY!
UH OH.
CHINK!
AAHHHHHH!!
WHUMPH!
OOOof
MY HAMMER.
WAY TO GO, JOHN!
BULLY!
UH, GUYS?

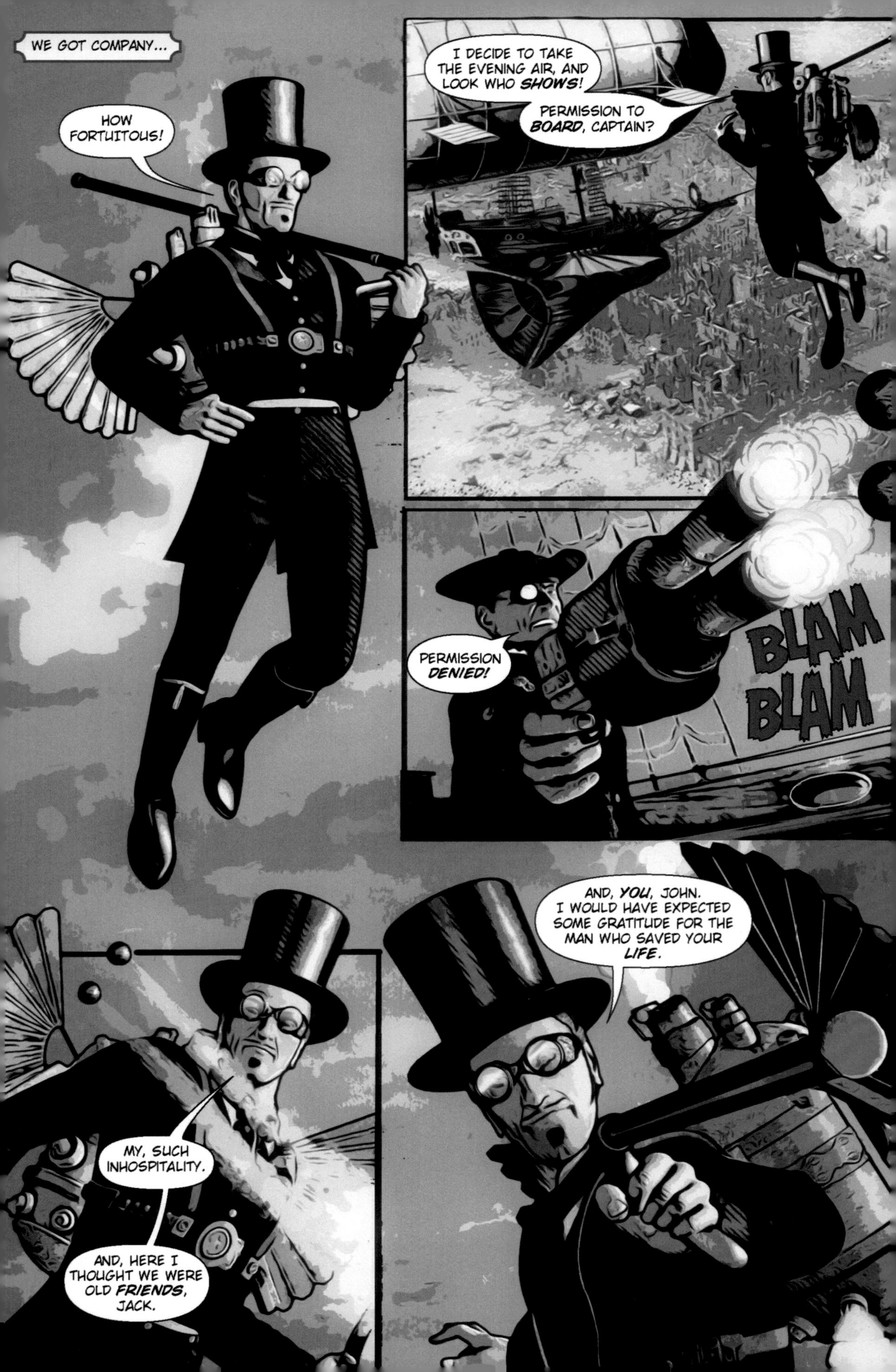

WE GOT COMPANY...
HOW FORTUITOUS!
I DECIDE TO TAKE THE EVENING AIR, AND LOOK WHO SHOWS!
PERMISSION TO BOARD, CAPTAIN?
PERMISSION DENIED!
BLAM BLAM
MY, SUCH INHOSPITALITY.
AND, HERE I THOUGHT WE WERE OLD FRIENDS, JACK.
AND, YOU, JOHN. I WOULD HAVE EXPECTED SOME GRATITUDE FOR THE MAN WHO SAVED YOUR LIFE.

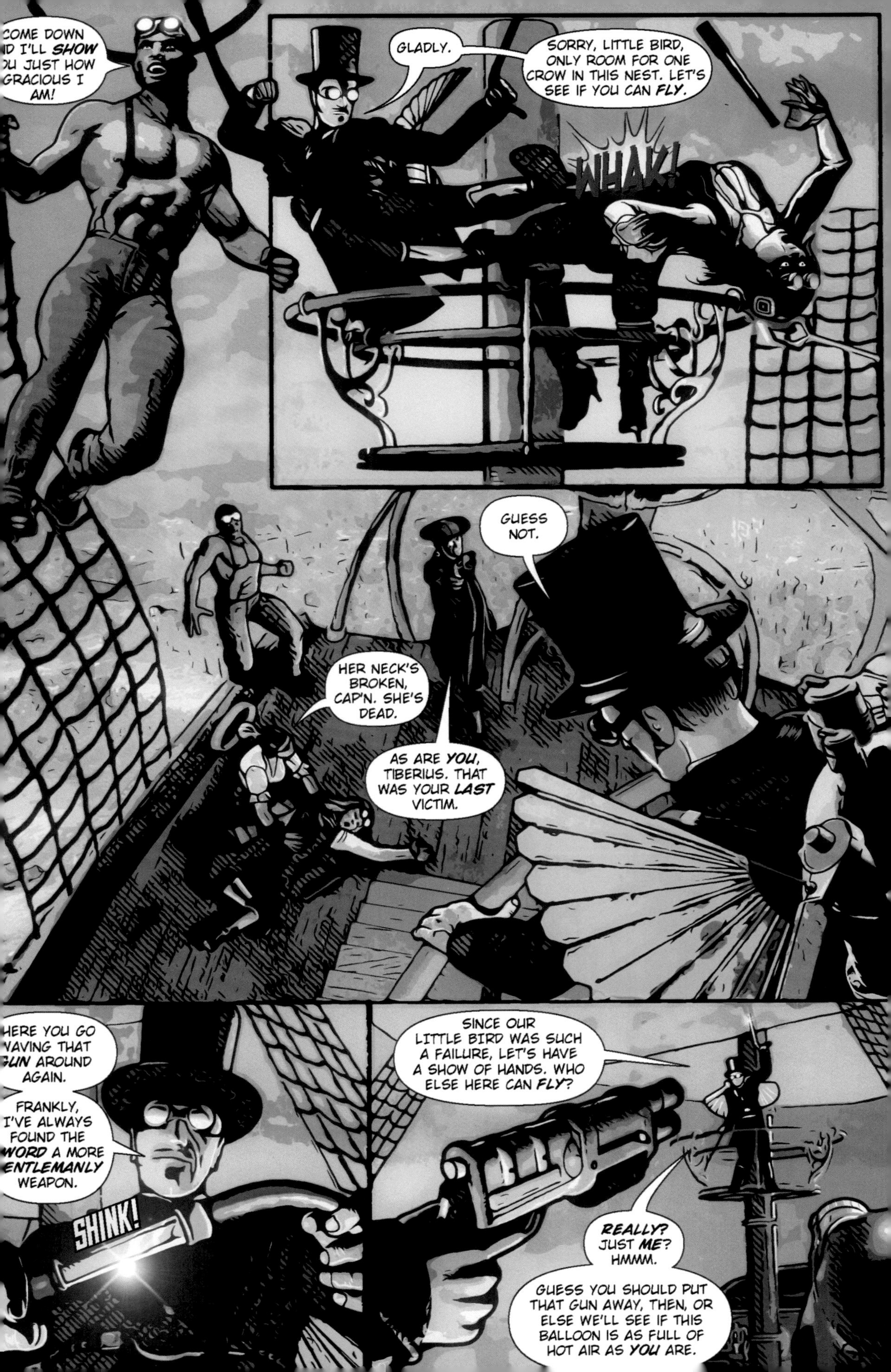

COME DOWN
ID I'LL SHOW
OU JUST HOW
GRACIOUS I
AM!
GLADLY.
SORRY, LITTLE BIRD, ONLY ROOM FOR ONE CROW IN THIS NEST. LET'S SEE IF YOU CAN FLY.
WHAK!
GUESS NOT.
HER NECK'S BROKEN, CAP'N. SHE'S DEAD.
AS ARE YOU, TIBERIUS. THAT WAS YOUR LAST VICTIM.
HERE YOU GO
VAVING THAT
GUN AROUND
AGAIN.
FRANKLY,
I'VE ALWAYS
FOUND THE
WORD A MORE
ENTLEMANLY
WEAPON.
SHINK!
SINCE OUR LITTLE BIRD WAS SUCH A FAILURE, LET'S HAVE A SHOW OF HANDS. WHO ELSE HERE CAN FLY?
REALLY? JUST ME? HMMM.
GUESS YOU SHOULD PUT THAT GUN AWAY, THEN, OR ELSE WE'LL SEE IF THIS BALLOON IS AS FULL OF HOT AIR AS YOU ARE.

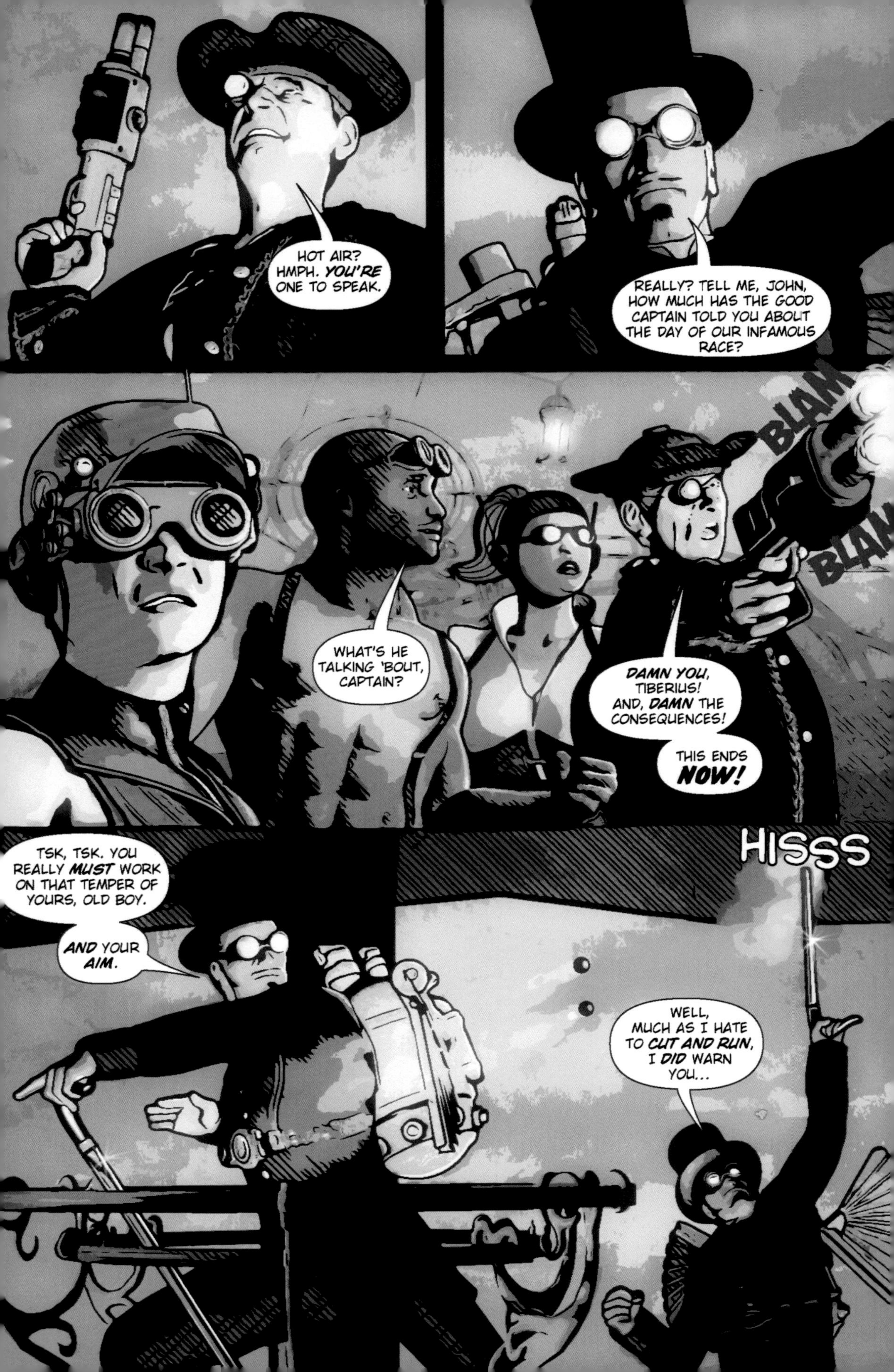
HOT AIR? HMPH. *YOU'RE* ONE TO SPEAK.
REALLY? TELL ME, JOHN, HOW MUCH HAS THE GOOD CAPTAIN TOLD YOU ABOUT THE DAY OF OUR INFAMOUS RACE?
WHAT'S HE TALKING 'BOUT, CAPTAIN?
DAMN YOU, TIBERIUS! AND, *DAMN* THE CONSEQUENCES!
THIS ENDS *NOW!*
HISSS
TSK, TSK. YOU REALLY *MUST* WORK ON THAT TEMPER OF YOURS, OLD BOY.
AND YOUR *AIM*.
WELL, MUCH AS I HATE TO *CUT AND RUN*, I *DID* WARN YOU...

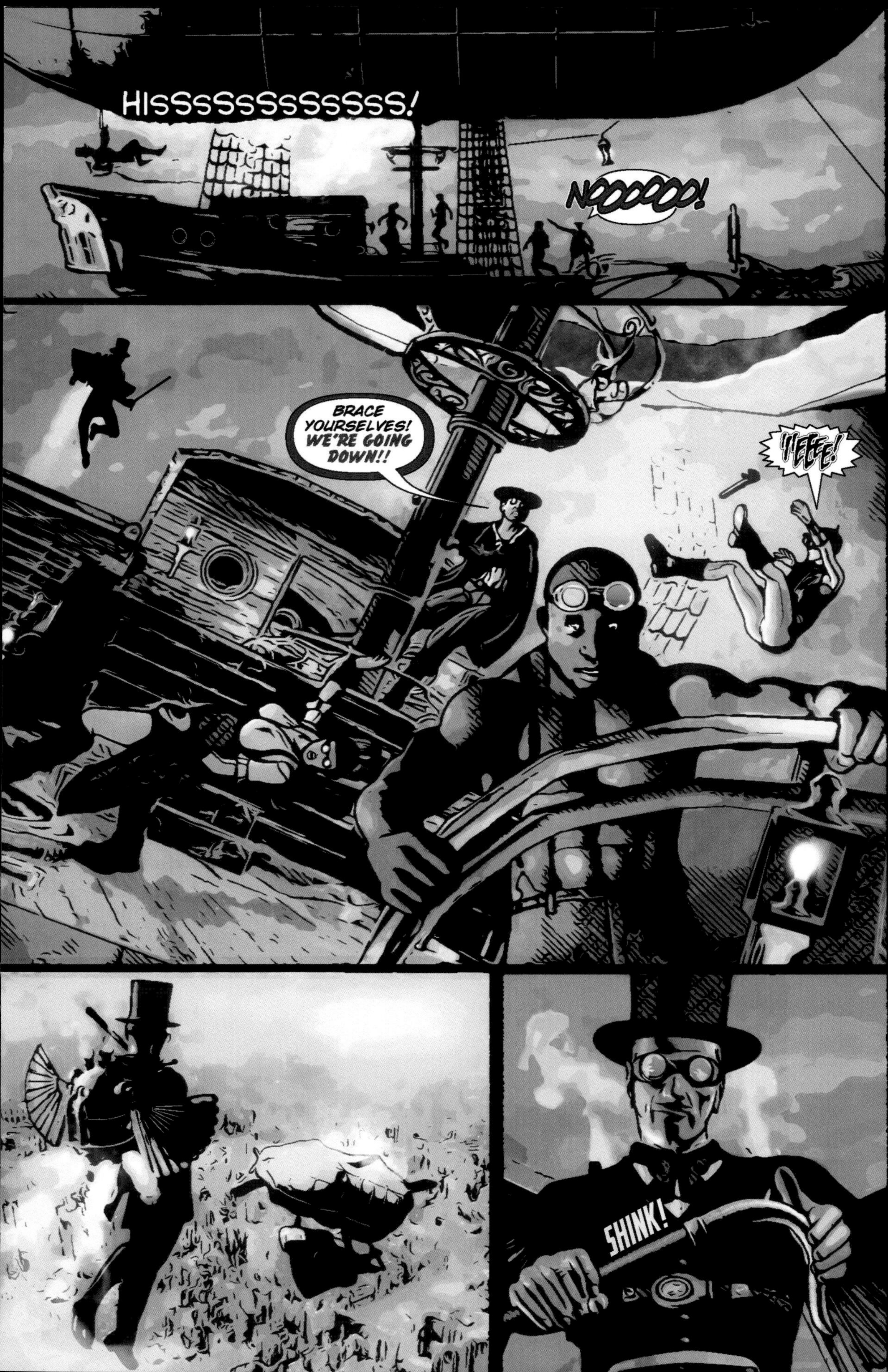
HISSSSSSSSSSSS!
NOOOOO!
BRACE YOURSELVES! WE'RE GOING DOWN!!
YIEEE!
SHINK!

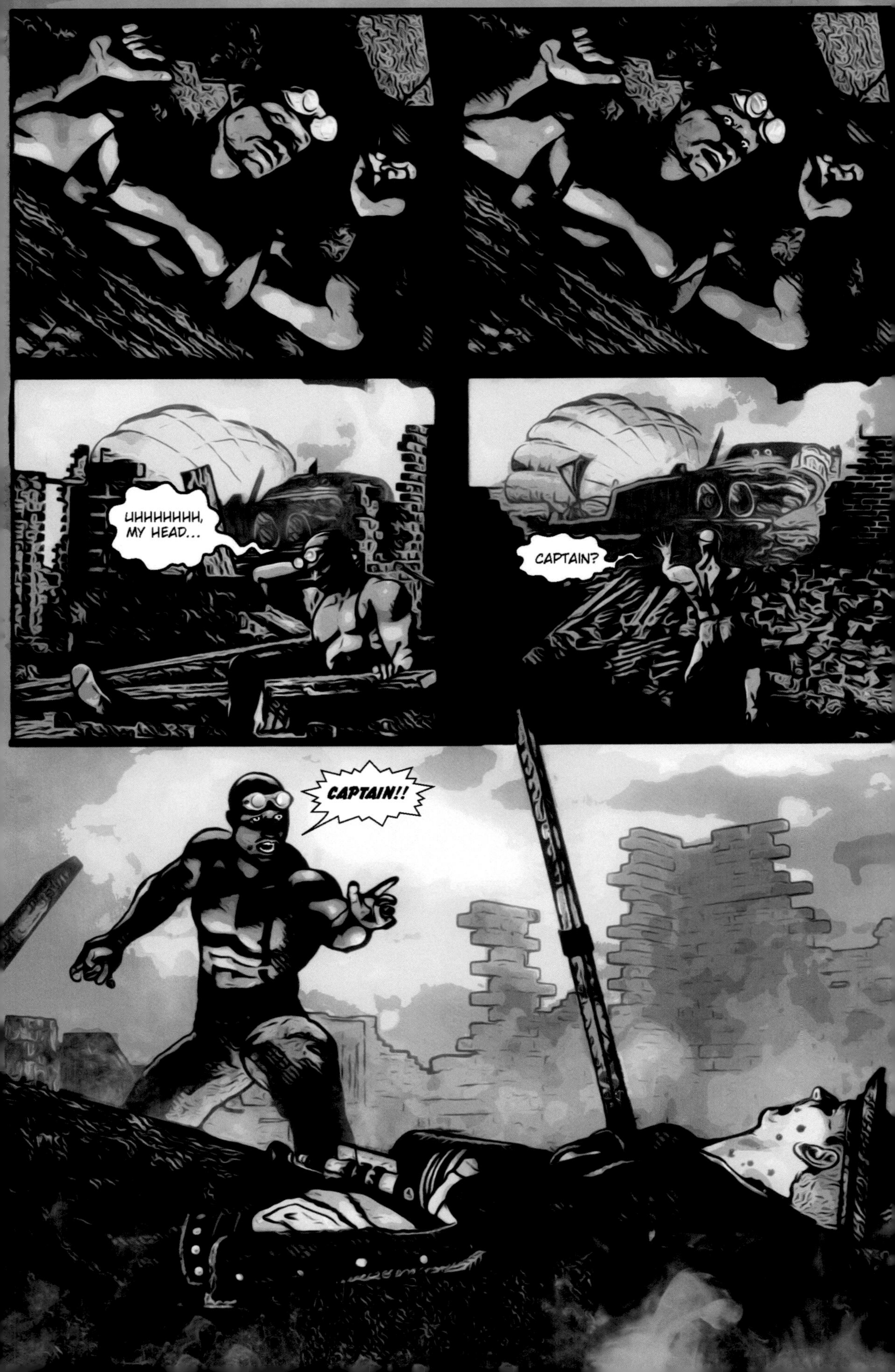
UHHHHHHH,
MY HEAD...
CAPTAIN?
CAPTAIN!!

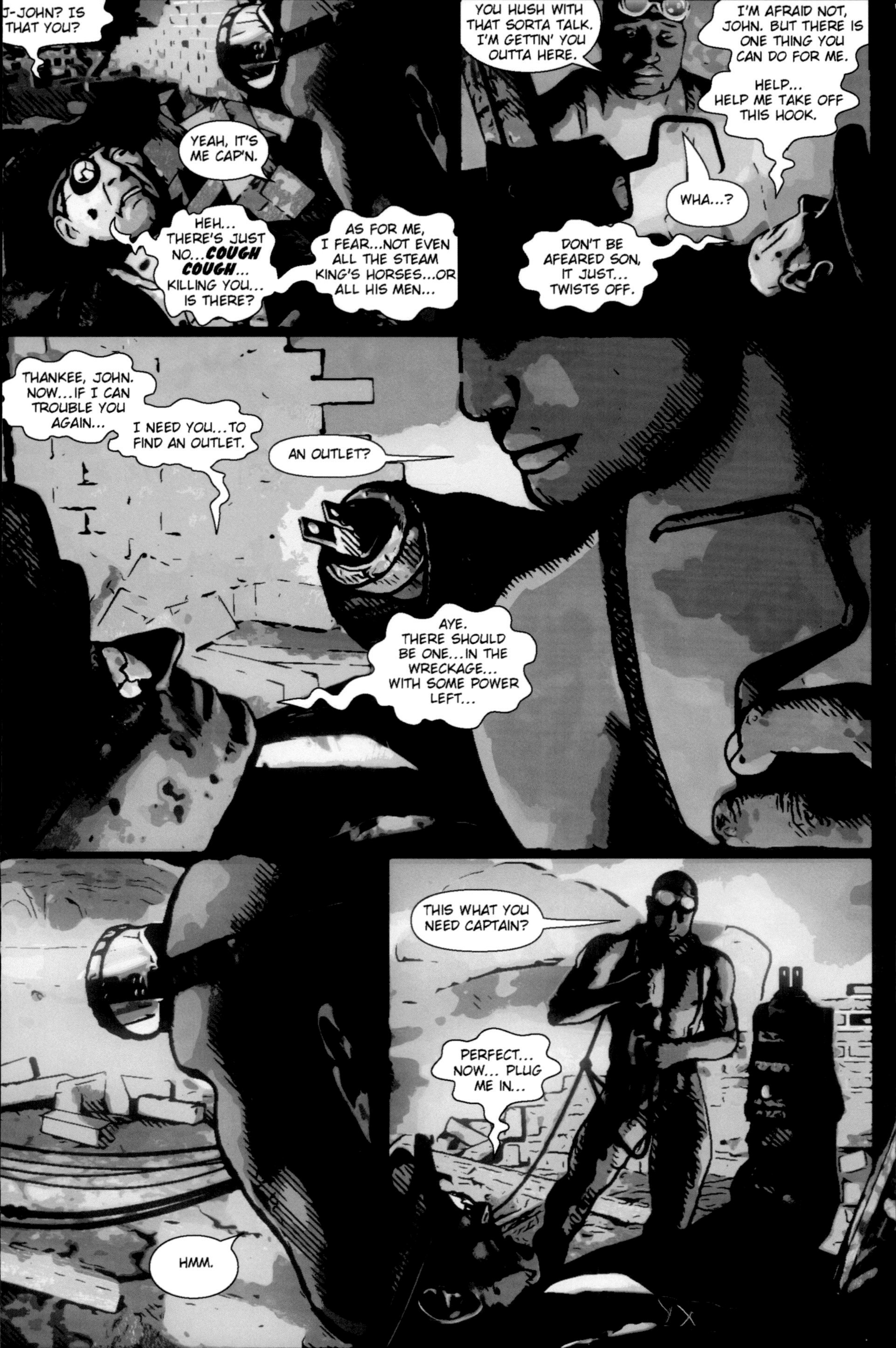
J-JOHN? IS THAT YOU?
YEAH, IT'S ME CAP'N.
HEH... THERE'S JUST NO...**COUGH COUGH**... KILLING YOU... IS THERE?
AS FOR ME, I FEAR...NOT EVEN ALL THE STEAM KING'S HORSES...OR ALL HIS MEN...
YOU HUSH WITH THAT SORTA TALK. I'M GETTIN' YOU OUTTA HERE.
I'M AFRAID NOT, JOHN. BUT THERE IS ONE THING YOU CAN DO FOR ME.
HELP... HELP ME TAKE OFF THIS HOOK.
WHA...?
DON'T BE AFEARED SON, IT JUST... TWISTS OFF.
THANKEE, JOHN. NOW...IF I CAN TROUBLE YOU AGAIN...
I NEED YOU...TO FIND AN OUTLET.
AN OUTLET?
AYE. THERE SHOULD BE ONE...IN THE WRECKAGE... WITH SOME POWER LEFT...
HMM.
THIS WHAT YOU NEED CAPTAIN?
PERFECT... NOW... PLUG ME IN...

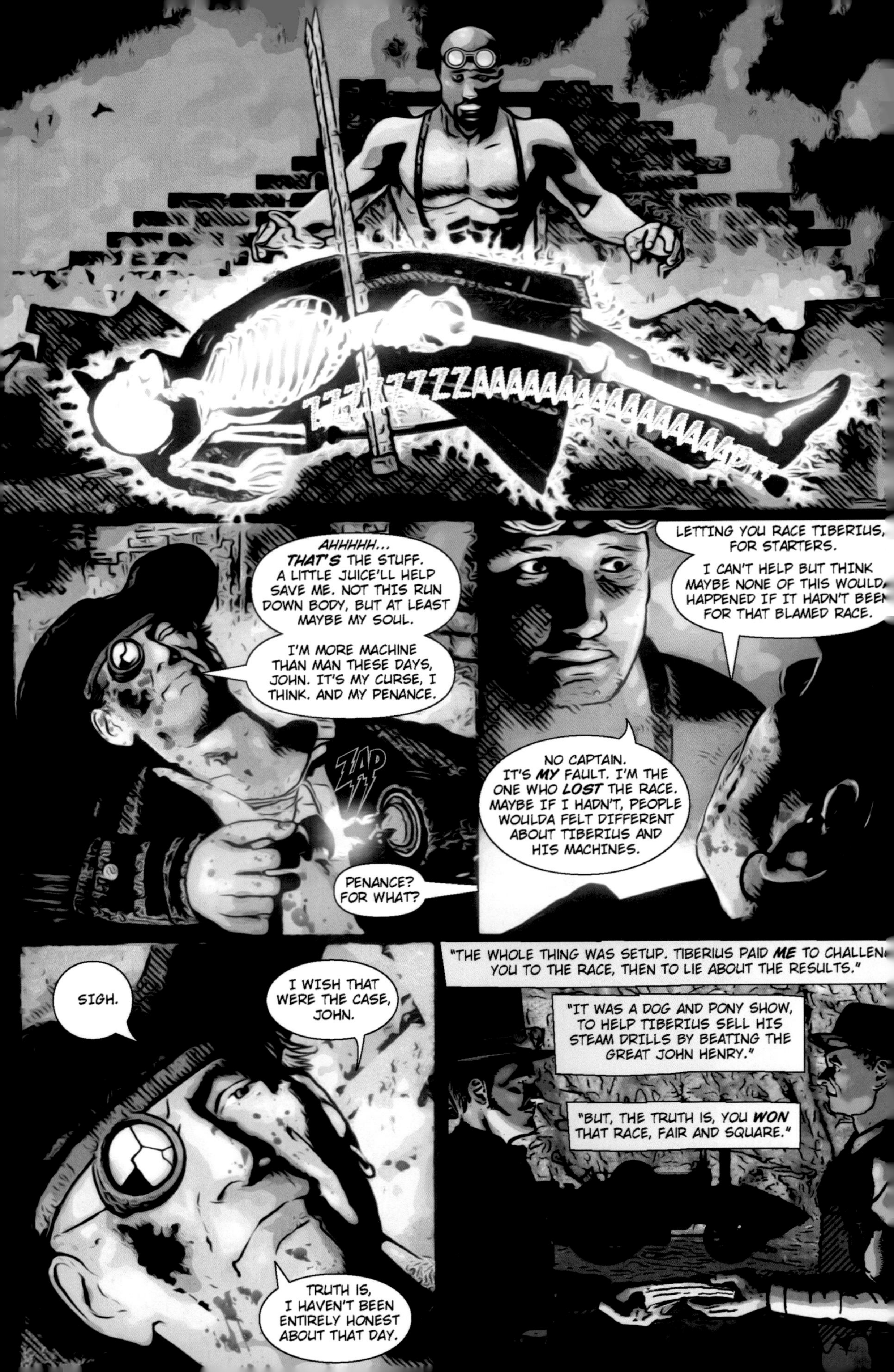
ZZZZZZZZAAAAAAAAAAAAAAAAAAAAAP!!
AHHHHH... THAT'S THE STUFF. A LITTLE JUICE'LL HELP SAVE ME. NOT THIS RUN DOWN BODY, BUT AT LEAST MAYBE MY SOUL.
I'M MORE MACHINE THAN MAN THESE DAYS, JOHN. IT'S MY CURSE, I THINK. AND MY PENANCE.
ZAP
PENANCE? FOR WHAT?
LETTING YOU RACE TIBERIUS, FOR STARTERS.
I CAN'T HELP BUT THINK MAYBE NONE OF THIS WOULD HAPPENED IF IT HADN'T BEEN FOR THAT BLAMED RACE.
NO CAPTAIN. IT'S MY FAULT. I'M THE ONE WHO LOST THE RACE. MAYBE IF I HADN'T, PEOPLE WOULDA FELT DIFFERENT ABOUT TIBERIUS AND HIS MACHINES.
SIGH.
I WISH THAT WERE THE CASE, JOHN.
TRUTH IS, I HAVEN'T BEEN ENTIRELY HONEST ABOUT THAT DAY.
"THE WHOLE THING WAS SETUP. TIBERIUS PAID ME TO CHALLENGE YOU TO THE RACE, THEN TO LIE ABOUT THE RESULTS."
"IT WAS A DOG AND PONY SHOW, TO HELP TIBERIUS SELL HIS STEAM DRILLS BY BEATING THE GREAT JOHN HENRY."
"BUT, THE TRUTH IS, YOU WON THAT RACE, FAIR AND SQUARE."

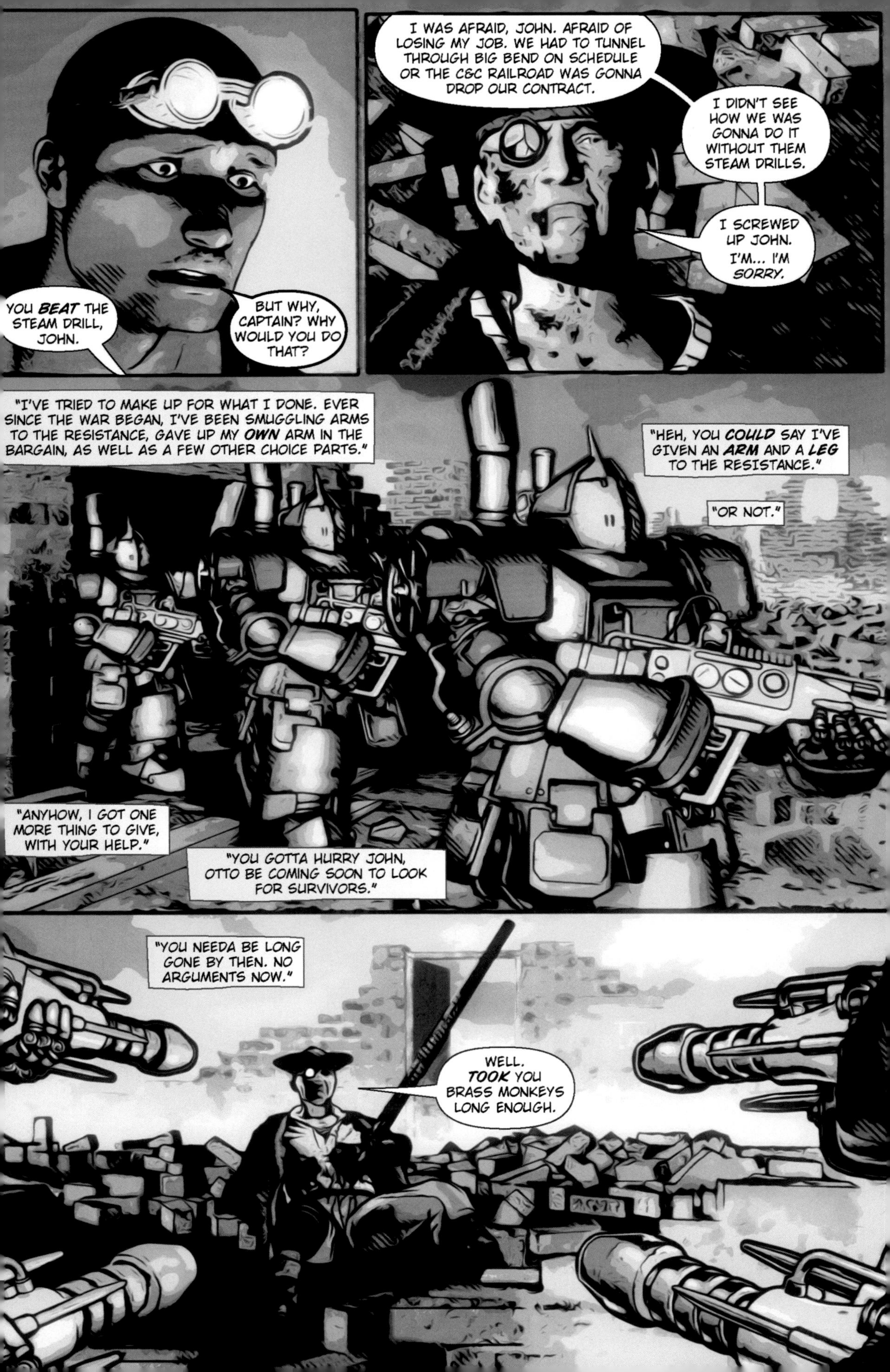
YOU *BEAT* THE STEAM DRILL, JOHN.
BUT WHY, CAPTAIN? WHY WOULD YOU DO THAT?
I WAS AFRAID, JOHN. AFRAID OF LOSING MY JOB. WE HAD TO TUNNEL THROUGH BIG BEND ON SCHEDULE OR THE C&C RAILROAD WAS GONNA DROP OUR CONTRACT.
I DIDN'T SEE HOW WE WAS GONNA DO IT WITHOUT THEM STEAM DRILLS.
I SCREWED UP JOHN.
I'M... I'M *SORRY.*
"I'VE TRIED TO MAKE UP FOR WHAT I DONE. EVER SINCE THE WAR BEGAN, I'VE BEEN SMUGGLING ARMS TO THE RESISTANCE, GAVE UP MY *OWN* ARM IN THE BARGAIN, AS WELL AS A FEW OTHER CHOICE PARTS."
"HEH, YOU *COULD* SAY I'VE GIVEN AN *ARM* AND A *LEG* TO THE RESISTANCE."
"OR NOT."
"ANYHOW, I GOT ONE MORE THING TO GIVE, WITH YOUR HELP."
"YOU GOTTA HURRY JOHN, OTTO BE COMING SOON TO LOOK FOR SURVIVORS."
"YOU NEEDA BE LONG GONE BY THEN. NO ARGUMENTS NOW."
WELL. *TOOK* YOU BRASS MONKEYS LONG ENOUGH.

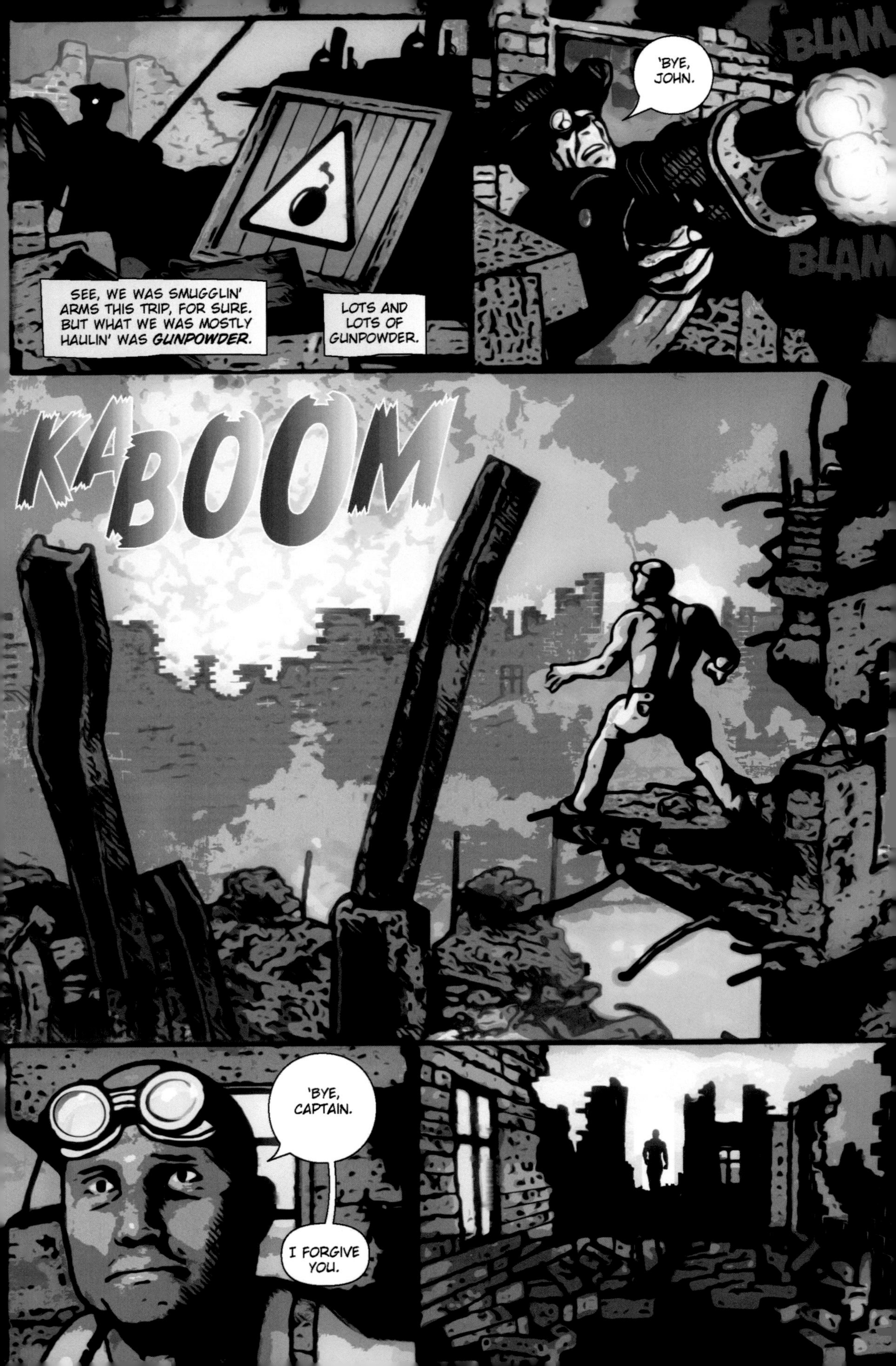
SEE, WE WAS SMUGGLIN' ARMS THIS TRIP, FOR SURE. BUT WHAT WE WAS MOSTLY HAULIN' WAS GUNPOWDER.
LOTS AND LOTS OF GUNPOWDER.
'BYE, JOHN.
BLAM
BLAM
KABOOM
'BYE, CAPTAIN.
I FORGIVE YOU.

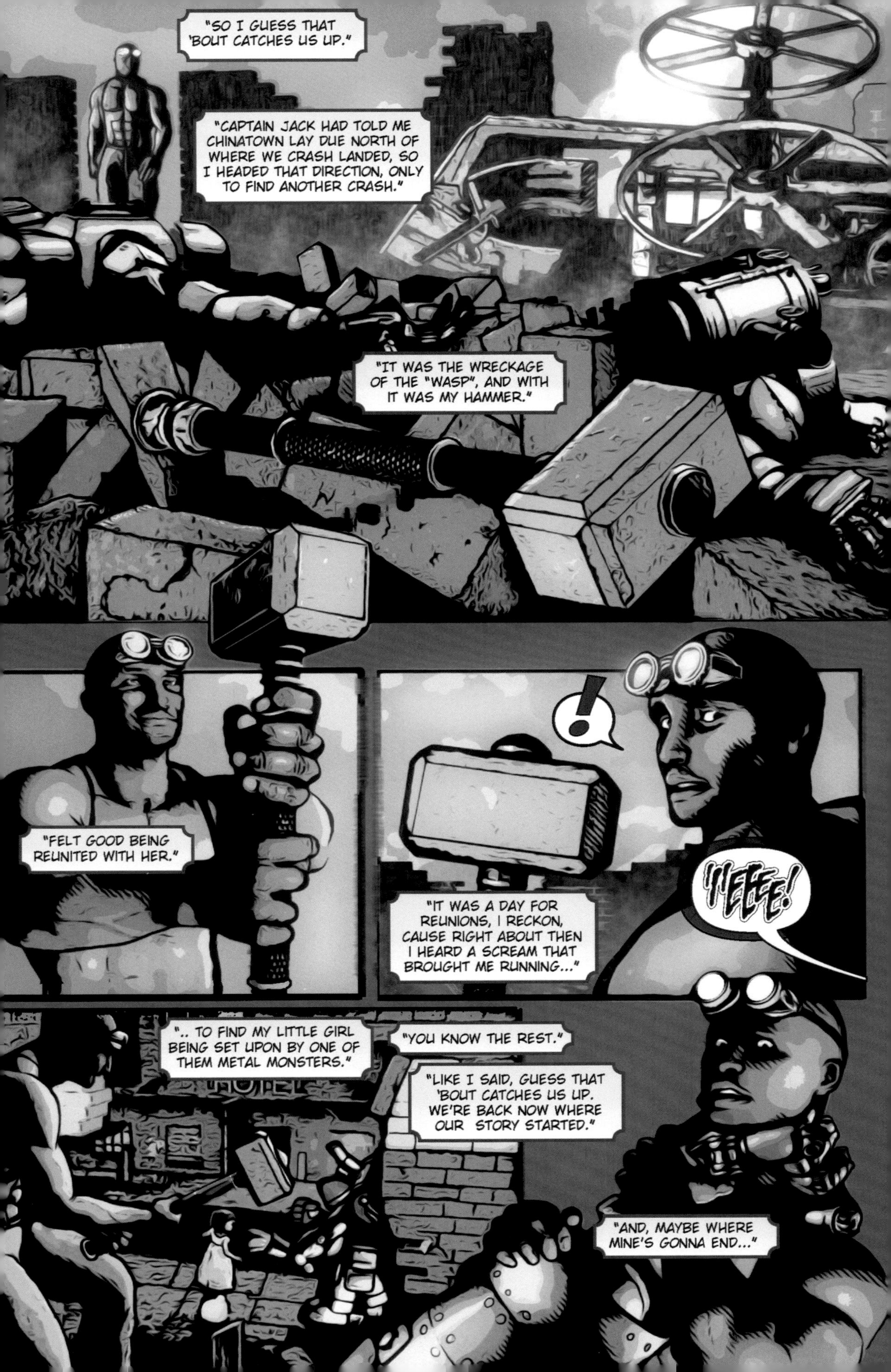
"SO I GUESS THAT 'BOUT CATCHES US UP."
"CAPTAIN JACK HAD TOLD ME CHINATOWN LAY DUE NORTH OF WHERE WE CRASH LANDED, SO I HEADED THAT DIRECTION, ONLY TO FIND ANOTHER CRASH."
"IT WAS THE WRECKAGE OF THE "WASP", AND WITH IT WAS MY HAMMER."
"FELT GOOD BEING REUNITED WITH HER."
!
"IT WAS A DAY FOR REUNIONS, I RECKON, CAUSE RIGHT ABOUT THEN I HEARD A SCREAM THAT BROUGHT ME RUNNING..."
"IEEEE!
".. TO FIND MY LITTLE GIRL BEING SET UPON BY ONE OF THEM METAL MONSTERS."
"YOU KNOW THE REST."
"LIKE I SAID, GUESS THAT 'BOUT CATCHES US UP. WE'RE BACK NOW WHERE OUR STORY STARTED."
"AND, MAYBE WHERE MINE'S GONNA END..."

CHAPTER THREE

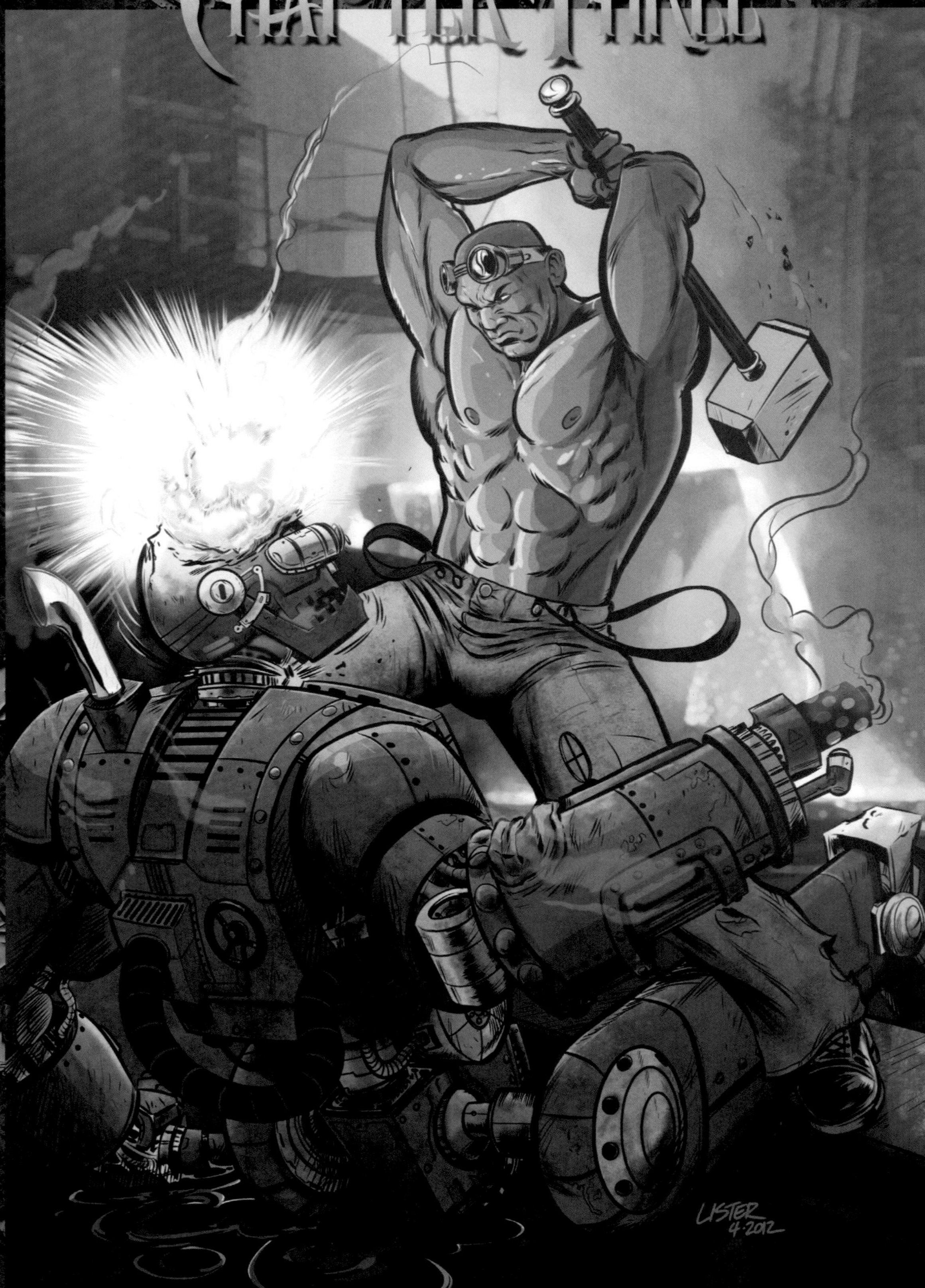
LISTER
4·2012

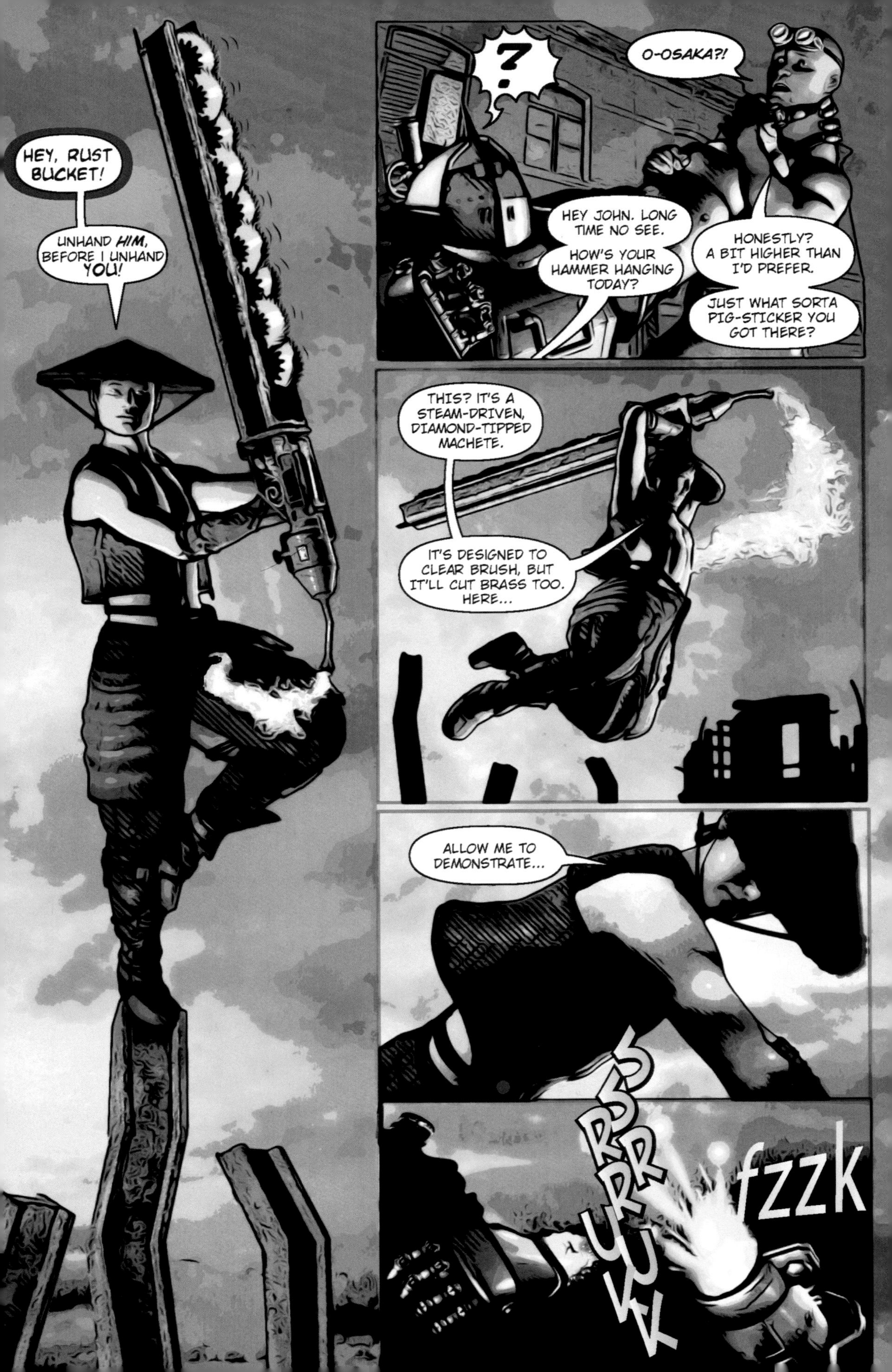
HEY, RUST BUCKET!
UNHAND HIM, BEFORE I UNHAND YOU!
?
O-OSAKA?!
HEY JOHN. LONG TIME NO SEE.
HOW'S YOUR HAMMER HANGING TODAY?
HONESTLY? A BIT HIGHER THAN I'D PREFER.
JUST WHAT SORTA PIG-STICKER YOU GOT THERE?
THIS? IT'S A STEAM-DRIVEN, DIAMOND-TIPPED MACHETE.
IT'S DESIGNED TO CLEAR BRUSH, BUT IT'LL CUT BRASS TOO. HERE...
ALLOW ME TO DEMONSTRATE...
fzzk

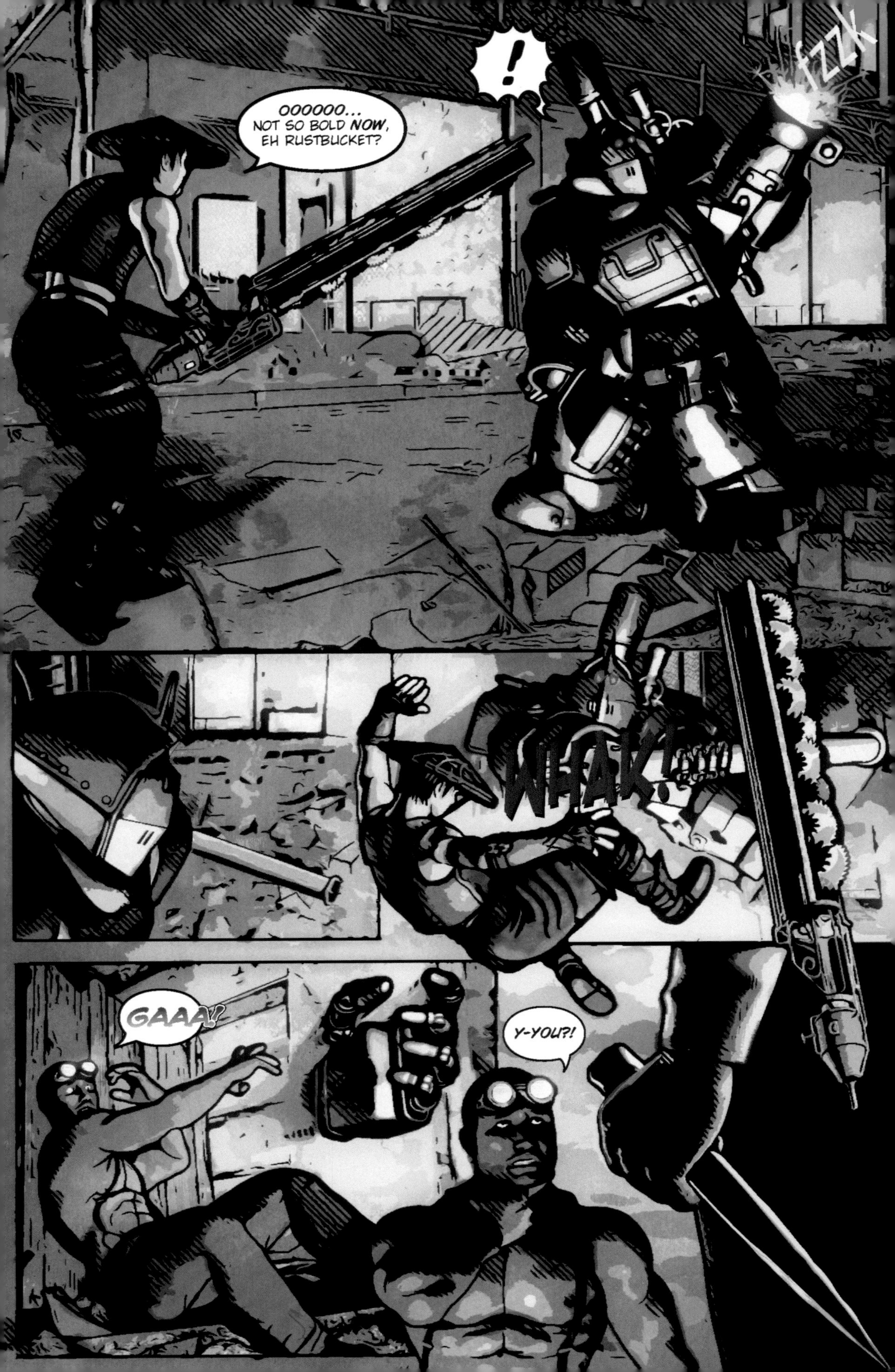
!
fzzk
OOOOOO...
NOT SO BOLD NOW,
EH RUSTBUCKET?
WHAK!
GAAA!
Y-YOU?!

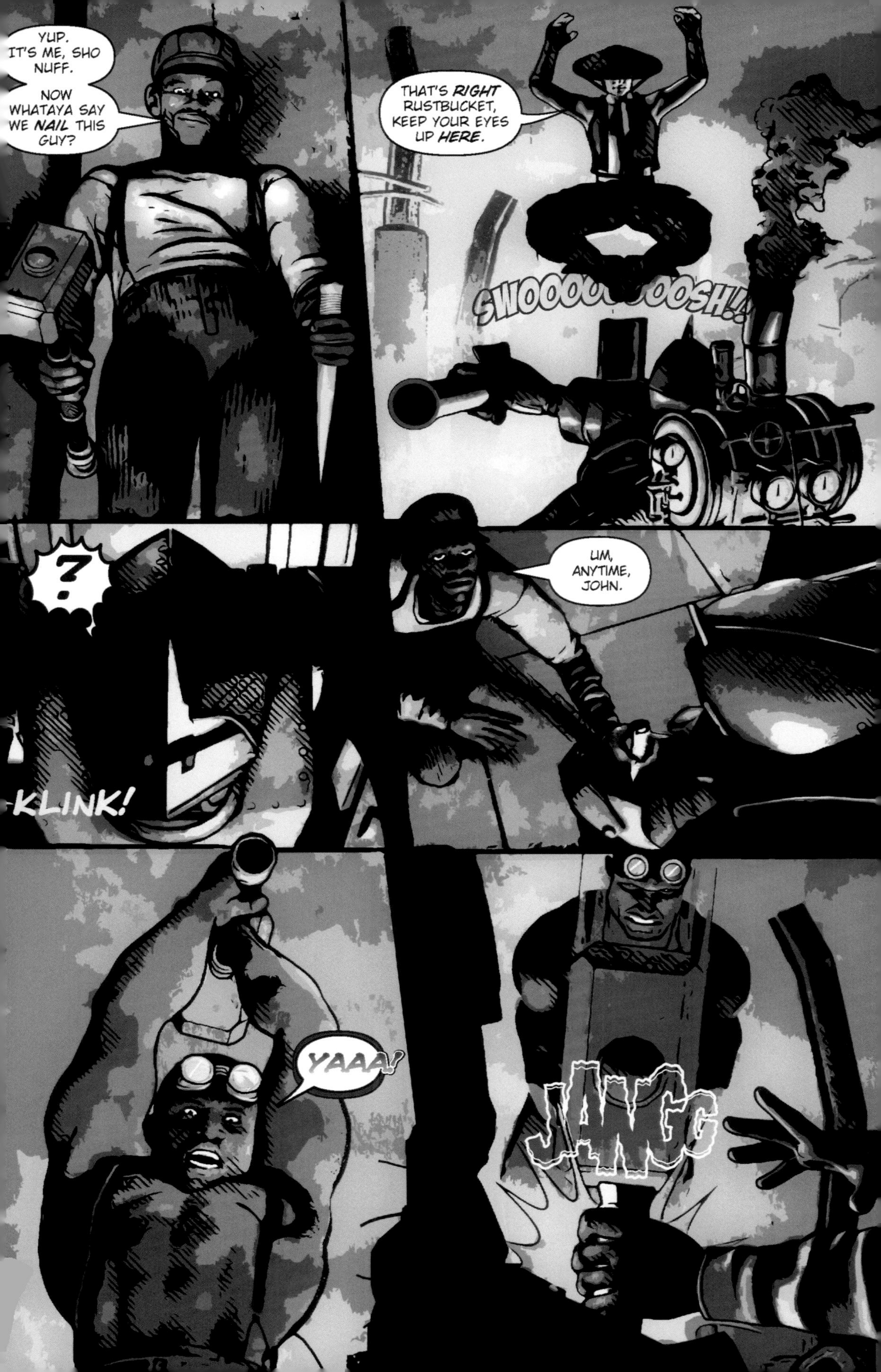
YUP. IT'S ME, SHO NUFF.
NOW WHATAYA SAY WE NAIL THIS GUY?
THAT'S RIGHT RUSTBUCKET, KEEP YOUR EYES UP HERE.
SWOOOO
OOSH!!
?
KLINK!
UM, ANYTIME, JOHN.
YAAA!
JANGG

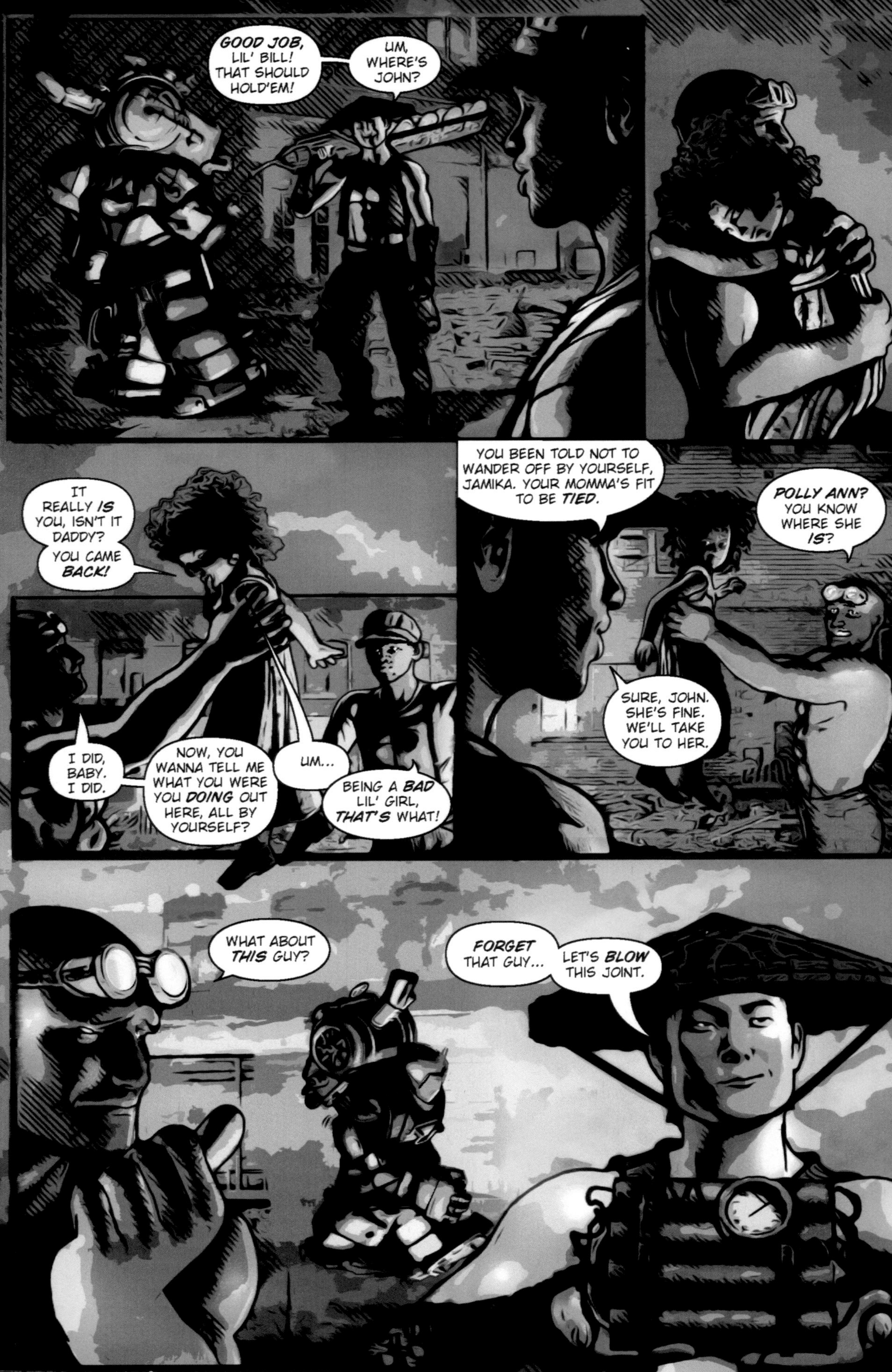
GOOD JOB, LIL' BILL! THAT SHOULD HOLD'EM!
UM, WHERE'S JOHN?
IT REALLY IS YOU, ISN'T IT DADDY?
YOU CAME BACK!
I DID, BABY. I DID.
NOW, YOU WANNA TELL ME WHAT YOU WERE YOU DOING OUT HERE, ALL BY YOURSELF?
UM...
BEING A BAD LIL' GIRL, THAT'S WHAT!
YOU BEEN TOLD NOT TO WANDER OFF BY YOURSELF, JAMIKA. YOUR MOMMA'S FIT TO BE TIED.
POLLY ANN? YOU KNOW WHERE SHE IS?
SURE, JOHN. SHE'S FINE. WE'LL TAKE YOU TO HER.
WHAT ABOUT THIS GUY?
FORGET THAT GUY...
LET'S BLOW THIS JOINT.

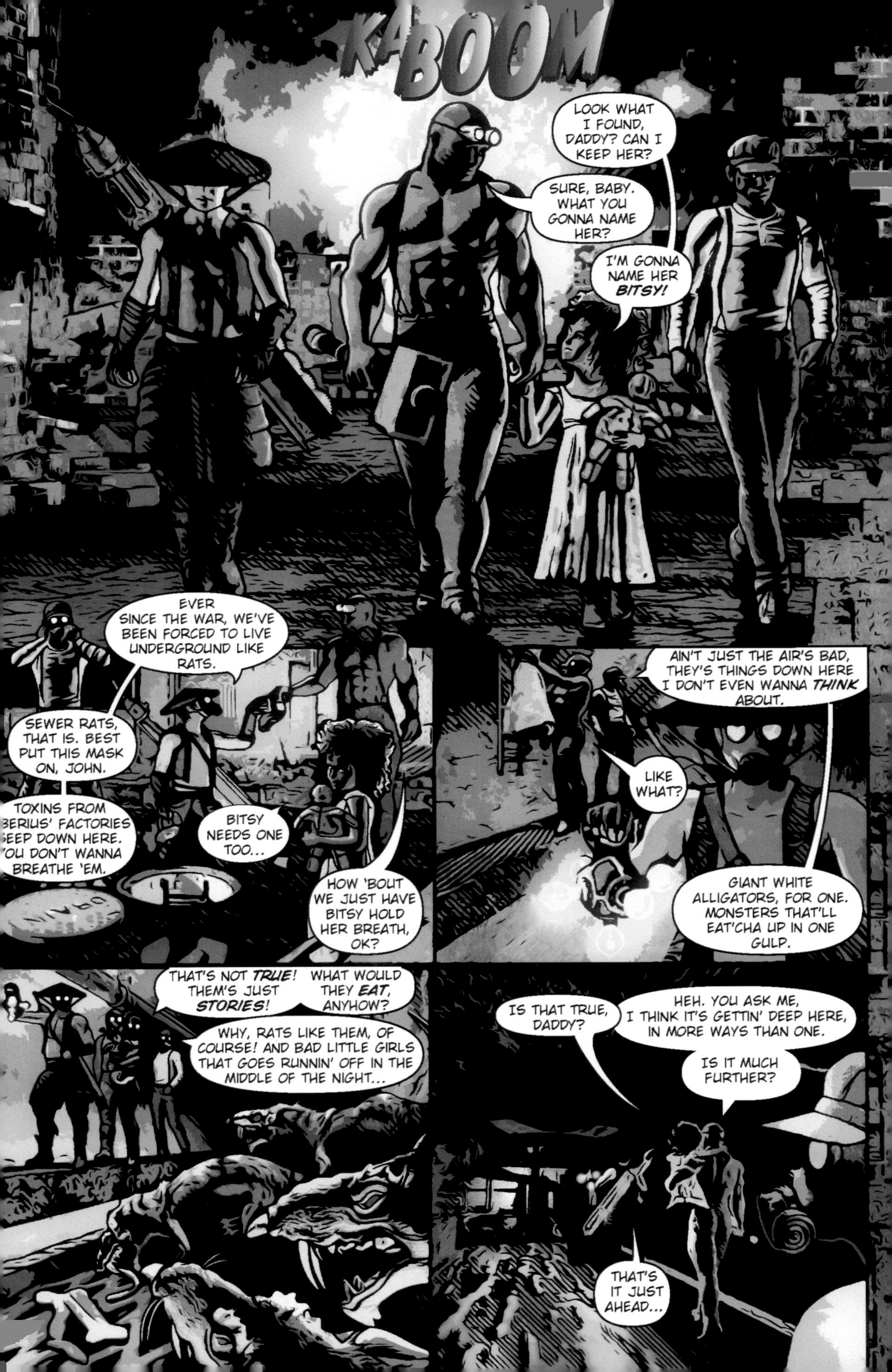
KABOOM
LOOK WHAT I FOUND, DADDY? CAN I KEEP HER?
SURE, BABY. WHAT YOU GONNA NAME HER?
I'M GONNA NAME HER BITSY!
EVER SINCE THE WAR, WE'VE BEEN FORCED TO LIVE UNDERGROUND LIKE RATS.
SEWER RATS, THAT IS. BEST PUT THIS MASK ON, JOHN.
TOXINS FROM BERIUS' FACTORIES SEEP DOWN HERE. YOU DON'T WANNA BREATHE 'EM.
BITSY NEEDS ONE TOO...
HOW 'BOUT WE JUST HAVE BITSY HOLD HER BREATH, OK?
AIN'T JUST THE AIR'S BAD, THEY'S THINGS DOWN HERE I DON'T EVEN WANNA THINK ABOUT.
LIKE WHAT?
GIANT WHITE ALLIGATORS, FOR ONE. MONSTERS THAT'LL EAT'CHA UP IN ONE GULP.
THAT'S NOT TRUE! THEM'S JUST STORIES!
WHAT WOULD THEY EAT, ANYHOW?
WHY, RATS LIKE THEM, OF COURSE! AND BAD LITTLE GIRLS THAT GOES RUNNIN' OFF IN THE MIDDLE OF THE NIGHT...
IS THAT TRUE, DADDY?
HEH. YOU ASK ME, I THINK IT'S GETTIN' DEEP HERE, IN MORE WAYS THAN ONE.
IS IT MUCH FURTHER?
THAT'S IT JUST AHEAD...

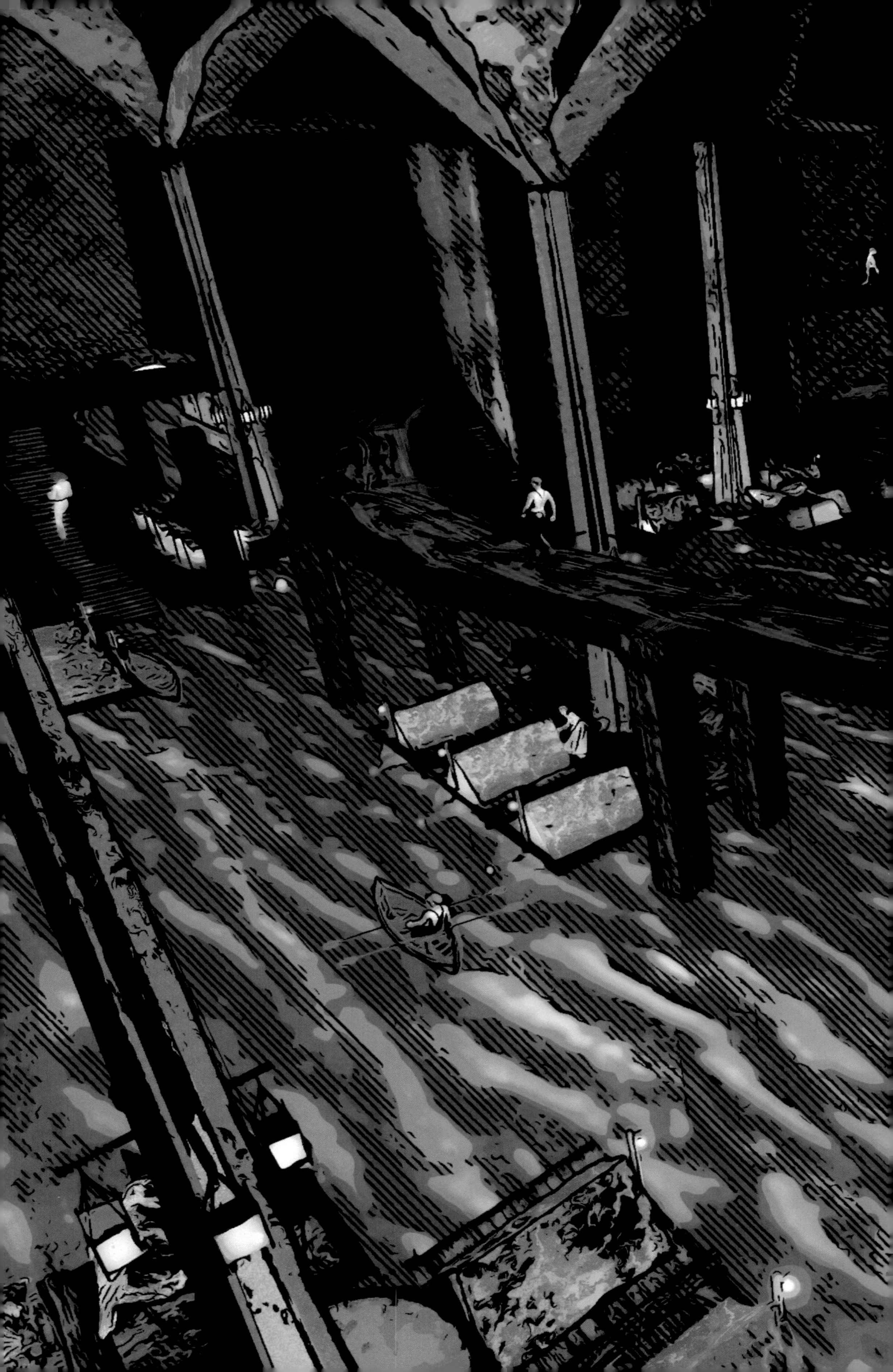

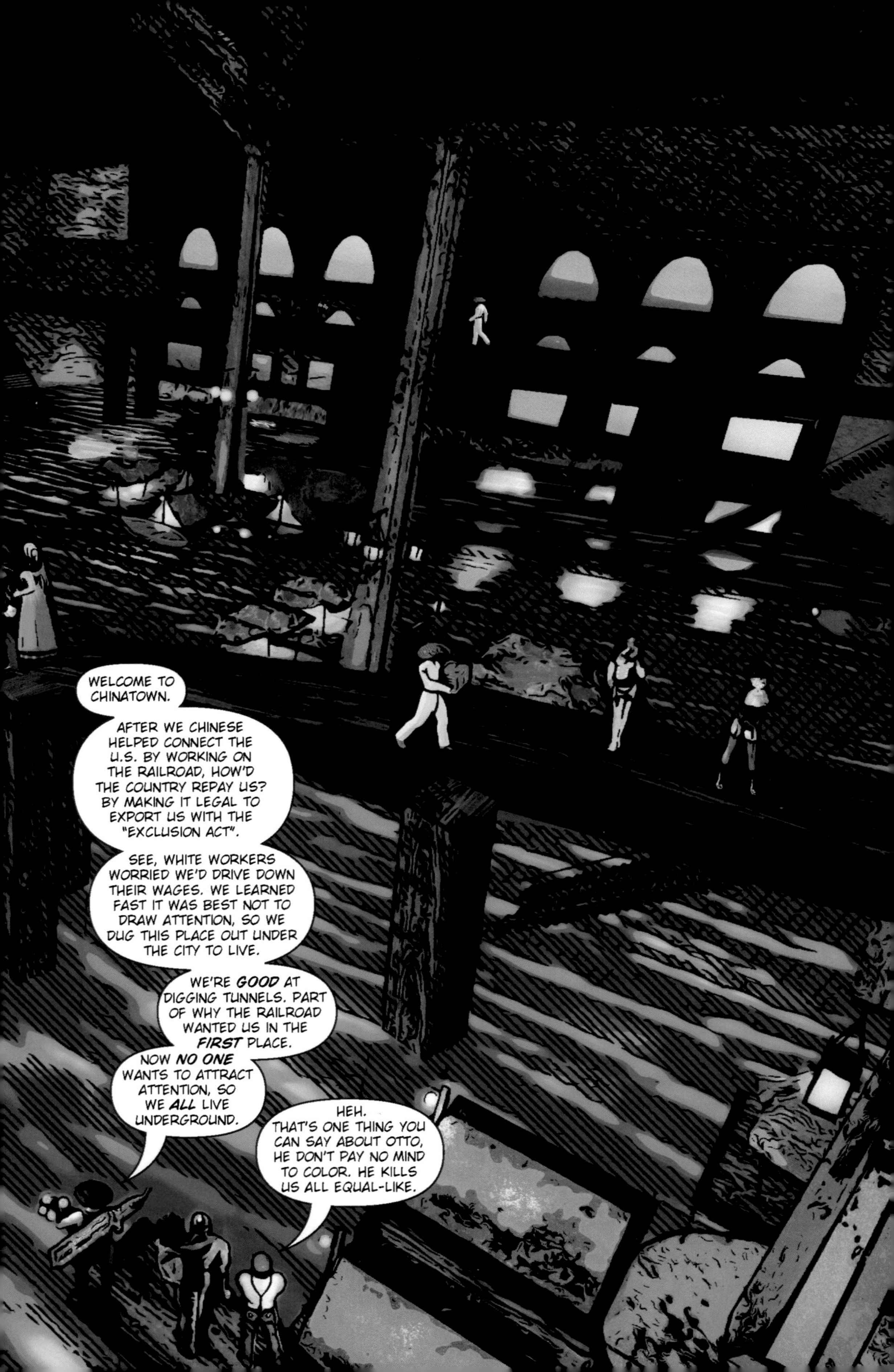
WELCOME TO CHINATOWN.
AFTER WE CHINESE HELPED CONNECT THE U.S. BY WORKING ON THE RAILROAD, HOW'D THE COUNTRY REPAY US? BY MAKING IT LEGAL TO EXPORT US WITH THE "EXCLUSION ACT".
SEE, WHITE WORKERS WORRIED WE'D DRIVE DOWN THEIR WAGES. WE LEARNED FAST IT WAS BEST NOT TO DRAW ATTENTION, SO WE DUG THIS PLACE OUT UNDER THE CITY TO LIVE.
WE'RE *GOOD* AT DIGGING TUNNELS. PART OF WHY THE RAILROAD WANTED US IN THE *FIRST* PLACE.
NOW *NO ONE* WANTS TO ATTRACT ATTENTION, SO WE *ALL* LIVE UNDERGROUND.
HEH. THAT'S ONE THING YOU CAN SAY ABOUT OTTO, HE DON'T PAY NO MIND TO COLOR. HE KILLS US ALL EQUAL-LIKE.

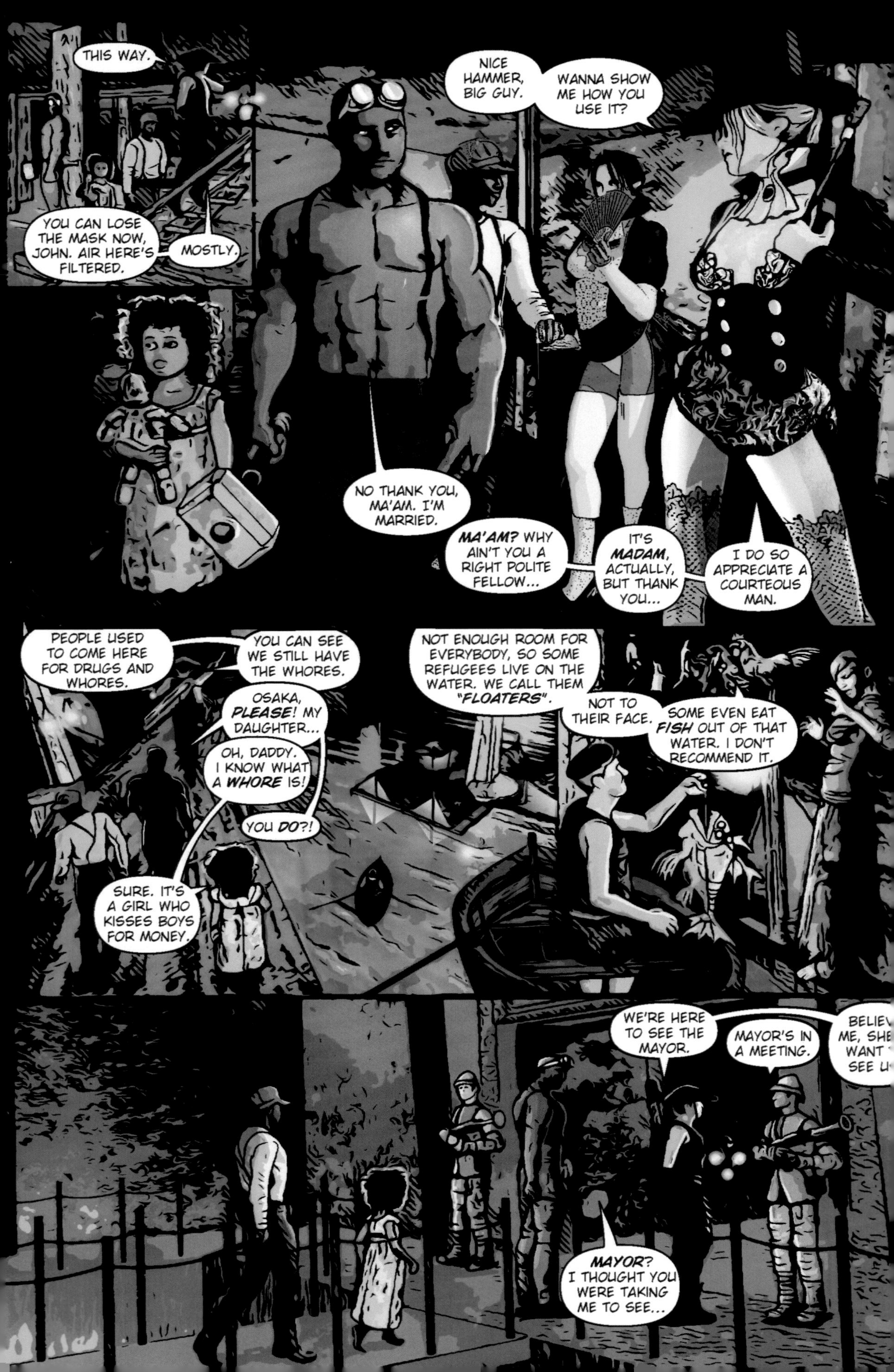
THIS WAY.
YOU CAN LOSE THE MASK NOW, JOHN. AIR HERE'S FILTERED.
MOSTLY.
NICE HAMMER, BIG GUY.
WANNA SHOW ME HOW YOU USE IT?
NO THANK YOU, MA'AM. I'M MARRIED.
MA'AM? WHY AIN'T YOU A RIGHT POLITE FELLOW...
IT'S MADAM, ACTUALLY, BUT THANK YOU...
I DO SO APPRECIATE A COURTEOUS MAN.
PEOPLE USED TO COME HERE FOR DRUGS AND WHORES.
YOU CAN SEE WE STILL HAVE THE WHORES.
OSAKA, PLEASE! MY DAUGHTER...
OH, DADDY. I KNOW WHAT A WHORE IS!
YOU DO?!
SURE. IT'S A GIRL WHO KISSES BOYS FOR MONEY.
NOT ENOUGH ROOM FOR EVERYBODY, SO SOME REFUGEES LIVE ON THE WATER. WE CALL THEM "FLOATERS".
NOT TO THEIR FACE.
SOME EVEN EAT FISH OUT OF THAT WATER. I DON'T RECOMMEND IT.
WE'RE HERE TO SEE THE MAYOR.
MAYOR'S IN A MEETING.
BELIEV ME, SHE WANT SEE U
MAYOR? I THOUGHT YOU WERE TAKING ME TO SEE...

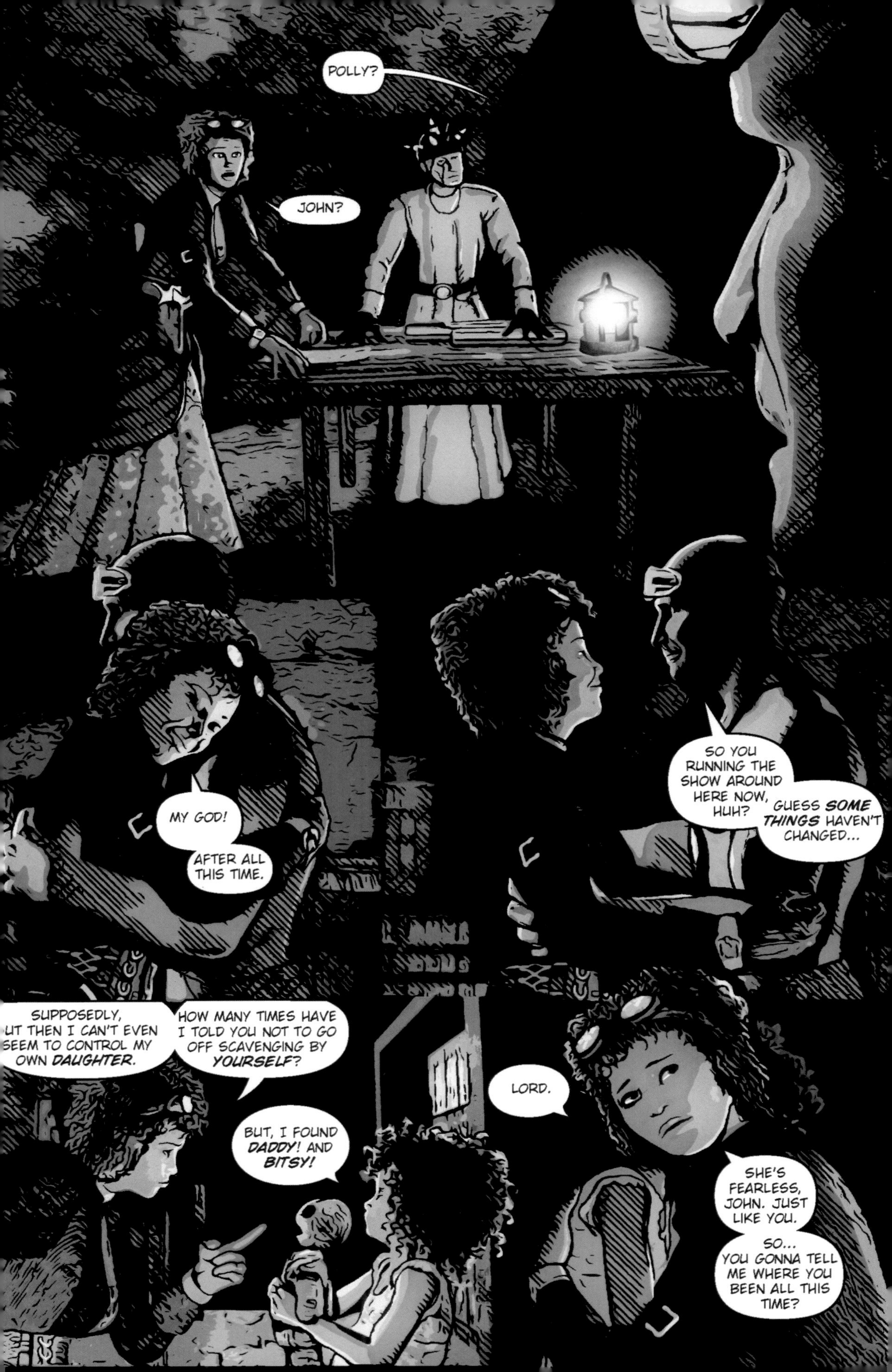
POLLY?
JOHN?
MY GOD!
AFTER ALL THIS TIME.
SO YOU RUNNING THE SHOW AROUND HERE NOW, HUH?
GUESS **SOME THINGS** HAVEN'T CHANGED...
SUPPOSEDLY, UT THEN I CAN'T EVEN SEEM TO CONTROL MY OWN **DAUGHTER**.
HOW MANY TIMES HAVE I TOLD YOU NOT TO GO OFF SCAVENGING BY **YOURSELF**?
BUT, I FOUND **DADDY**! AND **BITSY!**
LORD.
SHE'S FEARLESS, JOHN. JUST LIKE YOU.
SO... YOU GONNA TELL ME WHERE YOU BEEN ALL THIS TIME?

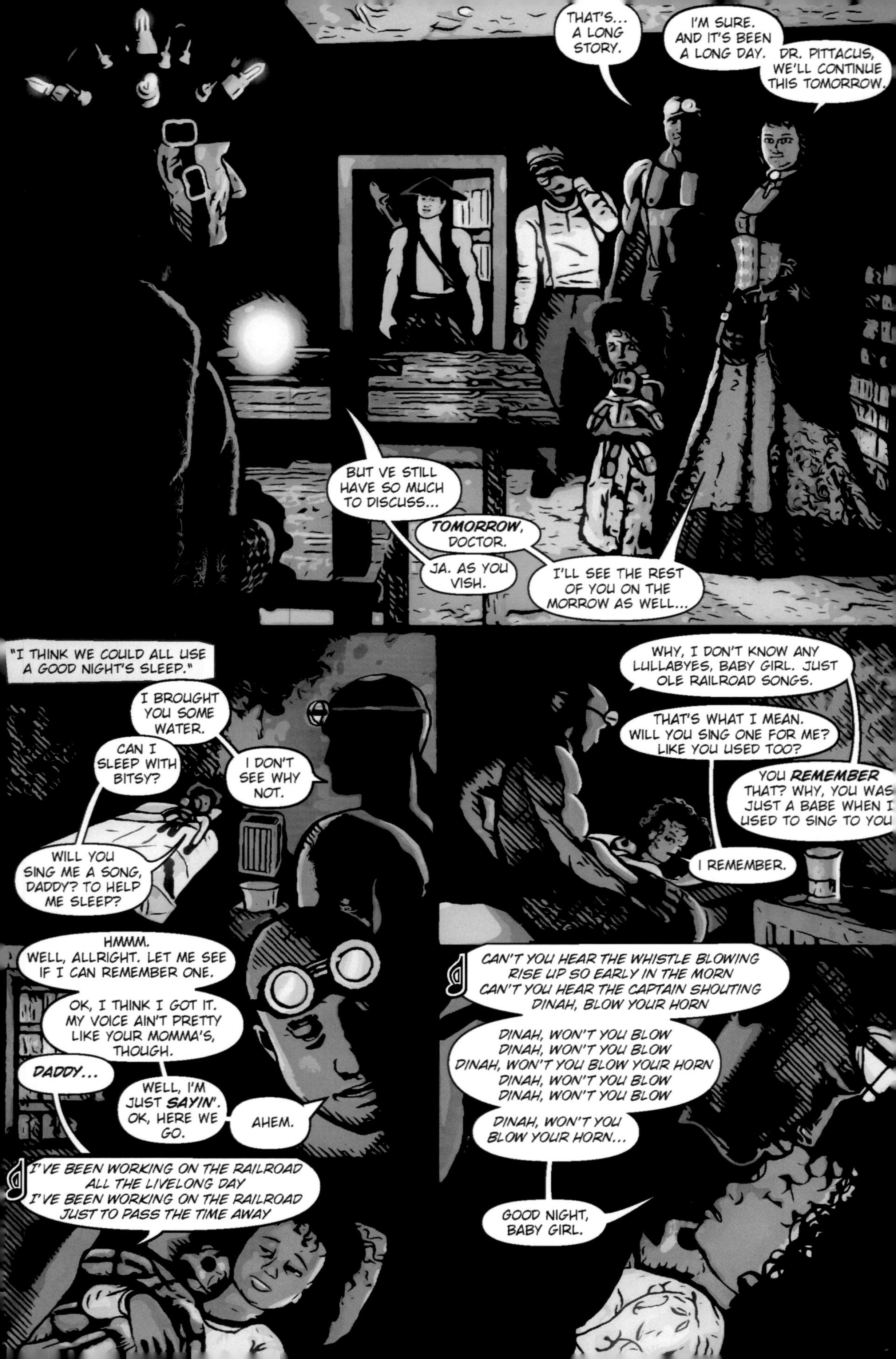
THAT'S... A LONG STORY.
I'M SURE. AND IT'S BEEN A LONG DAY.
DR. PITTACUS, WE'LL CONTINUE THIS TOMORROW.
BUT VE STILL HAVE SO MUCH TO DISCUSS...
TOMORROW, DOCTOR.
JA. AS YOU VISH.
I'LL SEE THE REST OF YOU ON THE MORROW AS WELL...
"I THINK WE COULD ALL USE A GOOD NIGHT'S SLEEP."
I BROUGHT YOU SOME WATER.
CAN I SLEEP WITH BITSY?
I DON'T SEE WHY NOT.
WILL YOU SING ME A SONG, DADDY? TO HELP ME SLEEP?
WHY, I DON'T KNOW ANY LULLABYES, BABY GIRL. JUST OLE RAILROAD SONGS.
THAT'S WHAT I MEAN. WILL YOU SING ONE FOR ME? LIKE YOU USED TOO?
YOU REMEMBER THAT? WHY, YOU WAS JUST A BABE WHEN I USED TO SING TO YOU
I REMEMBER.
HMMM. WELL, ALLRIGHT. LET ME SEE IF I CAN REMEMBER ONE.
OK, I THINK I GOT IT. MY VOICE AIN'T PRETTY LIKE YOUR MOMMA'S, THOUGH.
DADDY...
WELL, I'M JUST SAYIN'. OK, HERE WE GO.
AHEM.
I'VE BEEN WORKING ON THE RAILROAD ALL THE LIVELONG DAY I'VE BEEN WORKING ON THE RAILROAD JUST TO PASS THE TIME AWAY
CAN'T YOU HEAR THE WHISTLE BLOWING RISE UP SO EARLY IN THE MORN CAN'T YOU HEAR THE CAPTAIN SHOUTING DINAH, BLOW YOUR HORN
DINAH, WON'T YOU BLOW DINAH, WON'T YOU BLOW DINAH, WON'T YOU BLOW YOUR HORN DINAH, WON'T YOU BLOW DINAH, WON'T YOU BLOW
DINAH, WON'T YOU BLOW YOUR HORN...
GOOD NIGHT, BABY GIRL.

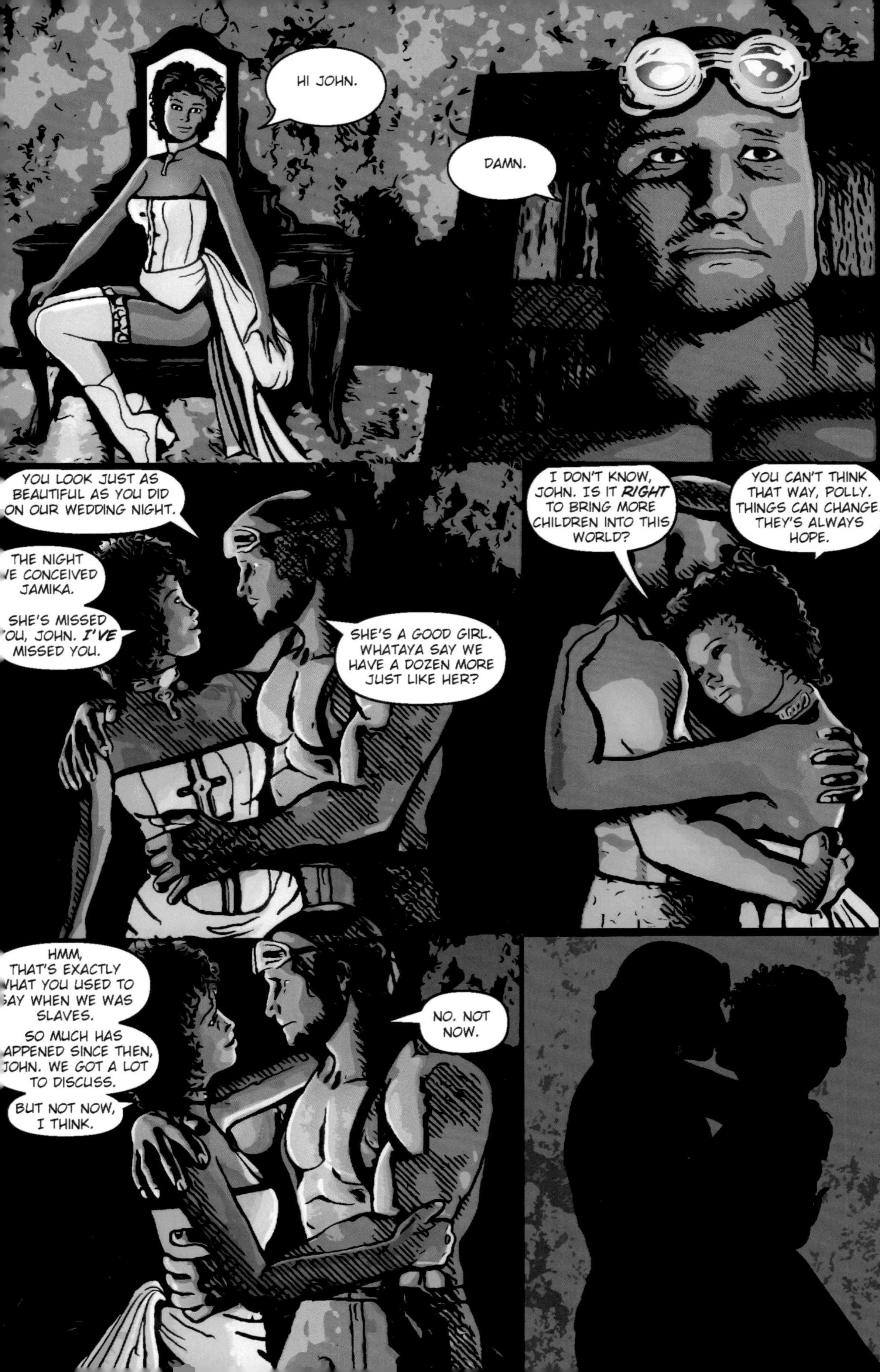
HI JOHN.
DAMN.
YOU LOOK JUST AS BEAUTIFUL AS YOU DID ON OUR WEDDING NIGHT.
THE NIGHT E CONCEIVED JAMIKA.
SHE'S MISSED OU, JOHN. I'VE MISSED YOU.
SHE'S A GOOD GIRL. WHATAYA SAY WE HAVE A DOZEN MORE JUST LIKE HER?
I DON'T KNOW, JOHN. IS IT RIGHT TO BRING MORE CHILDREN INTO THIS WORLD?
YOU CAN'T THINK THAT WAY, POLLY. THINGS CAN CHANGE. THEY'S ALWAYS HOPE.
HMM, THAT'S EXACTLY HAT YOU USED TO AY WHEN WE WAS SLAVES.
SO MUCH HAS APPENED SINCE THEN, JOHN. WE GOT A LOT TO DISCUSS.
BUT NOT NOW, I THINK.
NO. NOT NOW.

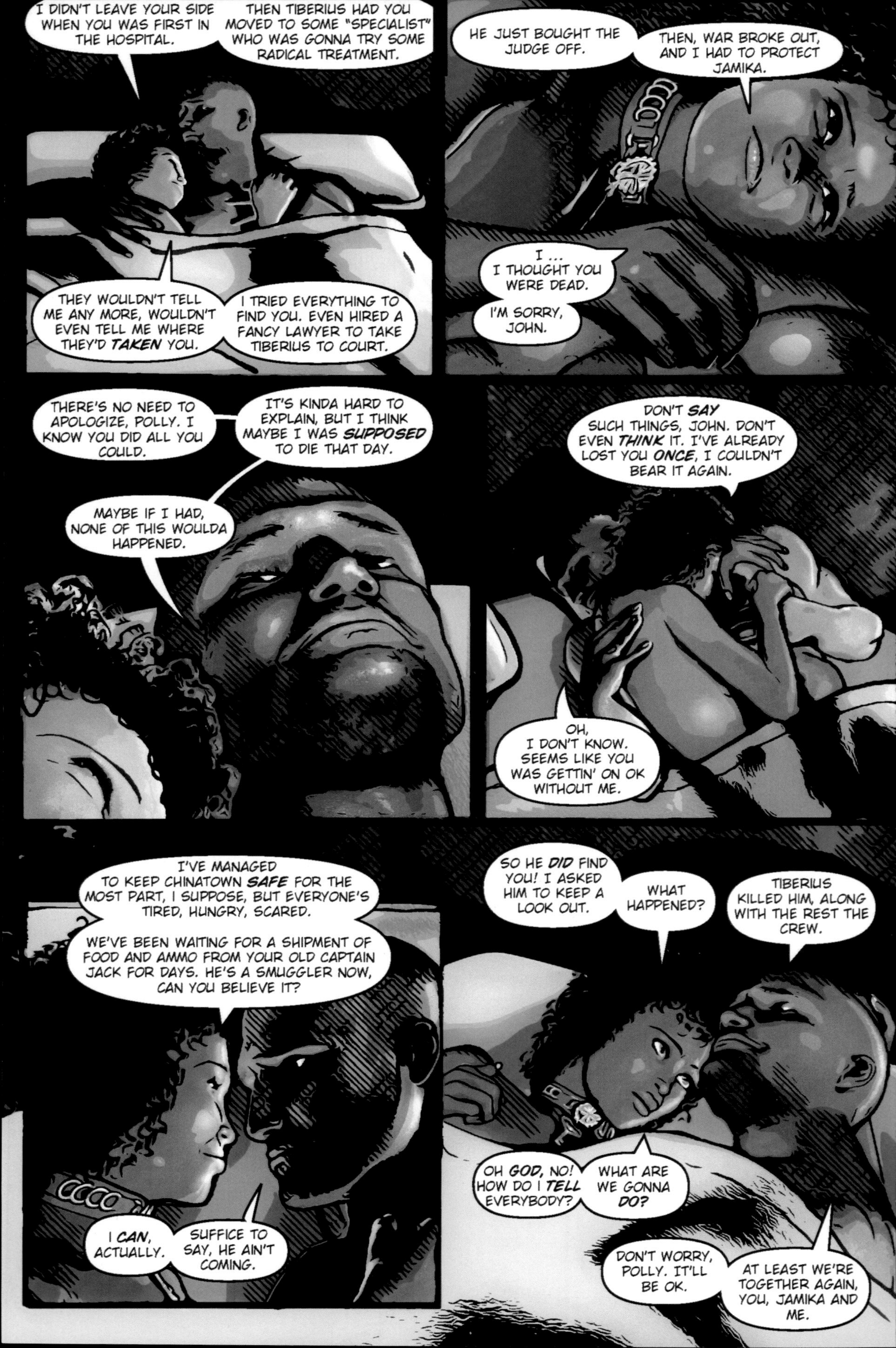
I DIDN'T LEAVE YOUR SIDE WHEN YOU WAS FIRST IN THE HOSPITAL.
THEN TIBERIUS HAD YOU MOVED TO SOME "SPECIALIST" WHO WAS GONNA TRY SOME RADICAL TREATMENT.
THEY WOULDN'T TELL ME ANY MORE, WOULDN'T EVEN TELL ME WHERE THEY'D *TAKEN* YOU.
I TRIED EVERYTHING TO FIND YOU. EVEN HIRED A FANCY LAWYER TO TAKE TIBERIUS TO COURT.
HE JUST BOUGHT THE JUDGE OFF.
THEN, WAR BROKE OUT, AND I HAD TO PROTECT JAMIKA.
I ... I THOUGHT YOU WERE DEAD.
I'M SORRY, JOHN.
THERE'S NO NEED TO APOLOGIZE, POLLY. I KNOW YOU DID ALL YOU COULD.
IT'S KINDA HARD TO EXPLAIN, BUT I THINK MAYBE I WAS *SUPPOSED* TO DIE THAT DAY.
MAYBE IF I HAD, NONE OF THIS WOULDA HAPPENED.
DON'T *SAY* SUCH THINGS, JOHN. DON'T EVEN *THINK* IT. I'VE ALREADY LOST YOU *ONCE*, I COULDN'T BEAR IT AGAIN.
OH, I DON'T KNOW. SEEMS LIKE YOU WAS GETTIN' ON OK WITHOUT ME.
I'VE MANAGED TO KEEP CHINATOWN *SAFE* FOR THE MOST PART, I SUPPOSE, BUT EVERYONE'S TIRED, HUNGRY, SCARED.
WE'VE BEEN WAITING FOR A SHIPMENT OF FOOD AND AMMO FROM YOUR OLD CAPTAIN JACK FOR DAYS. HE'S A SMUGGLER NOW, CAN YOU BELIEVE IT?
I *CAN*, ACTUALLY.
SUFFICE TO SAY, HE AIN'T COMING.
SO HE *DID* FIND YOU! I ASKED HIM TO KEEP A LOOK OUT.
WHAT HAPPENED?
TIBERIUS KILLED HIM, ALONG WITH THE REST THE CREW.
OH *GOD*, NO! HOW DO I *TELL* EVERYBODY?
WHAT ARE WE GONNA *DO?*
DON'T WORRY, POLLY. IT'LL BE OK.
AT LEAST WE'RE TOGETHER AGAIN, YOU, JAMIKA AND ME.

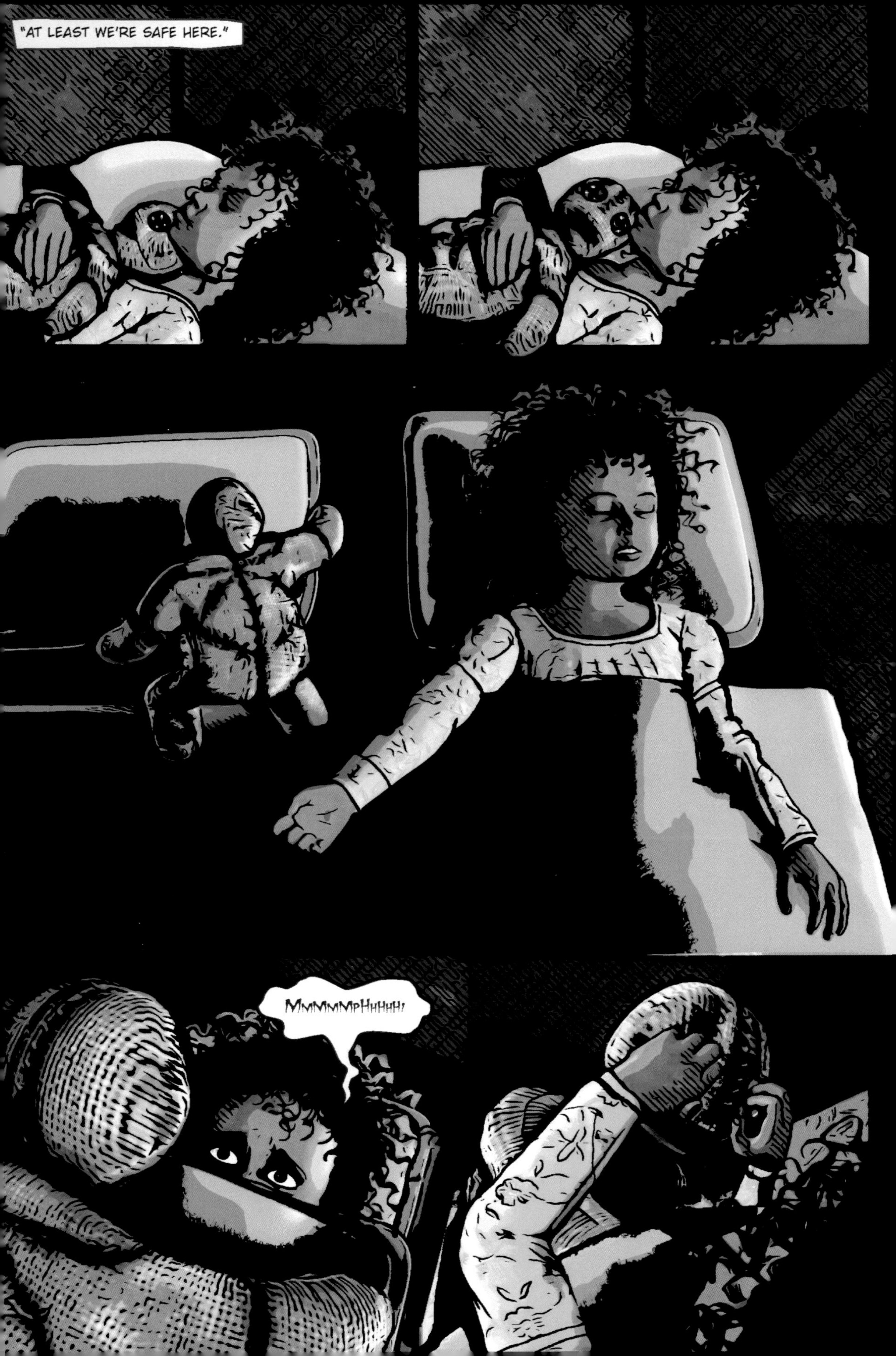
"AT LEAST WE'RE SAFE HERE."
MMMMMMPHHHHH!

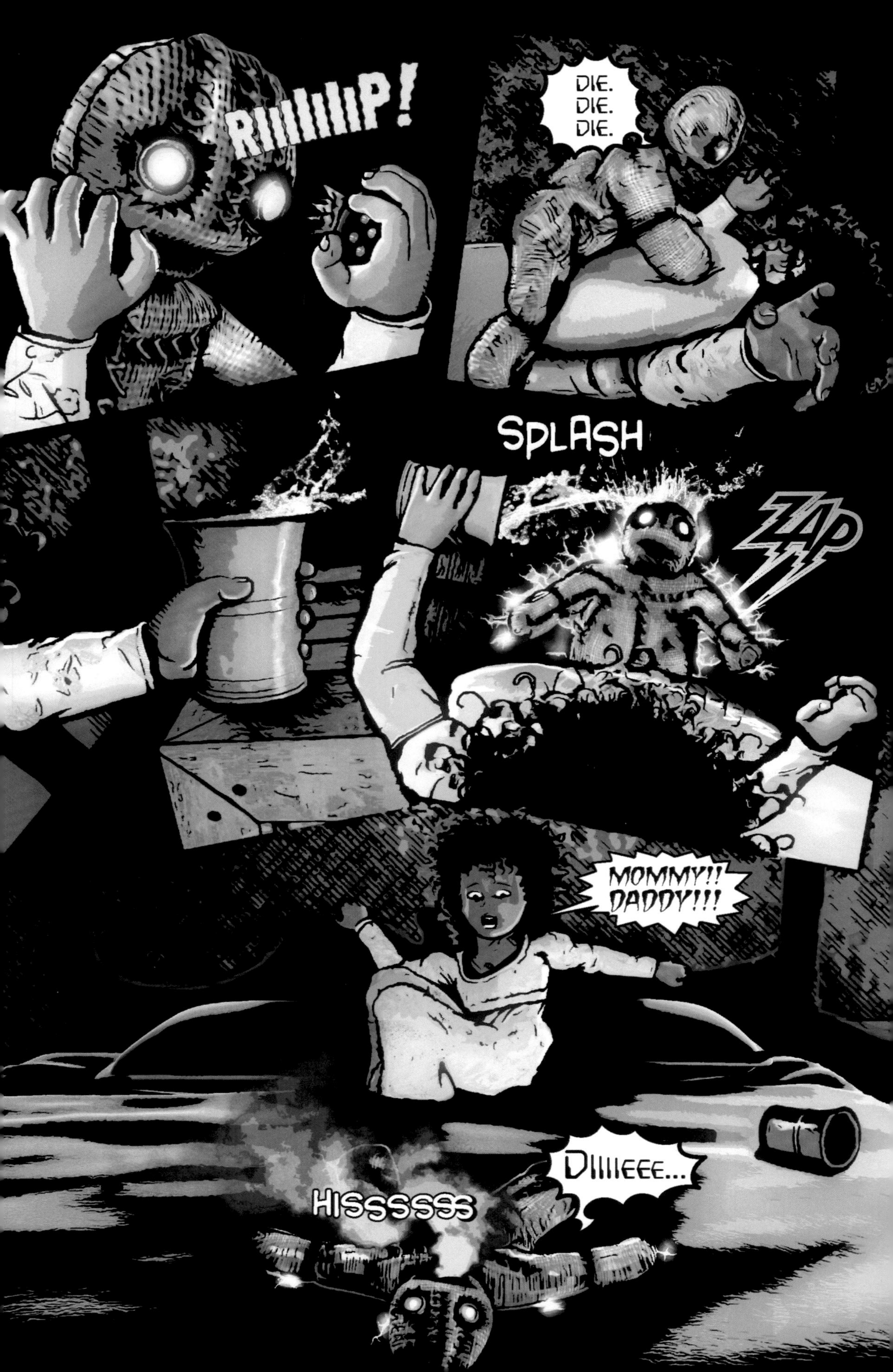
RIIIIIIP!
DIE.
DIE.
DIE.
SPLASH
ZAP
MOMMY!!
DADDY!!!
DIIIIEEE...
HISSSSSS

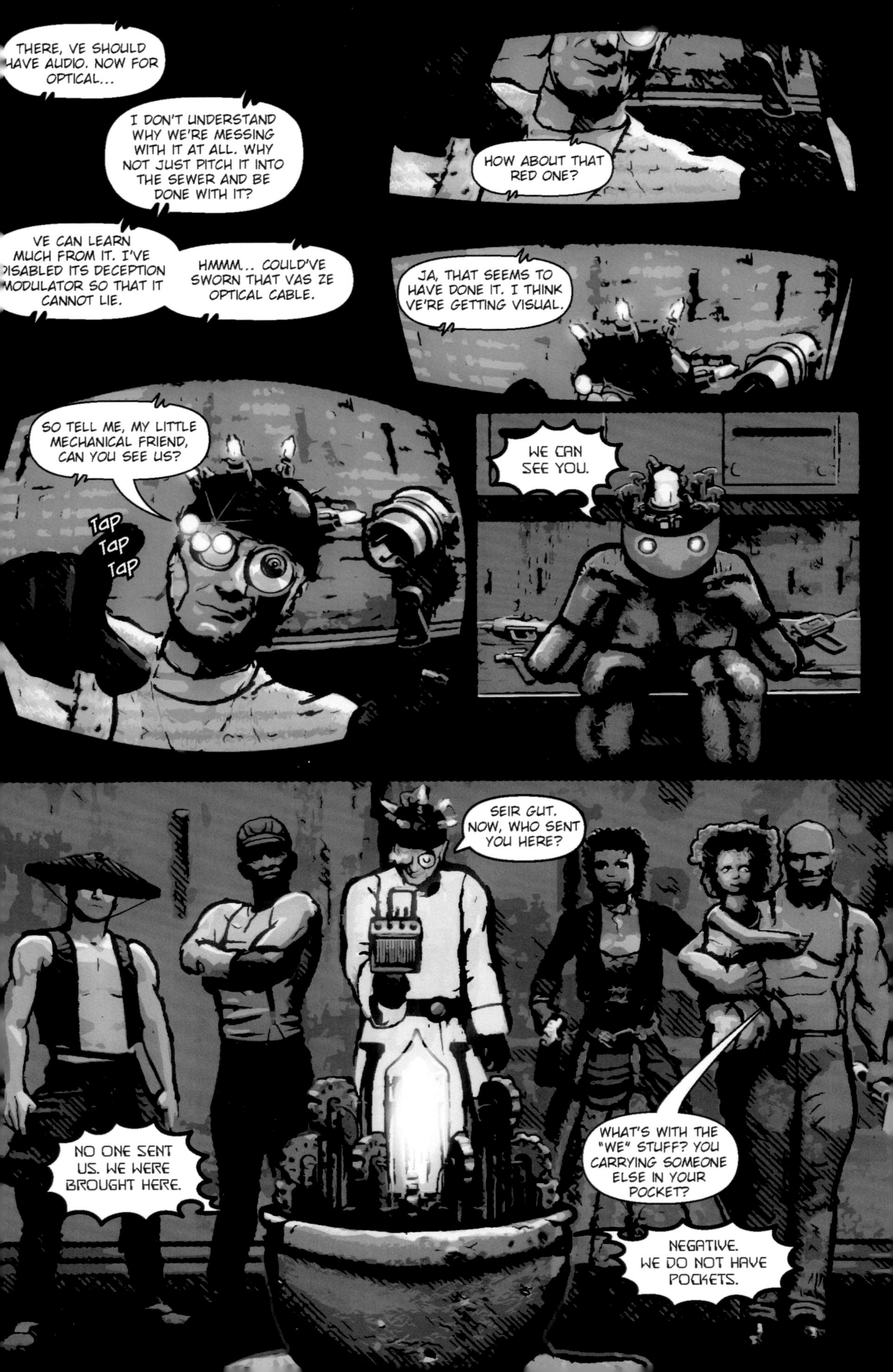

THERE, VE SHOULD HAVE AUDIO. NOW FOR OPTICAL...
I DON'T UNDERSTAND WHY WE'RE MESSING WITH IT AT ALL. WHY NOT JUST PITCH IT INTO THE SEWER AND BE DONE WITH IT?
HOW ABOUT THAT RED ONE?
VE CAN LEARN MUCH FROM IT. I'VE DISABLED ITS DECEPTION MODULATOR SO THAT IT CANNOT LIE.
HMMM... COULD'VE SWORN THAT VAS ZE OPTICAL CABLE.
JA, THAT SEEMS TO HAVE DONE IT. I THINK VE'RE GETTING VISUAL.
SO TELL ME, MY LITTLE MECHANICAL FRIEND, CAN YOU SEE US?
Tap
Tap
Tap
WE CAN SEE YOU.
SEIR GUT. NOW, WHO SENT YOU HERE?
NO ONE SENT US. WE WERE BROUGHT HERE.
WHAT'S WITH THE "WE" STUFF? YOU CARRYING SOMEONE ELSE IN YOUR POCKET?
NEGATIVE. WE DO NOT HAVE POCKETS.

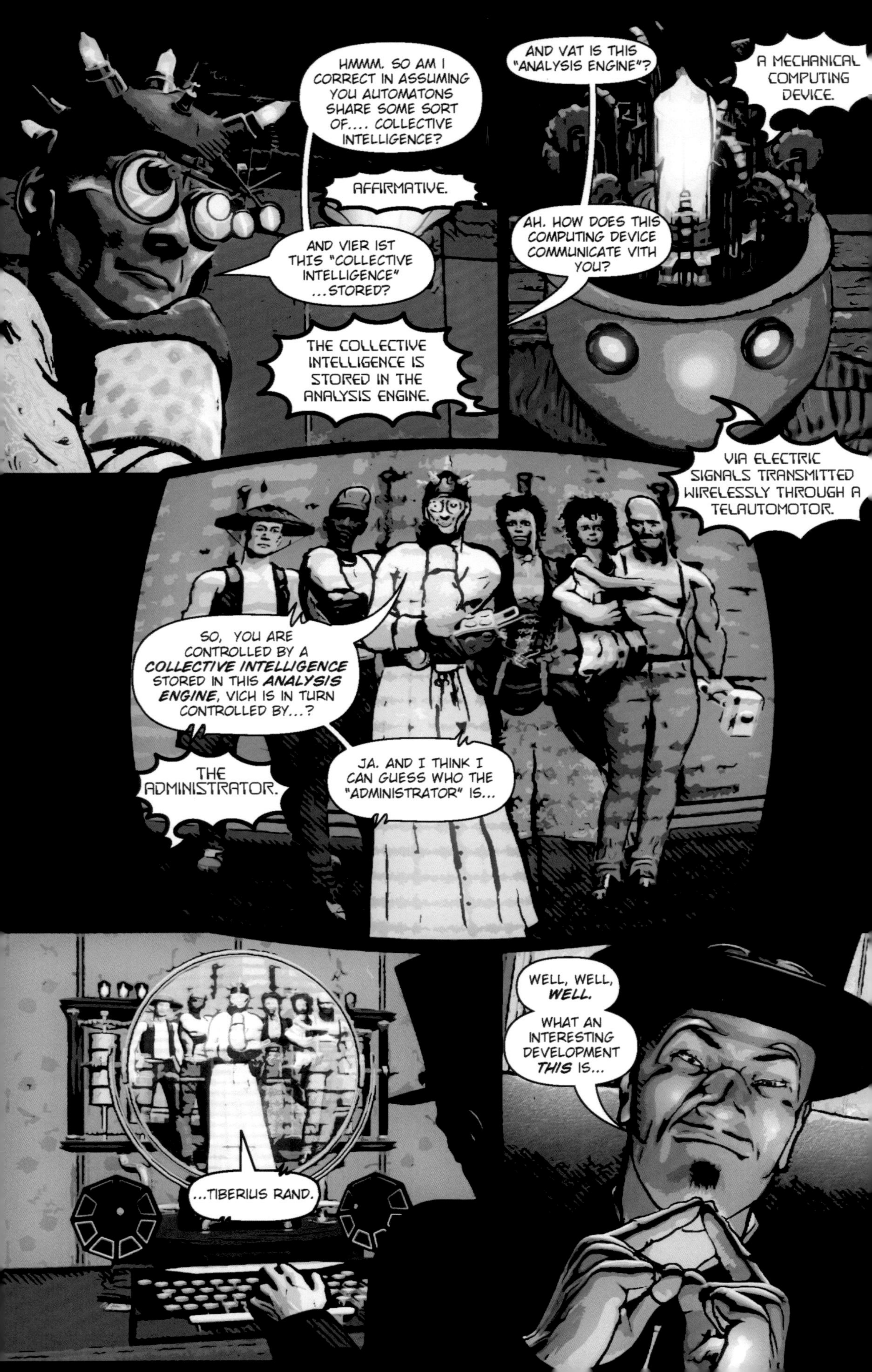
HMMM. SO AM I CORRECT IN ASSUMING YOU AUTOMATONS SHARE SOME SORT OF.... COLLECTIVE INTELLIGENCE?
AFFIRMATIVE.
AND VIER IST THIS "COLLECTIVE INTELLIGENCE" ...STORED?
THE COLLECTIVE INTELLIGENCE IS STORED IN THE ANALYSIS ENGINE.
AND VAT IS THIS "ANALYSIS ENGINE"?
A MECHANICAL COMPUTING DEVICE.
AH. HOW DOES THIS COMPUTING DEVICE COMMUNICATE VITH YOU?
VIA ELECTRIC SIGNALS TRANSMITTED WIRELESSLY THROUGH A TELAUTOMOTOR.
SO, YOU ARE CONTROLLED BY A COLLECTIVE INTELLIGENCE STORED IN THIS ANALYSIS ENGINE, VICH IS IN TURN CONTROLLED BY...?
THE ADMINISTRATOR.
JA. AND I THINK I CAN GUESS WHO THE "ADMINISTRATOR" IS...
...TIBERIUS RAND.
WELL, WELL, WELL.
WHAT AN INTERESTING DEVELOPMENT THIS IS...

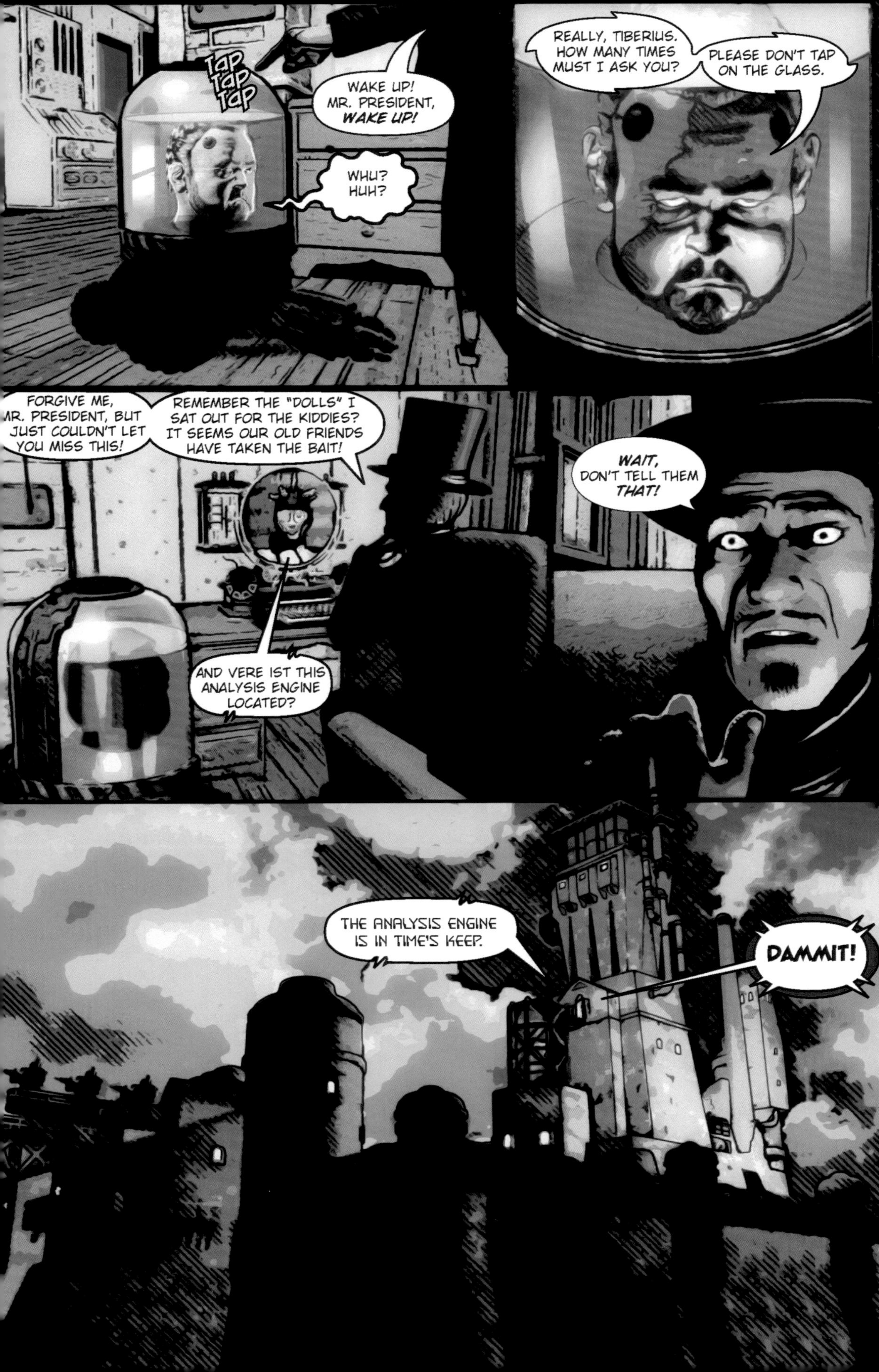
TAP TAP TAP
WAKE UP! MR. PRESIDENT, WAKE UP!
WHU? HUH?
REALLY, TIBERIUS. HOW MANY TIMES MUST I ASK YOU?
PLEASE DON'T TAP ON THE GLASS.
FORGIVE ME, MR. PRESIDENT, BUT I JUST COULDN'T LET YOU MISS THIS!
REMEMBER THE "DOLLS" I SAT OUT FOR THE KIDDIES? IT SEEMS OUR OLD FRIENDS HAVE TAKEN THE BAIT!
AND VERE IST THIS ANALYSIS ENGINE LOCATED?
WAIT, DON'T TELL THEM THAT!
THE ANALYSIS ENGINE IS IN TIME'S KEEP.
DAMMIT!

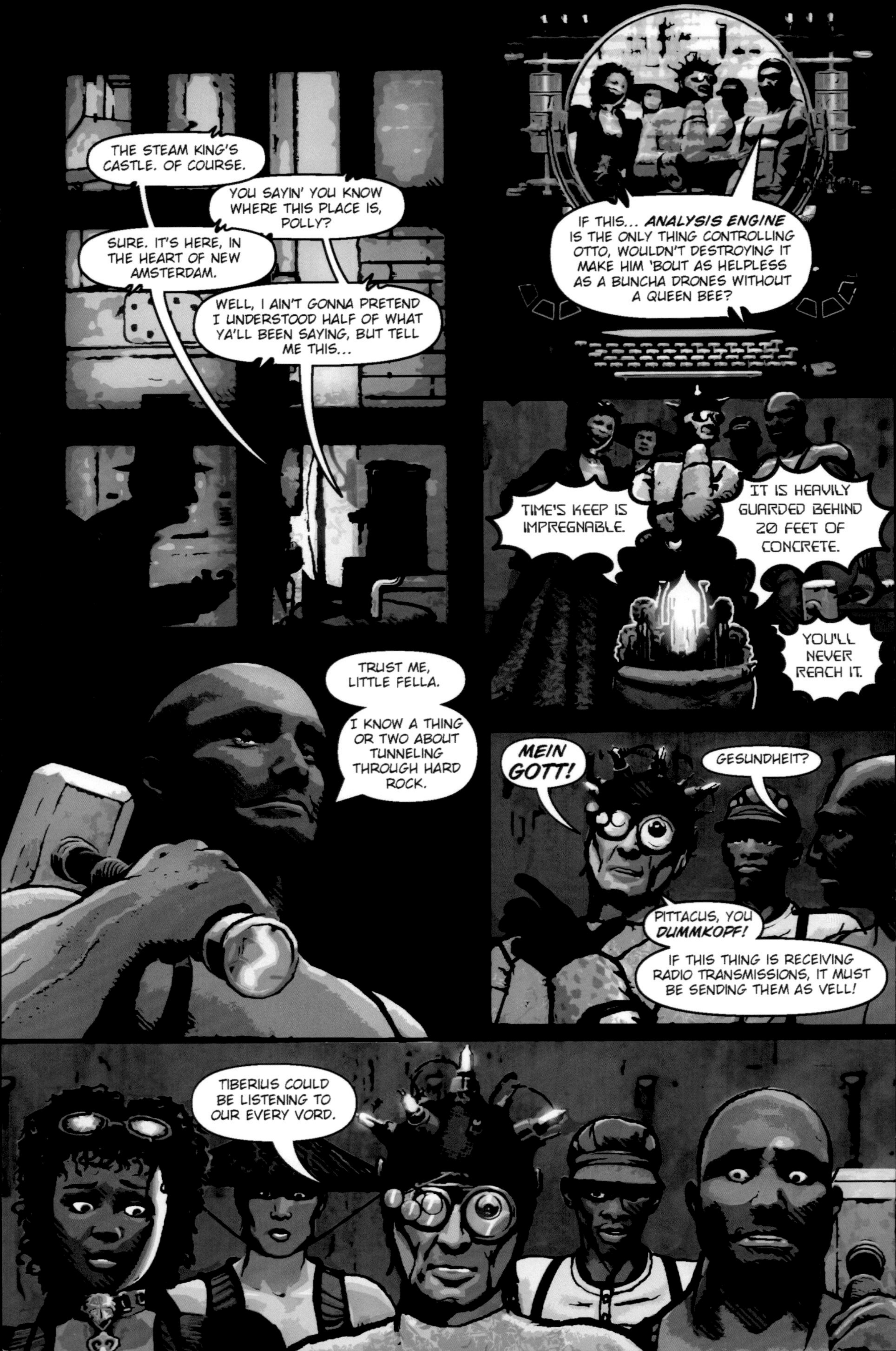
THE STEAM KING'S CASTLE. OF COURSE.
YOU SAYIN' YOU KNOW WHERE THIS PLACE IS, POLLY?
SURE. IT'S HERE, IN THE HEART OF NEW AMSTERDAM.
WELL, I AIN'T GONNA PRETEND I UNDERSTOOD HALF OF WHAT YA'LL BEEN SAYING, BUT TELL ME THIS...
IF THIS... ANALYSIS ENGINE IS THE ONLY THING CONTROLLING OTTO, WOULDN'T DESTROYING IT MAKE HIM 'BOUT AS HELPLESS AS A BUNCHA DRONES WITHOUT A QUEEN BEE?
TIME'S KEEP IS IMPREGNABLE.
IT IS HEAVILY GUARDED BEHIND 20 FEET OF CONCRETE.
YOU'LL NEVER REACH IT.
TRUST ME, LITTLE FELLA.
I KNOW A THING OR TWO ABOUT TUNNELING THROUGH HARD ROCK.
MEIN GOTT!
GESUNDHEIT?
PITTACUS, YOU DUMMKOPF!
IF THIS THING IS RECEIVING RADIO TRANSMISSIONS, IT MUST BE SENDING THEM AS VELL!
TIBERIUS COULD BE LISTENING TO OUR EVERY VORD.

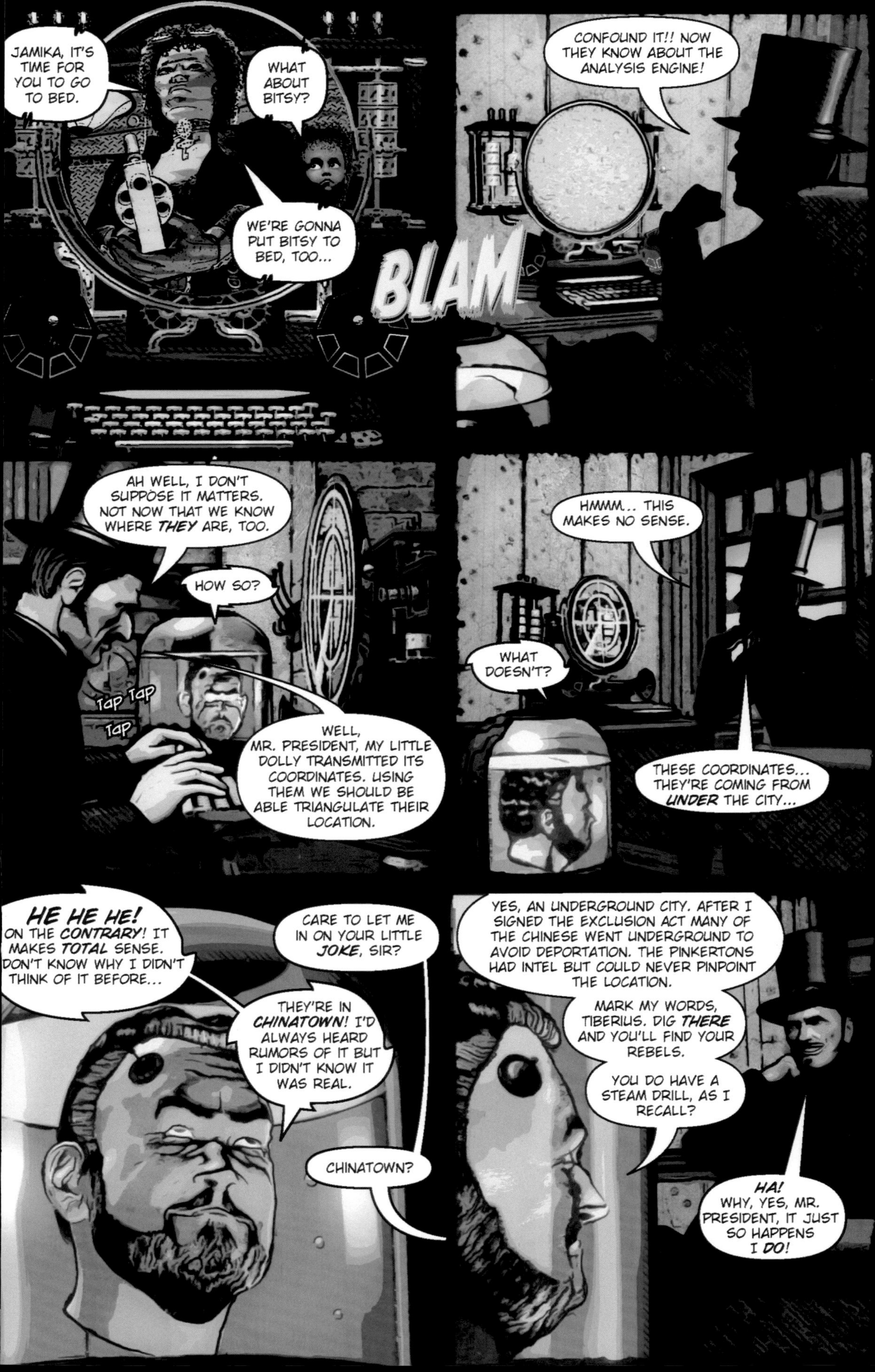
JAMIKA, IT'S TIME FOR YOU TO GO TO BED.
WHAT ABOUT BITSY?
WE'RE GONNA PUT BITSY TO BED, TOO...
BLAM
CONFOUND IT!! NOW THEY KNOW ABOUT THE ANALYSIS ENGINE!
AH WELL, I DON'T SUPPOSE IT MATTERS. NOT NOW THAT WE KNOW WHERE THEY ARE, TOO.
HOW SO?
Tap Tap Tap
WELL, MR. PRESIDENT, MY LITTLE DOLLY TRANSMITTED ITS COORDINATES. USING THEM WE SHOULD BE ABLE TRIANGULATE THEIR LOCATION.
HMMM... THIS MAKES NO SENSE.
WHAT DOESN'T?
THESE COORDINATES... THEY'RE COMING FROM UNDER THE CITY...
HE HE HE! ON THE CONTRARY! IT MAKES TOTAL SENSE. DON'T KNOW WHY I DIDN'T THINK OF IT BEFORE...
CARE TO LET ME IN ON YOUR LITTLE JOKE, SIR?
THEY'RE IN CHINATOWN! I'D ALWAYS HEARD RUMORS OF IT BUT I DIDN'T KNOW IT WAS REAL.
CHINATOWN?
YES, AN UNDERGROUND CITY. AFTER I SIGNED THE EXCLUSION ACT MANY OF THE CHINESE WENT UNDERGROUND TO AVOID DEPORTATION. THE PINKERTONS HAD INTEL BUT COULD NEVER PINPOINT THE LOCATION.
MARK MY WORDS, TIBERIUS. DIG THERE AND YOU'LL FIND YOUR REBELS.
YOU DO HAVE A STEAM DRILL, AS I RECALL?
HA! WHY, YES, MR. PRESIDENT, IT JUST SO HAPPENS I DO!

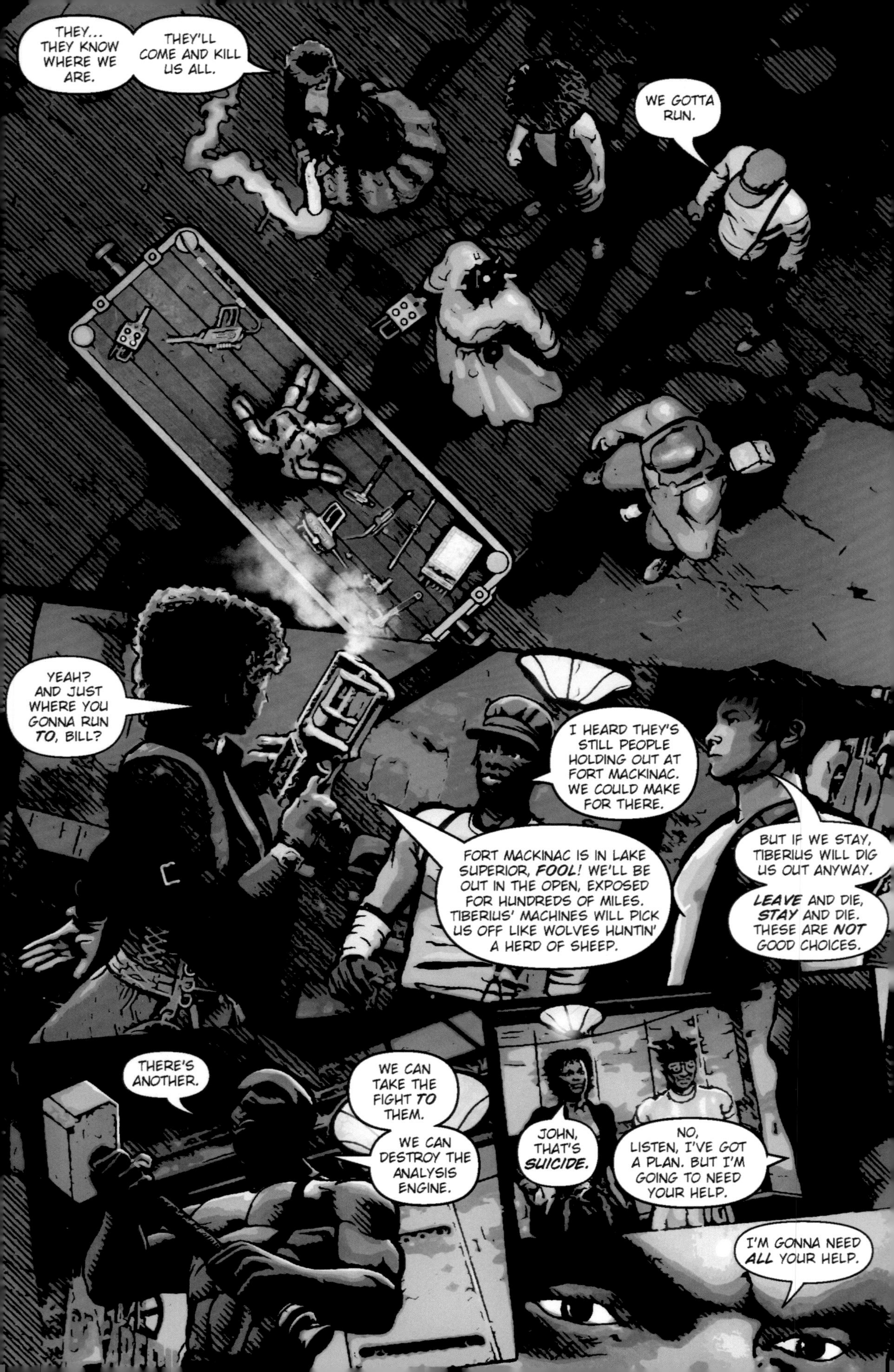
THEY... THEY KNOW WHERE WE ARE.
THEY'LL COME AND KILL US ALL.
WE GOTTA RUN.
YEAH? AND JUST WHERE YOU GONNA RUN *TO*, BILL?
I HEARD THEY'S STILL PEOPLE HOLDING OUT AT FORT MACKINAC. WE COULD MAKE FOR THERE.
FORT MACKINAC IS IN LAKE SUPERIOR, ***FOOL!*** WE'LL BE OUT IN THE OPEN, EXPOSED FOR HUNDREDS OF MILES. TIBERIUS' MACHINES WILL PICK US OFF LIKE WOLVES HUNTIN' A HERD OF SHEEP.
BUT IF WE STAY, TIBERIUS WILL DIG US OUT ANYWAY.
LEAVE AND DIE, ***STAY*** AND DIE. THESE ARE ***NOT*** GOOD CHOICES.
THERE'S ANOTHER.
WE CAN TAKE THE FIGHT ***TO*** THEM.
WE CAN DESTROY THE ANALYSIS ENGINE.
JOHN, THAT'S ***SUICIDE.***
NO, LISTEN, I'VE GOT A PLAN. BUT I'M GOING TO NEED YOUR HELP.
I'M GONNA NEED ***ALL*** YOUR HELP.

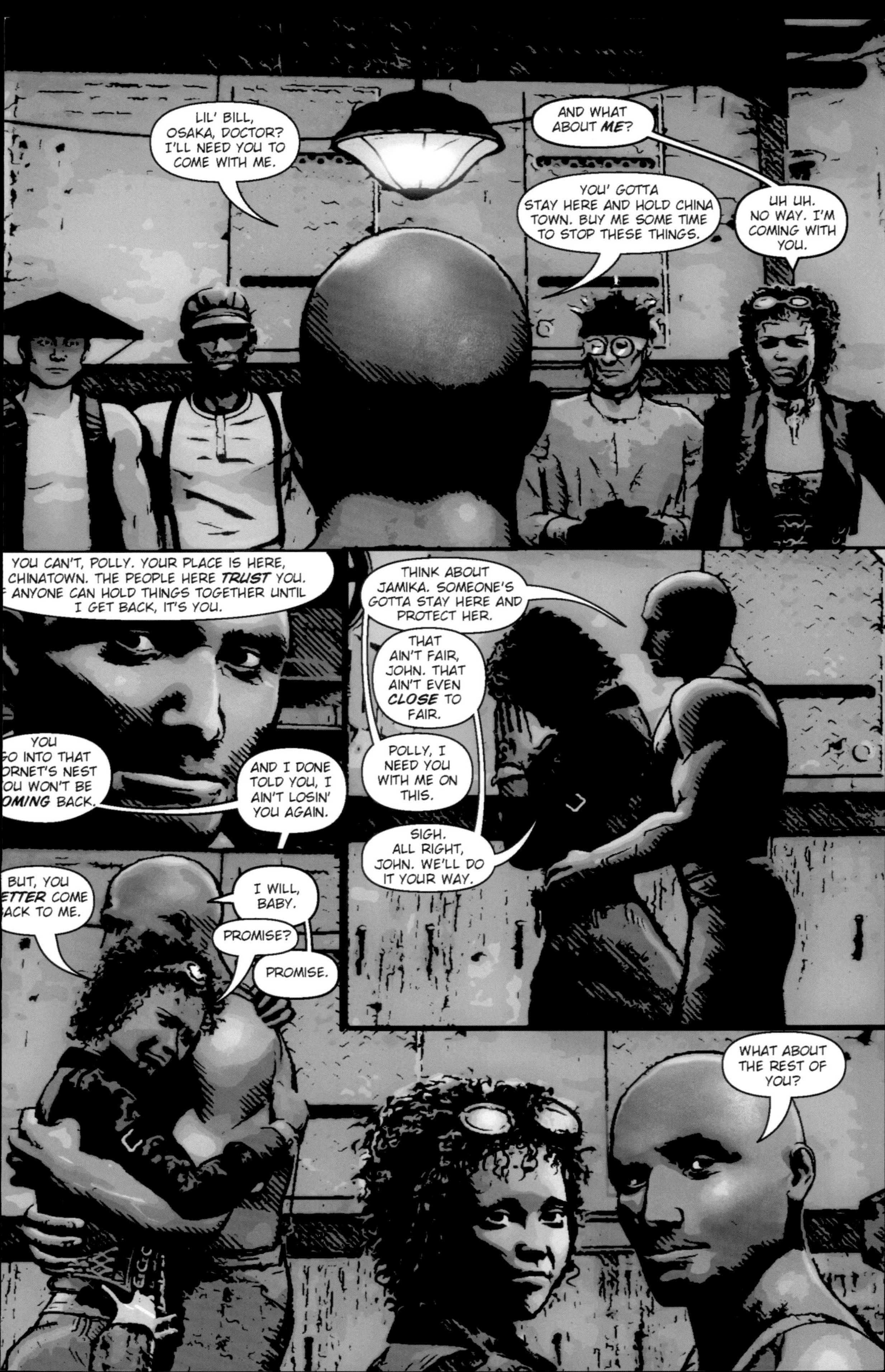
LIL' BILL, OSAKA, DOCTOR? I'LL NEED YOU TO COME WITH ME.
AND WHAT ABOUT ME?
YOU' GOTTA STAY HERE AND HOLD CHINA TOWN. BUY ME SOME TIME TO STOP THESE THINGS.
UH UH. NO WAY. I'M COMING WITH YOU.
YOU CAN'T, POLLY. YOUR PLACE IS HERE, CHINATOWN. THE PEOPLE HERE TRUST YOU. IF ANYONE CAN HOLD THINGS TOGETHER UNTIL I GET BACK, IT'S YOU.
YOU GO INTO THAT HORNET'S NEST YOU WON'T BE COMING BACK.
AND I DONE TOLD YOU, I AIN'T LOSIN' YOU AGAIN.
THINK ABOUT JAMIKA. SOMEONE'S GOTTA STAY HERE AND PROTECT HER.
THAT AIN'T FAIR, JOHN. THAT AIN'T EVEN CLOSE TO FAIR.
POLLY, I NEED YOU WITH ME ON THIS.
SIGH. ALL RIGHT, JOHN. WE'LL DO IT YOUR WAY.
BUT, YOU BETTER COME BACK TO ME.
I WILL, BABY.
PROMISE?
PROMISE.
WHAT ABOUT THE REST OF YOU?

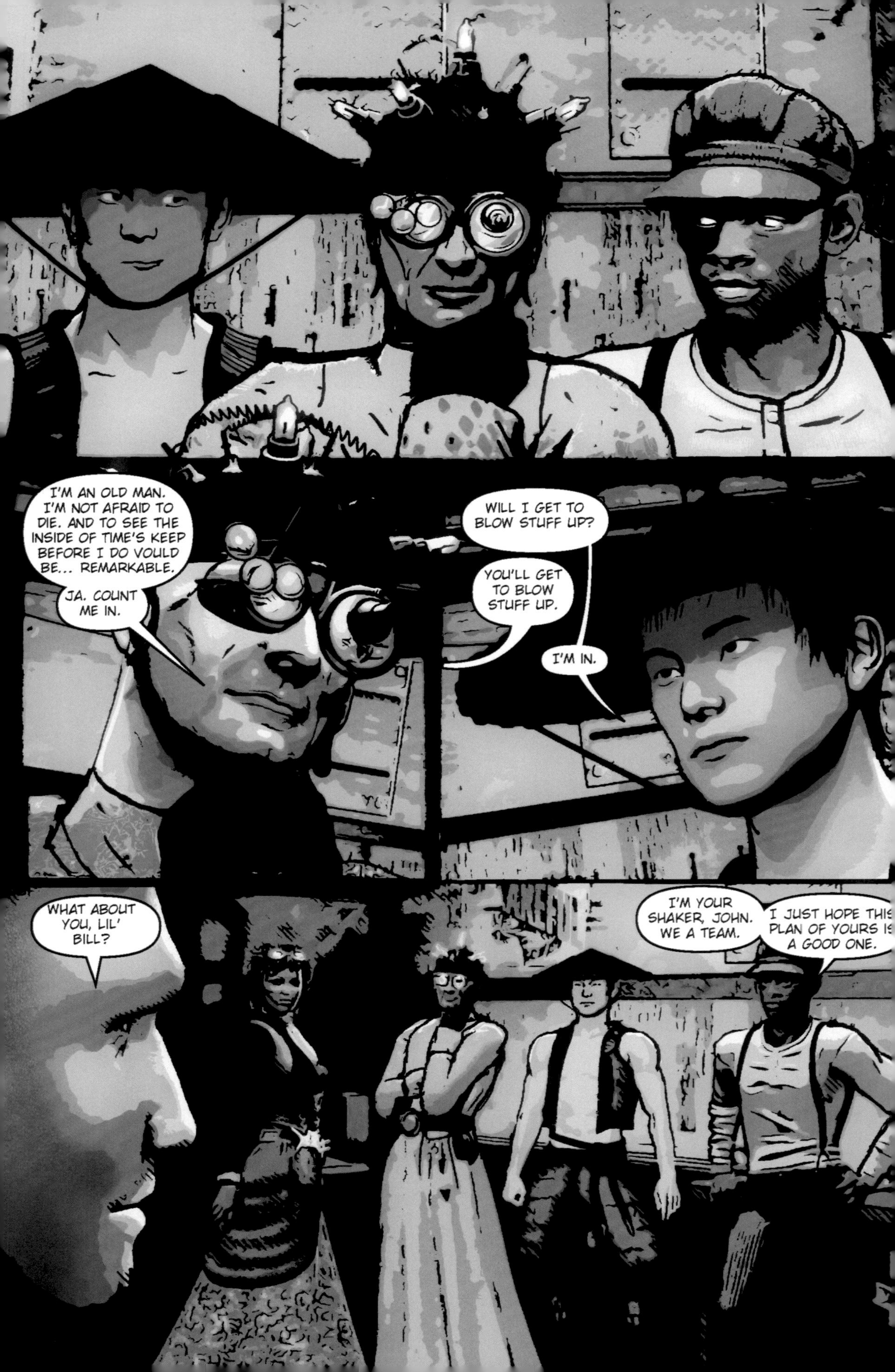
I'M AN OLD MAN. I'M NOT AFRAID TO DIE. AND TO SEE THE INSIDE OF TIME'S KEEP BEFORE I DO VOULD BE... REMARKABLE.
JA. COUNT ME IN.
WILL I GET TO BLOW STUFF UP?
YOU'LL GET TO BLOW STUFF UP.
I'M IN.
WHAT ABOUT YOU, LIL' BILL?
I'M YOUR SHAKER, JOHN. WE A TEAM.
I JUST HOPE THIS PLAN OF YOURS IS A GOOD ONE.

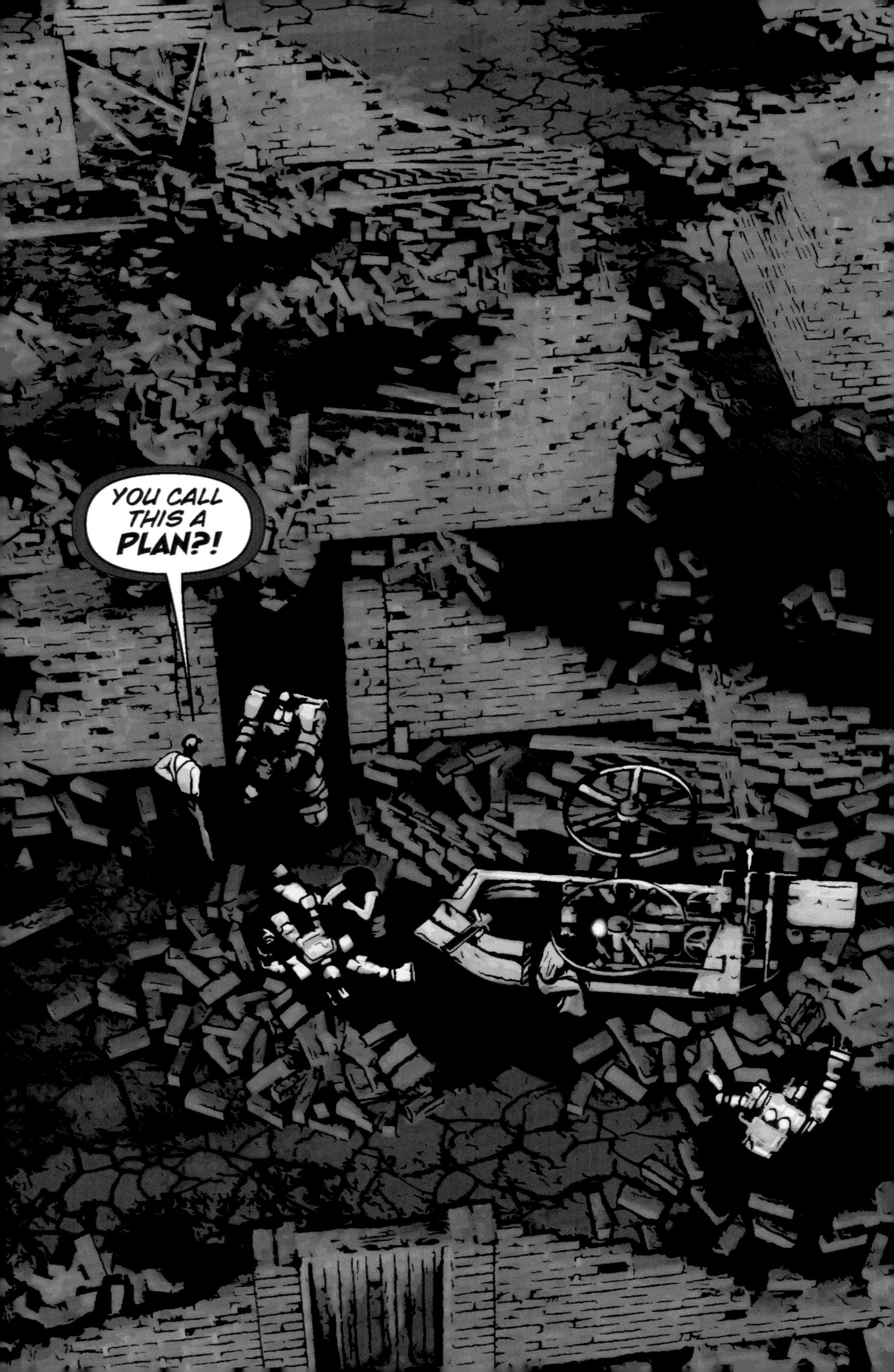
YOU CALL THIS A PLAN?!

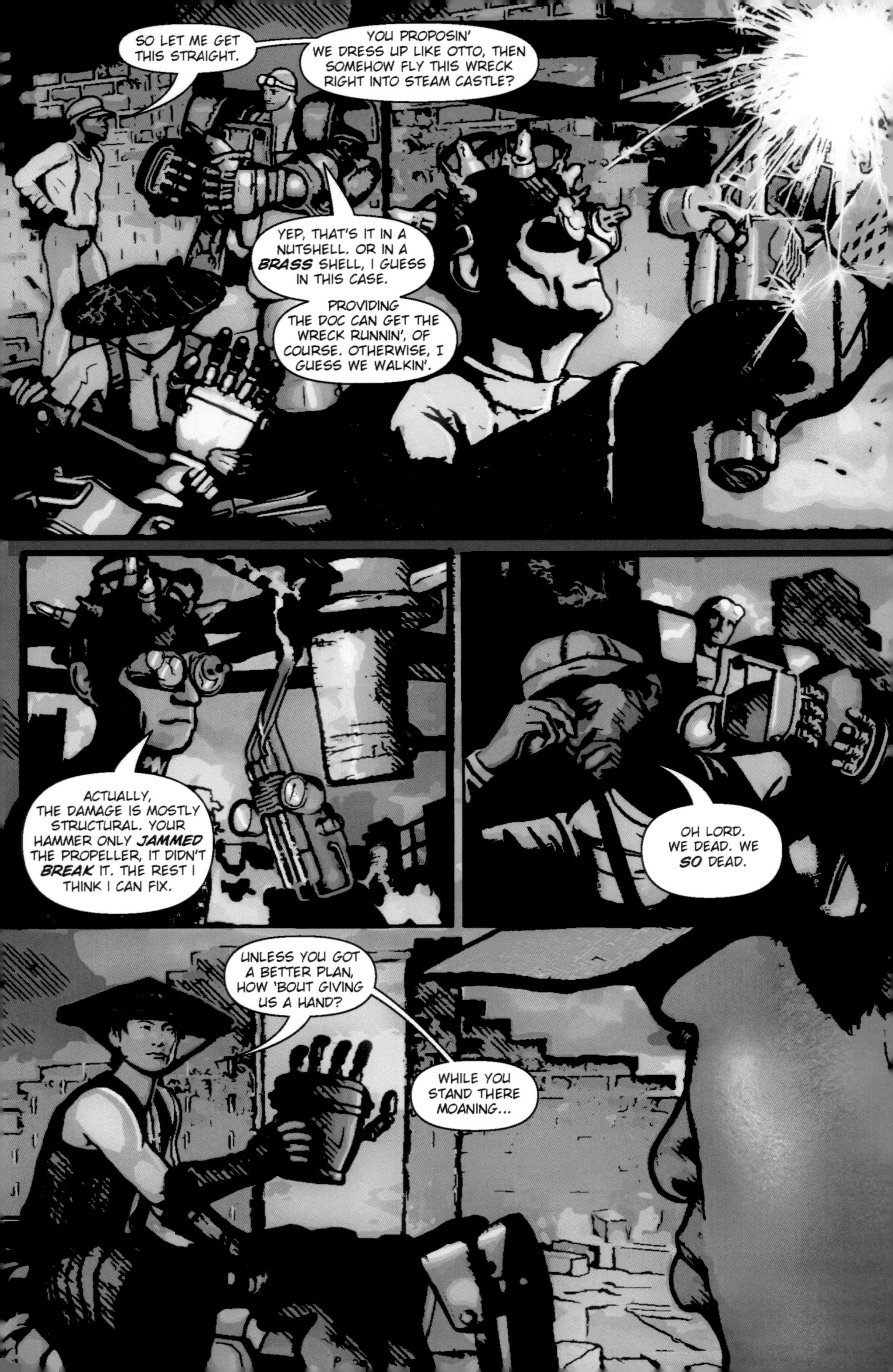
SO LET ME GET THIS STRAIGHT.
YOU PROPOSIN' WE DRESS UP LIKE OTTO, THEN SOMEHOW FLY THIS WRECK RIGHT INTO STEAM CASTLE?
YEP, THAT'S IT IN A NUTSHELL. OR IN A **BRASS** SHELL, I GUESS IN THIS CASE.
PROVIDING THE DOC CAN GET THE WRECK RUNNIN', OF COURSE. OTHERWISE, I GUESS WE WALKIN'.
ACTUALLY, THE DAMAGE IS MOSTLY STRUCTURAL. YOUR HAMMER ONLY **JAMMED** THE PROPELLER, IT DIDN'T **BREAK** IT. THE REST I THINK I CAN FIX.
OH LORD. WE DEAD. WE **SO** DEAD.
UNLESS YOU GOT A BETTER PLAN, HOW 'BOUT GIVING US A HAND?
WHILE YOU STAND THERE MOANING...

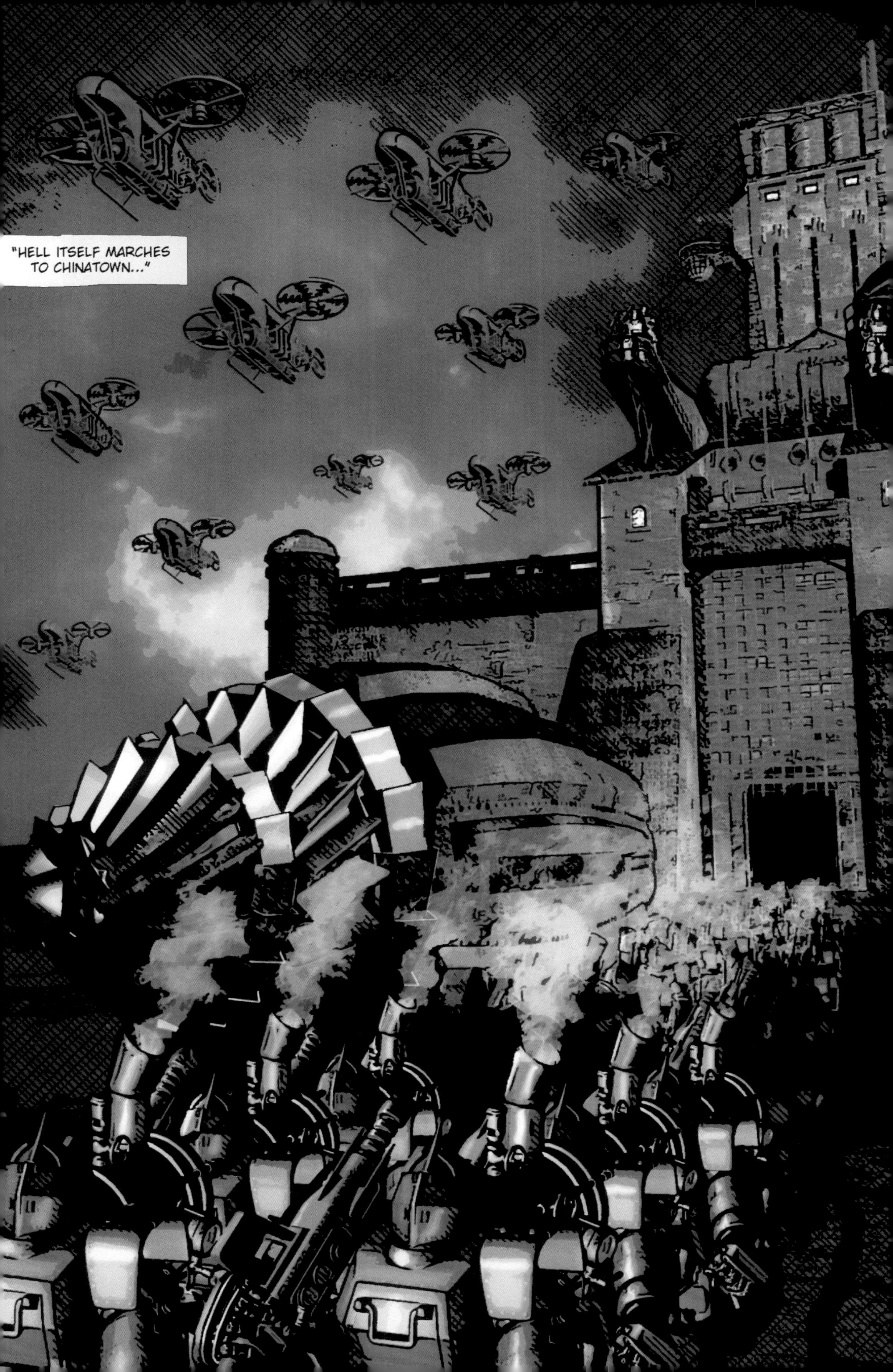
"HELL ITSELF MARCHES TO CHINATOWN..."

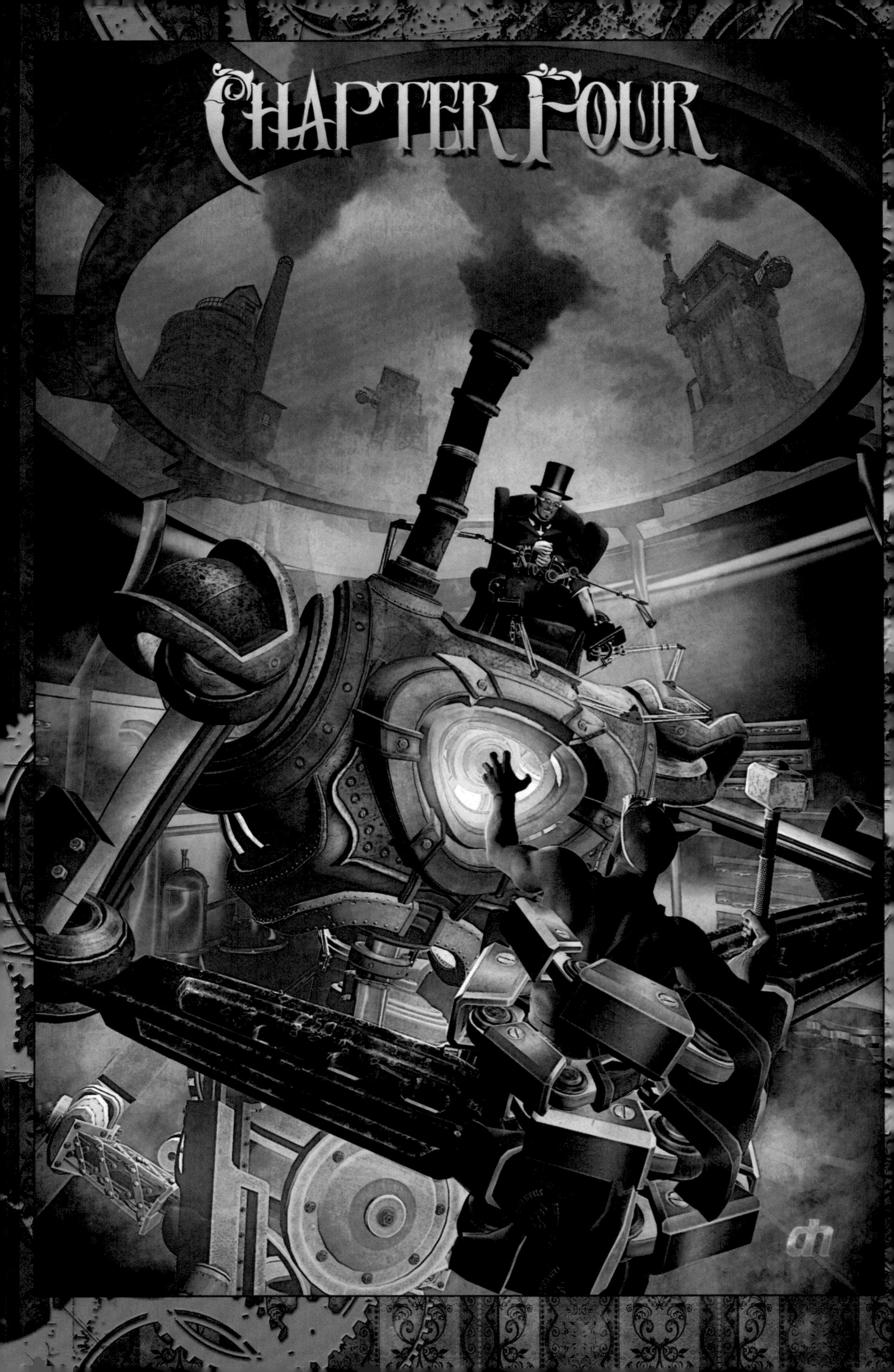
CHAPTER FOUR

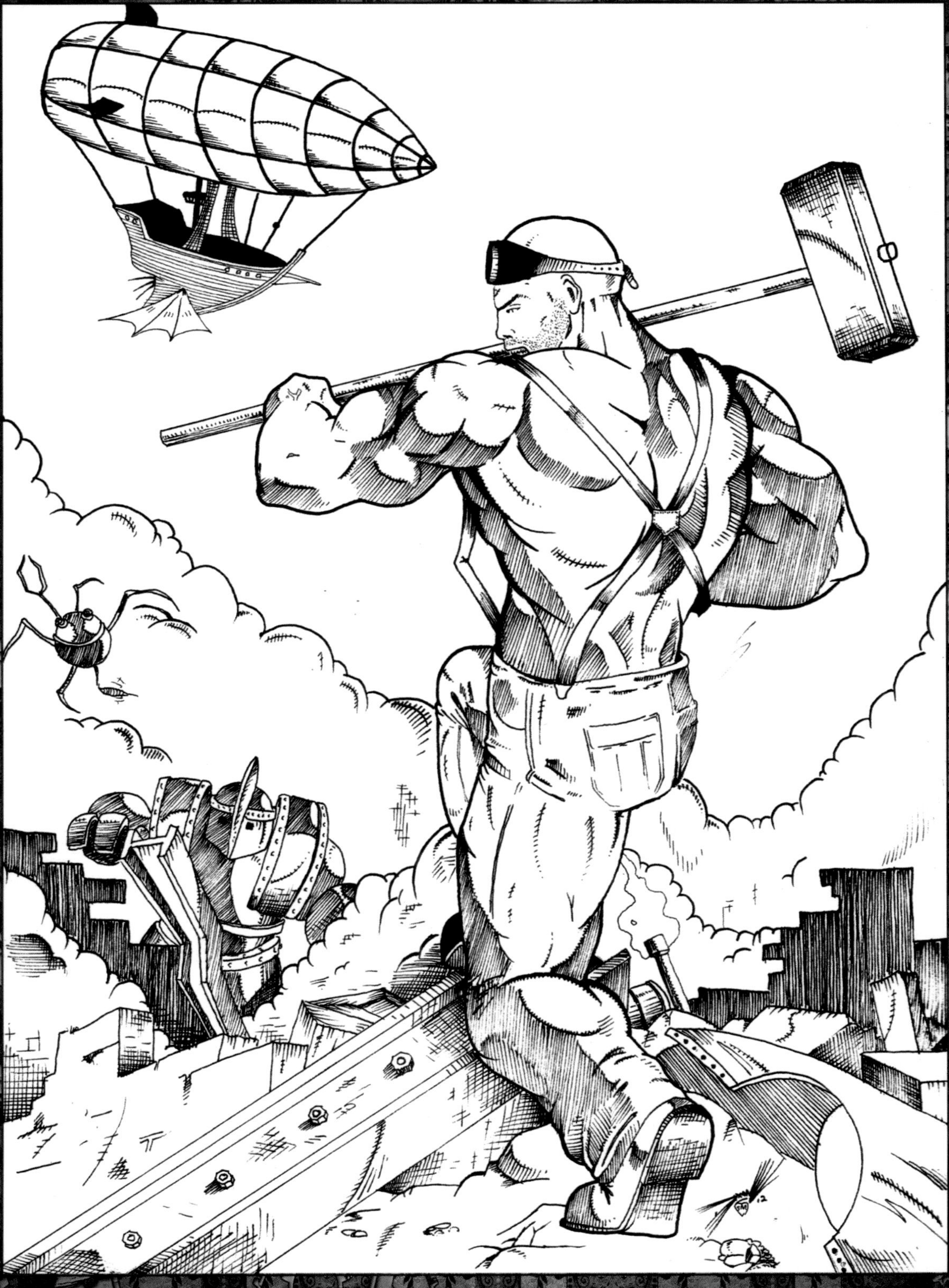

PIN-UP BY CHRIS DIXON

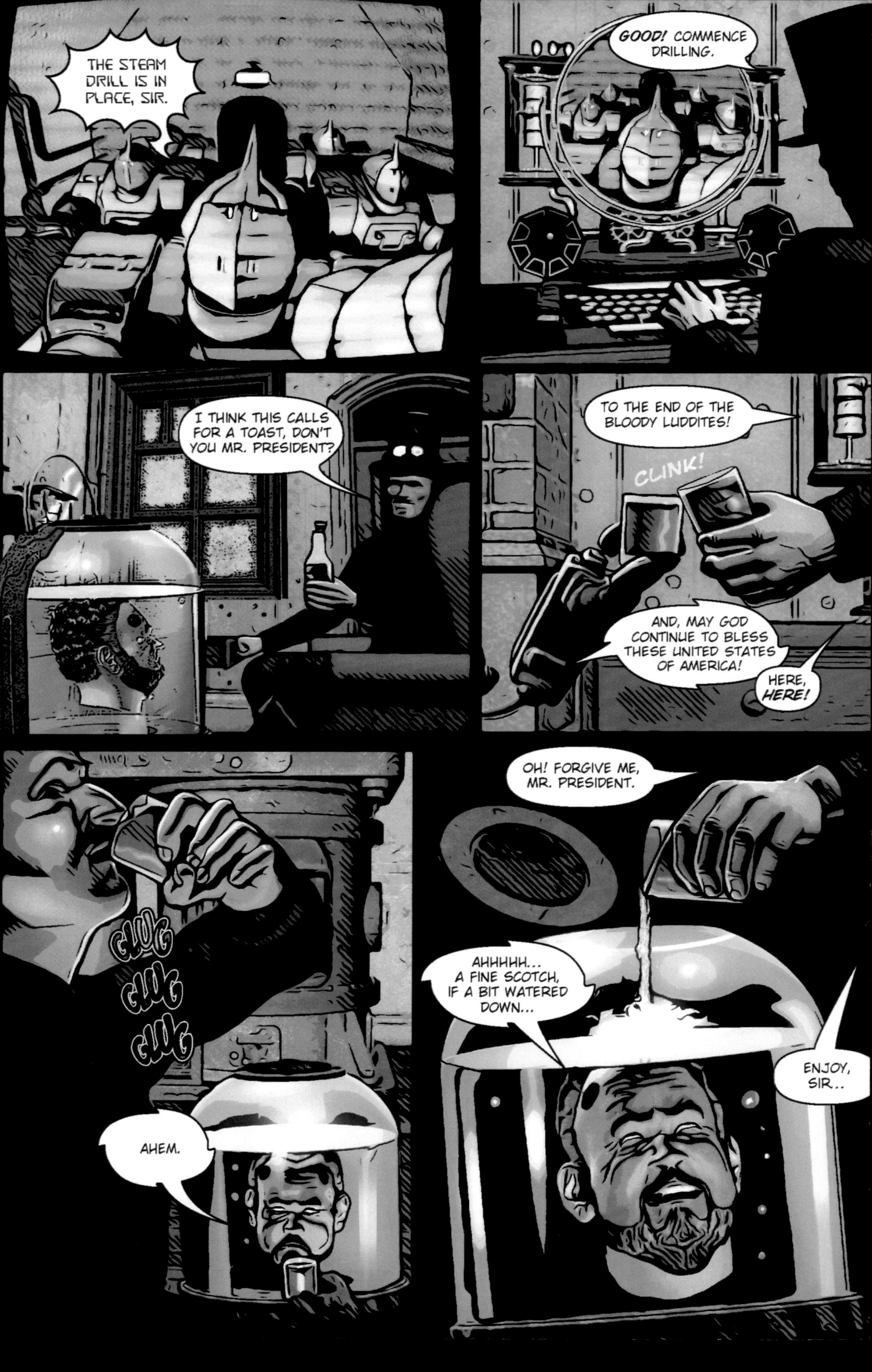
THE STEAM DRILL IS IN PLACE, SIR.
GOOD! COMMENCE DRILLING.
I THINK THIS CALLS FOR A TOAST, DON'T YOU MR. PRESIDENT?
TO THE END OF THE BLOODY LUDDITES!
CLINK!
AND, MAY GOD CONTINUE TO BLESS THESE UNITED STATES OF AMERICA!
HERE, HERE!
GLUG
GLUG
GLUG
AHEM.
OH! FORGIVE ME, MR. PRESIDENT.
AHHHHH... A FINE SCOTCH, IF A BIT WATERED DOWN...
ENJOY, SIR...

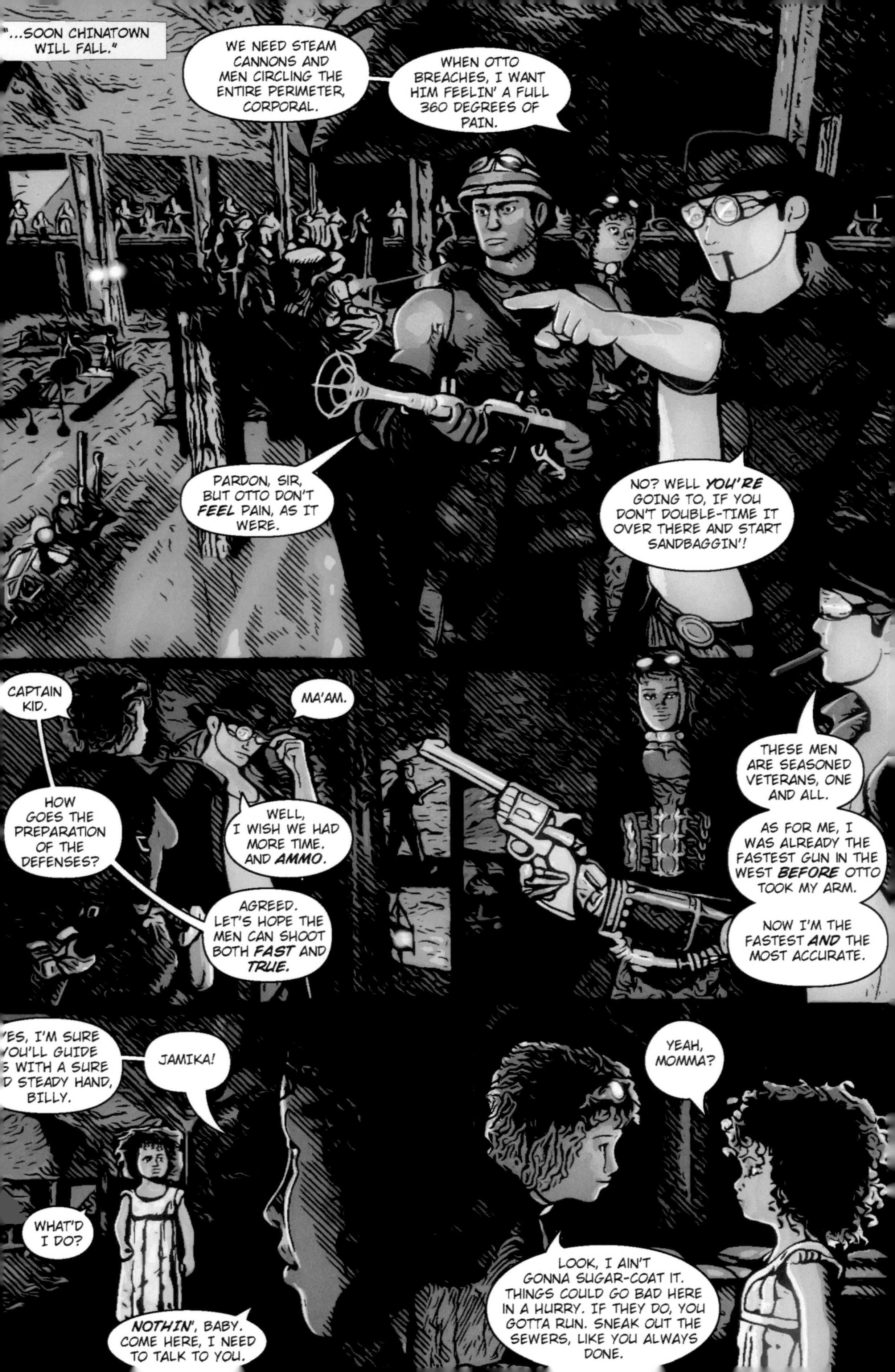
"...SOON CHINATOWN WILL FALL."
WE NEED STEAM CANNONS AND MEN CIRCLING THE ENTIRE PERIMETER, CORPORAL.
WHEN OTTO BREACHES, I WANT HIM FEELIN' A FULL 360 DEGREES OF PAIN.
PARDON, SIR, BUT OTTO DON'T FEEL PAIN, AS IT WERE.
NO? WELL YOU'RE GOING TO, IF YOU DON'T DOUBLE-TIME IT OVER THERE AND START SANDBAGGIN'!
CAPTAIN KID.
MA'AM.
HOW GOES THE PREPARATION OF THE DEFENSES?
WELL, I WISH WE HAD MORE TIME. AND AMMO.
AGREED. LET'S HOPE THE MEN CAN SHOOT BOTH FAST AND TRUE.
THESE MEN ARE SEASONED VETERANS, ONE AND ALL.
AS FOR ME, I WAS ALREADY THE FASTEST GUN IN THE WEST BEFORE OTTO TOOK MY ARM.
NOW I'M THE FASTEST AND THE MOST ACCURATE.
YES, I'M SURE YOU'LL GUIDE US WITH A SURE AND STEADY HAND, BILLY.
JAMIKA!
WHAT'D I DO?
NOTHIN', BABY. COME HERE, I NEED TO TALK TO YOU.
YEAH, MOMMA?
LOOK, I AIN'T GONNA SUGAR-COAT IT. THINGS COULD GO BAD HERE IN A HURRY. IF THEY DO, YOU GOTTA RUN. SNEAK OUT THE SEWERS, LIKE YOU ALWAYS DONE.

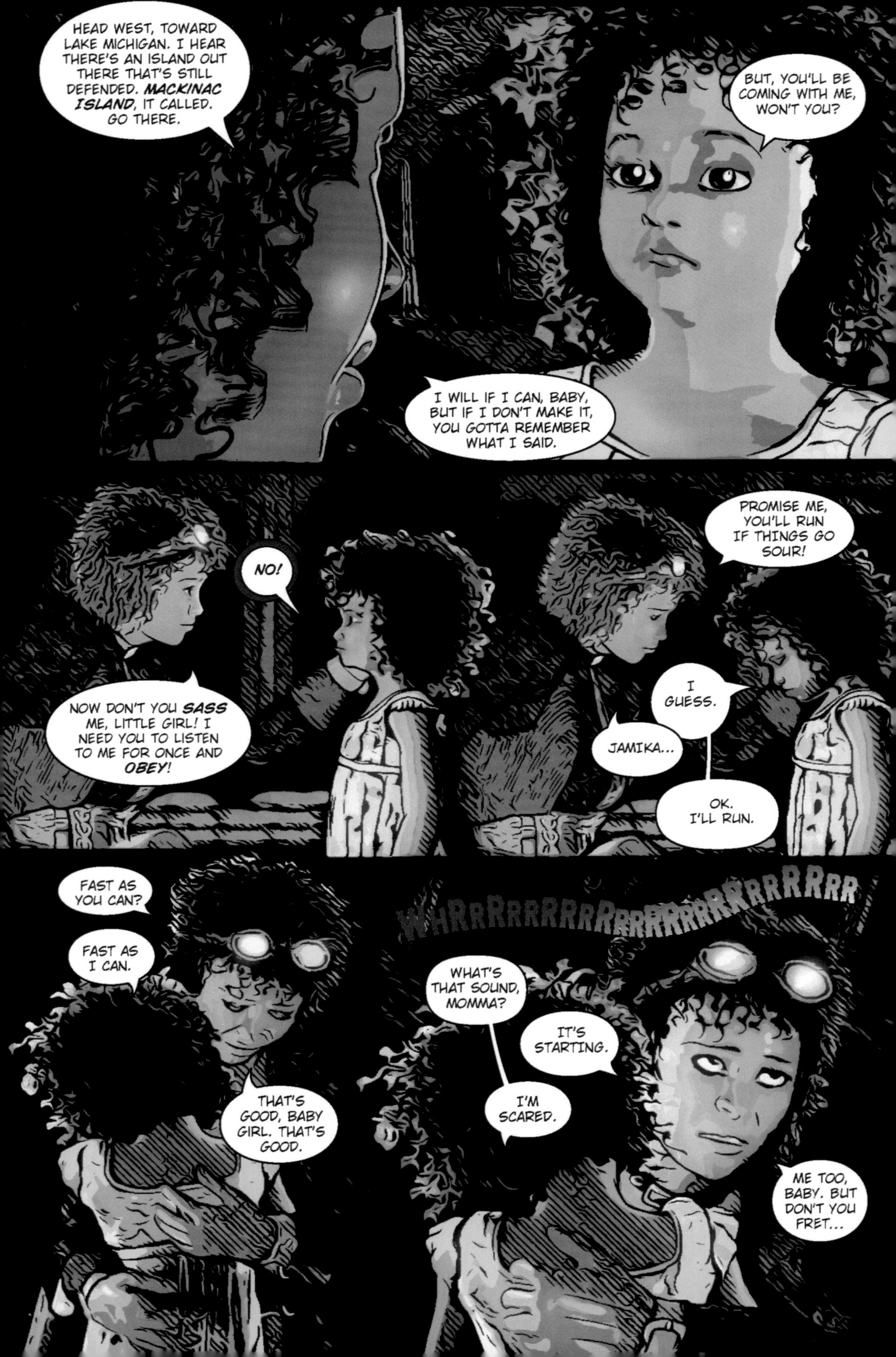
HEAD WEST, TOWARD LAKE MICHIGAN. I HEAR THERE'S AN ISLAND OUT THERE THAT'S STILL DEFENDED. MACKINAC ISLAND, IT CALLED. GO THERE.
BUT, YOU'LL BE COMING WITH ME, WON'T YOU?
I WILL IF I CAN, BABY, BUT IF I DON'T MAKE IT, YOU GOTTA REMEMBER WHAT I SAID.
NO!
NOW DON'T YOU SASS ME, LITTLE GIRL! I NEED YOU TO LISTEN TO ME FOR ONCE AND OBEY!
PROMISE ME, YOU'LL RUN IF THINGS GO SOUR!
I GUESS.
JAMIKA...
OK. I'LL RUN.
FAST AS YOU CAN?
FAST AS I CAN.
THAT'S GOOD, BABY GIRL. THAT'S GOOD.
WHRRRRRRRRRRRRRRRRRRRRRRRRRR
WHAT'S THAT SOUND, MOMMA?
IT'S STARTING.
I'M SCARED.
ME TOO, BABY. BUT DON'T YOU FRET...

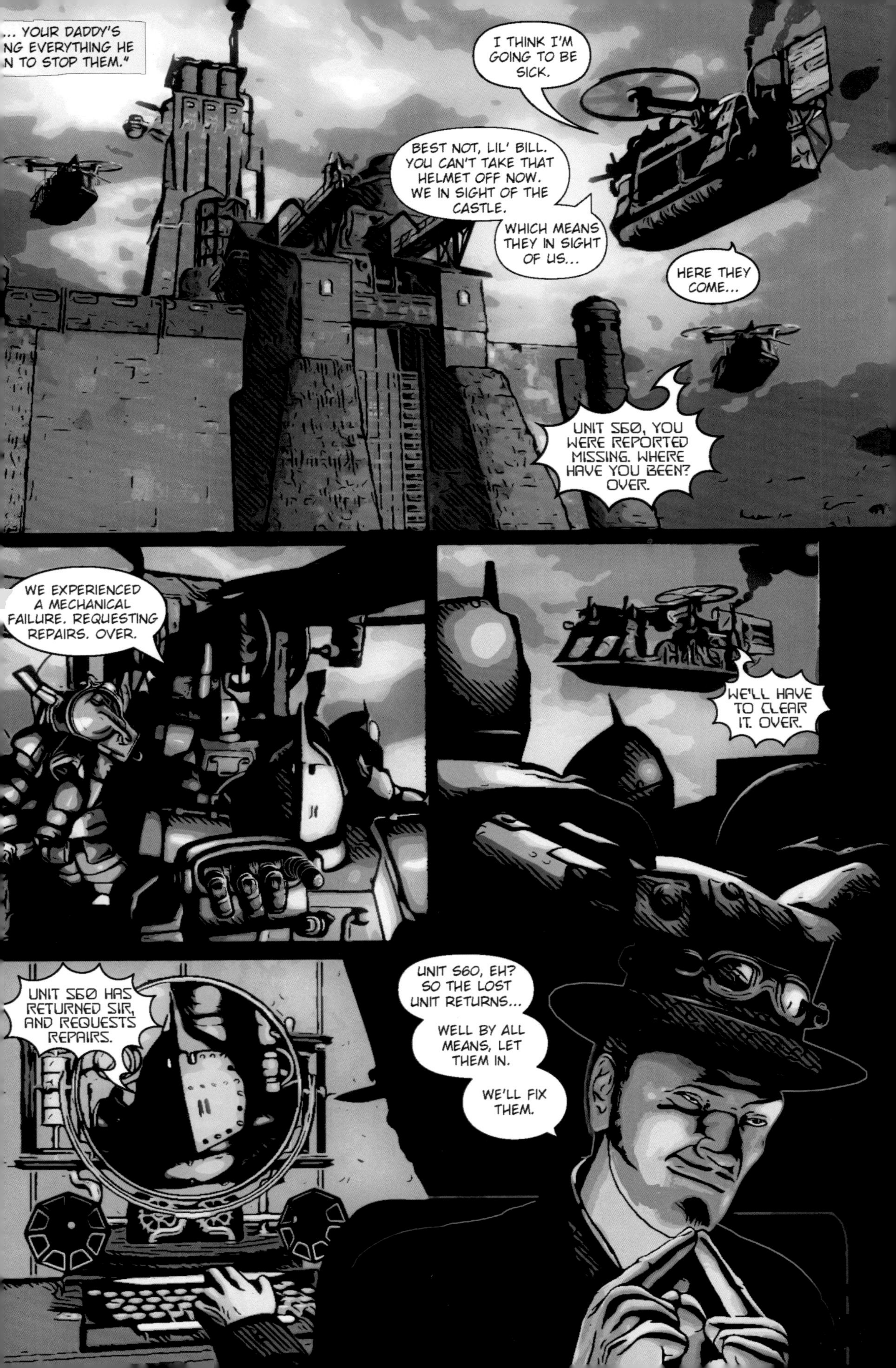
... YOUR DADDY'S
NG EVERYTHING HE
N TO STOP THEM."
I THINK I'M GOING TO BE SICK.
BEST NOT, LIL' BILL. YOU CAN'T TAKE THAT HELMET OFF NOW. WE IN SIGHT OF THE CASTLE.
WHICH MEANS THEY IN SIGHT OF US...
HERE THEY COME...
UNIT S60, YOU WERE REPORTED MISSING. WHERE HAVE YOU BEEN? OVER.
WE EXPERIENCED A MECHANICAL FAILURE. REQUESTING REPAIRS. OVER.
WE'LL HAVE TO CLEAR IT. OVER.
UNIT S60 HAS RETURNED SIR, AND REQUESTS REPAIRS.
UNIT S60, EH? SO THE LOST UNIT RETURNS...
WELL BY ALL MEANS, LET THEM IN.
WE'LL FIX THEM.

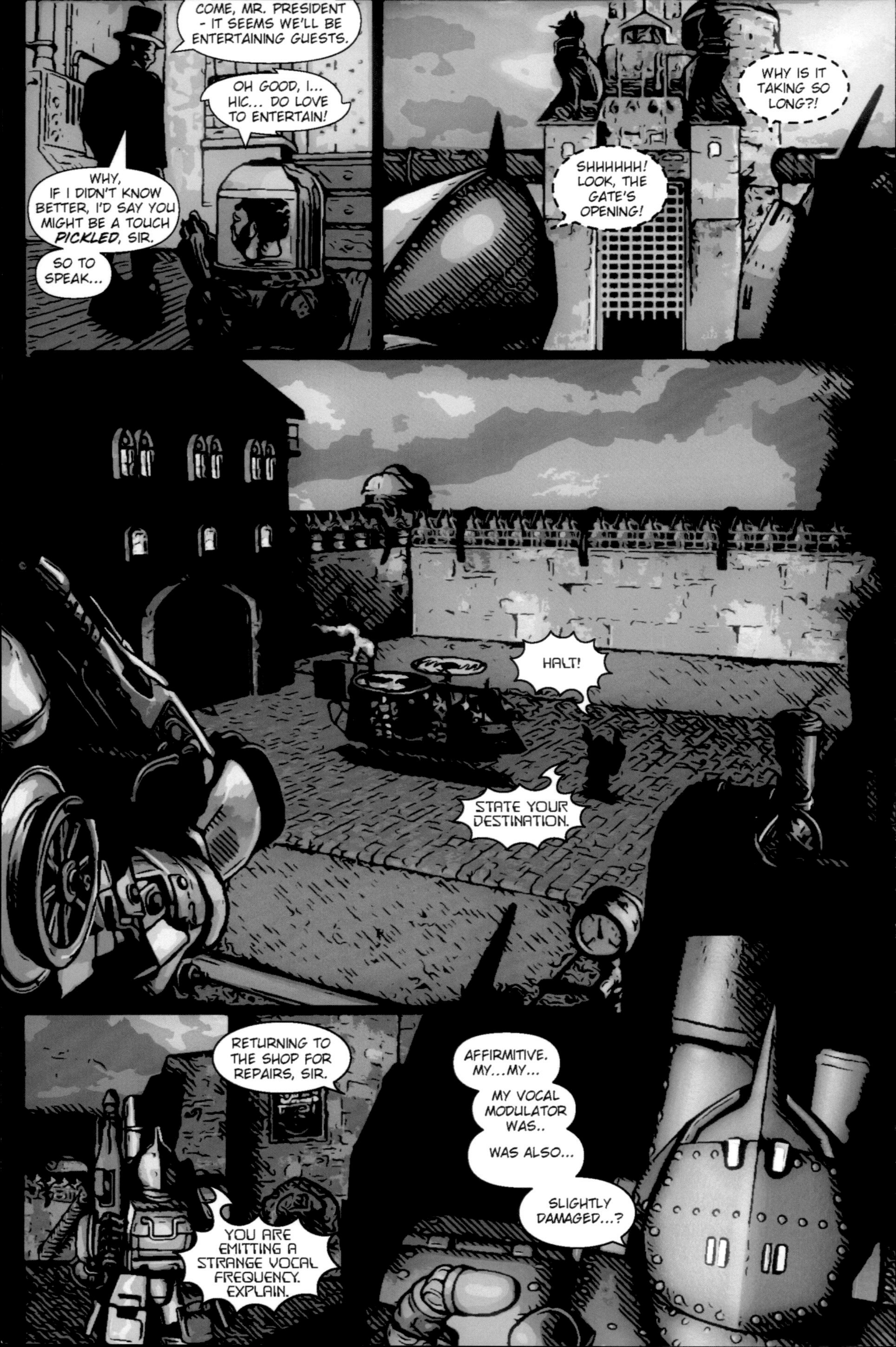
COME, MR. PRESIDENT - IT SEEMS WE'LL BE ENTERTAINING GUESTS.
OH GOOD, I... HIC... DO LOVE TO ENTERTAIN!
WHY, IF I DIDN'T KNOW BETTER, I'D SAY YOU MIGHT BE A TOUCH PICKLED, SIR.
SO TO SPEAK...
WHY IS IT TAKING SO LONG?!
SHHHHHH! LOOK, THE GATE'S OPENING!
HALT!
STATE YOUR DESTINATION.
RETURNING TO THE SHOP FOR REPAIRS, SIR.
YOU ARE EMITTING A STRANGE VOCAL FREQUENCY. EXPLAIN.
AFFIRMITIVE. MY...MY...
MY VOCAL MODULATOR WAS..
WAS ALSO...
SLIGHTLY DAMAGED...?

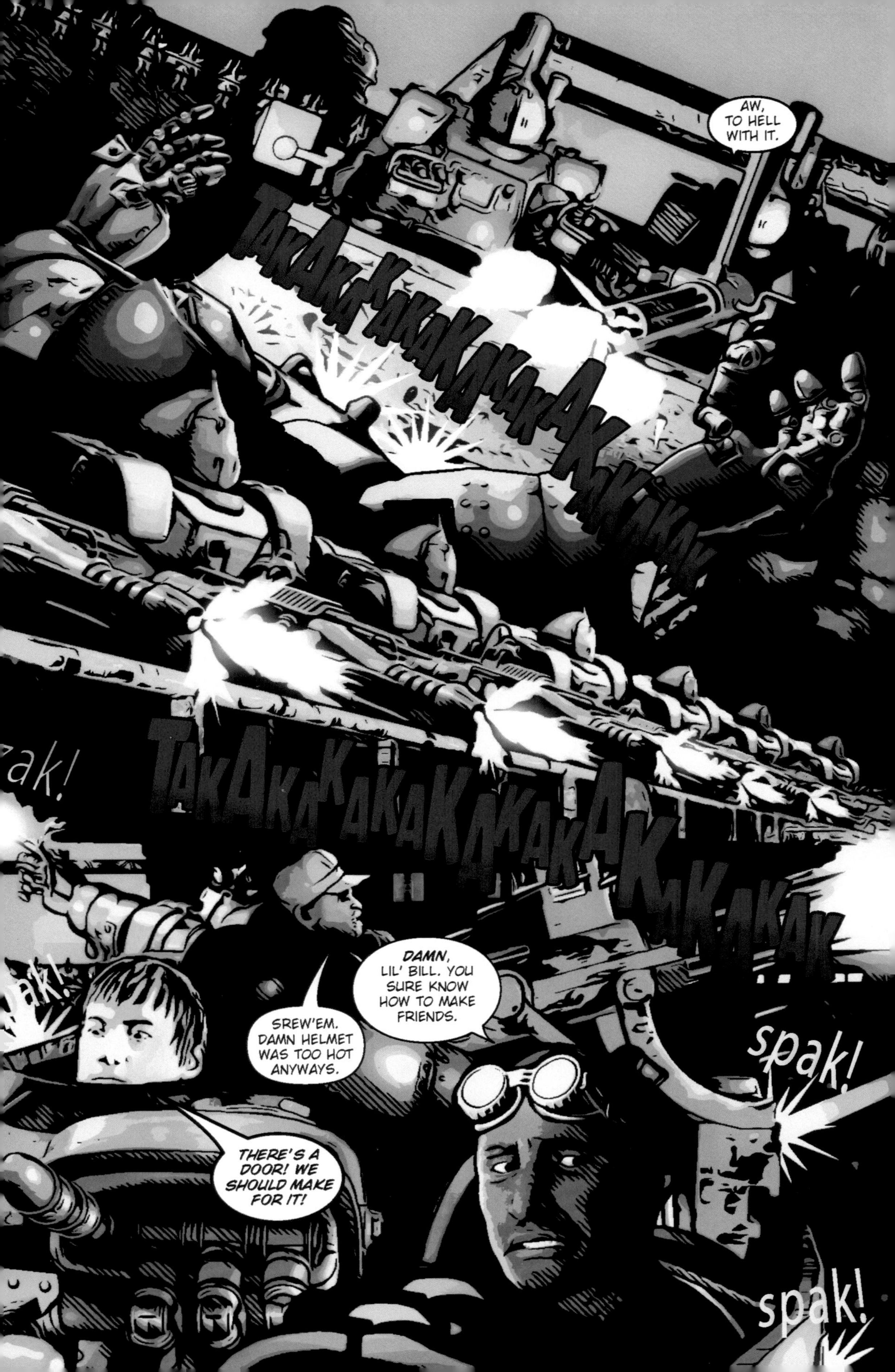
AW, TO HELL WITH IT.
TAKAKAKAKAKAKAKAKAKAKAKAKAK
TAKAKAKAKAKAKAKAKAKAKAKAKAK
ak!
pak!
SREW'EM. DAMN HELMET WAS TOO HOT ANYWAYS.
DAMN, LIL' BILL. YOU SURE KNOW HOW TO MAKE FRIENDS.
spak!
THERE'S A DOOR! WE SHOULD MAKE FOR IT!
spak!

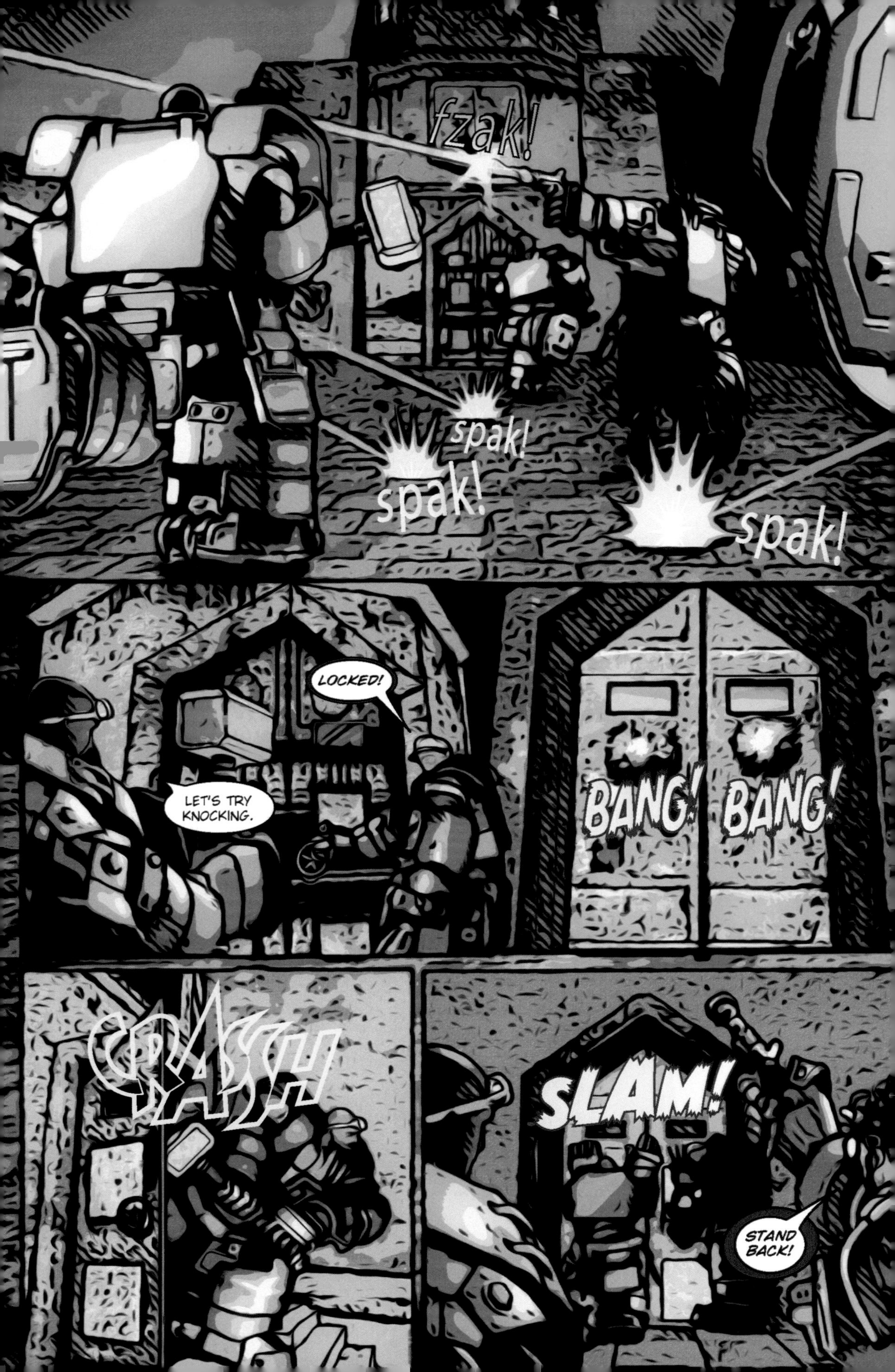
fzak!
spak!
spak!
spak!
LOCKED!
LET'S TRY KNOCKING.
BANG! BANG!
CRASH
SLAM!
STAND BACK!

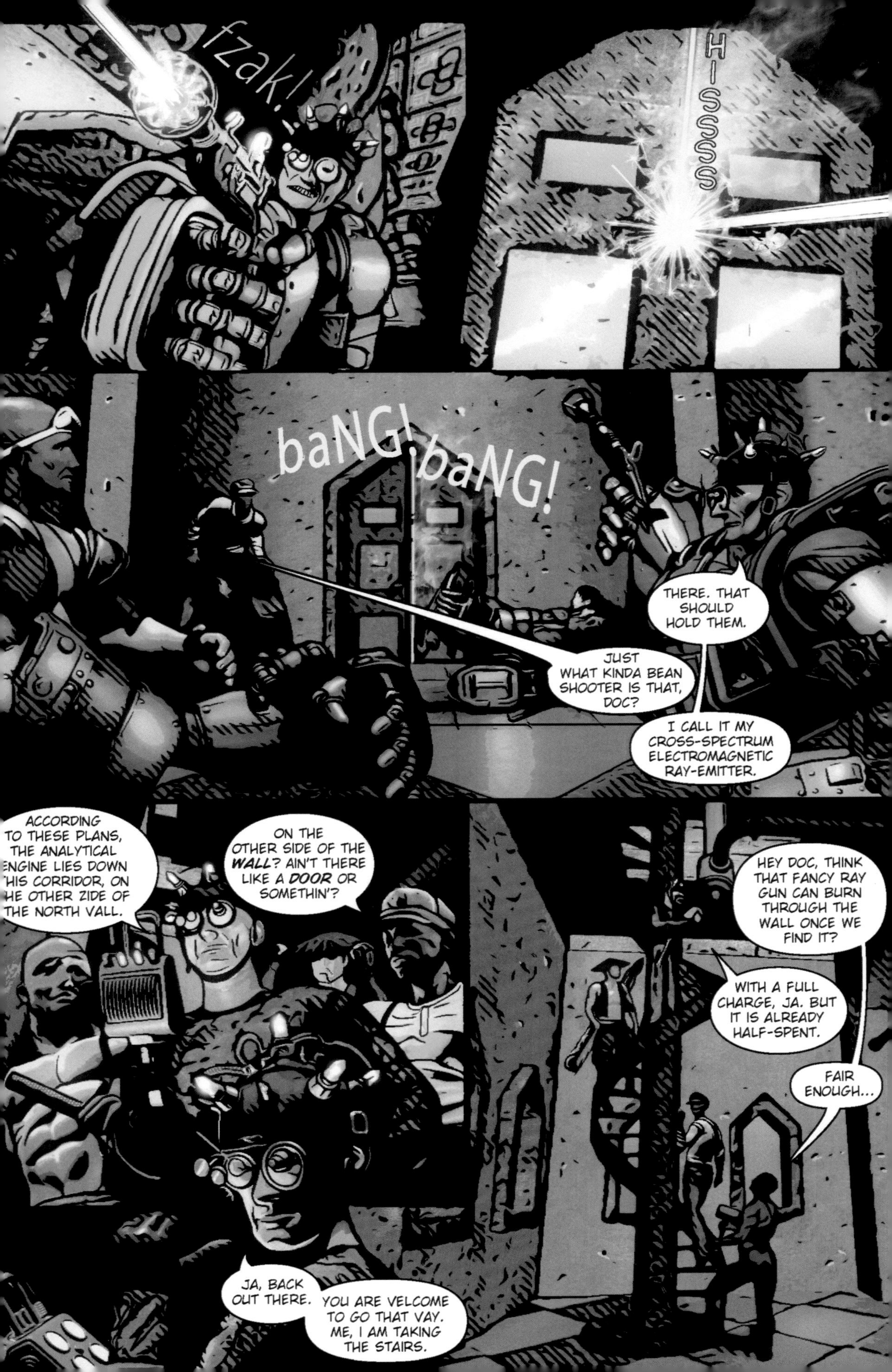
fzak!
HISSSS
baNG! baNG!
THERE. THAT SHOULD HOLD THEM.
JUST WHAT KINDA BEAN SHOOTER IS THAT, DOC?
I CALL IT MY CROSS-SPECTRUM ELECTROMAGNETIC RAY-EMITTER.
ACCORDING TO THESE PLANS, THE ANALYTICAL ENGINE LIES DOWN THIS CORRIDOR, ON THE OTHER ZIDE OF THE NORTH VALL.
ON THE OTHER SIDE OF THE WALL? AIN'T THERE LIKE A DOOR OR SOMETHIN'?
JA, BACK OUT THERE.
YOU ARE VELCOME TO GO THAT VAY. ME, I AM TAKING THE STAIRS.
HEY DOC, THINK THAT FANCY RAY GUN CAN BURN THROUGH THE WALL ONCE WE FIND IT?
WITH A FULL CHARGE, JA. BUT IT IS ALREADY HALF-SPENT.
FAIR ENOUGH...

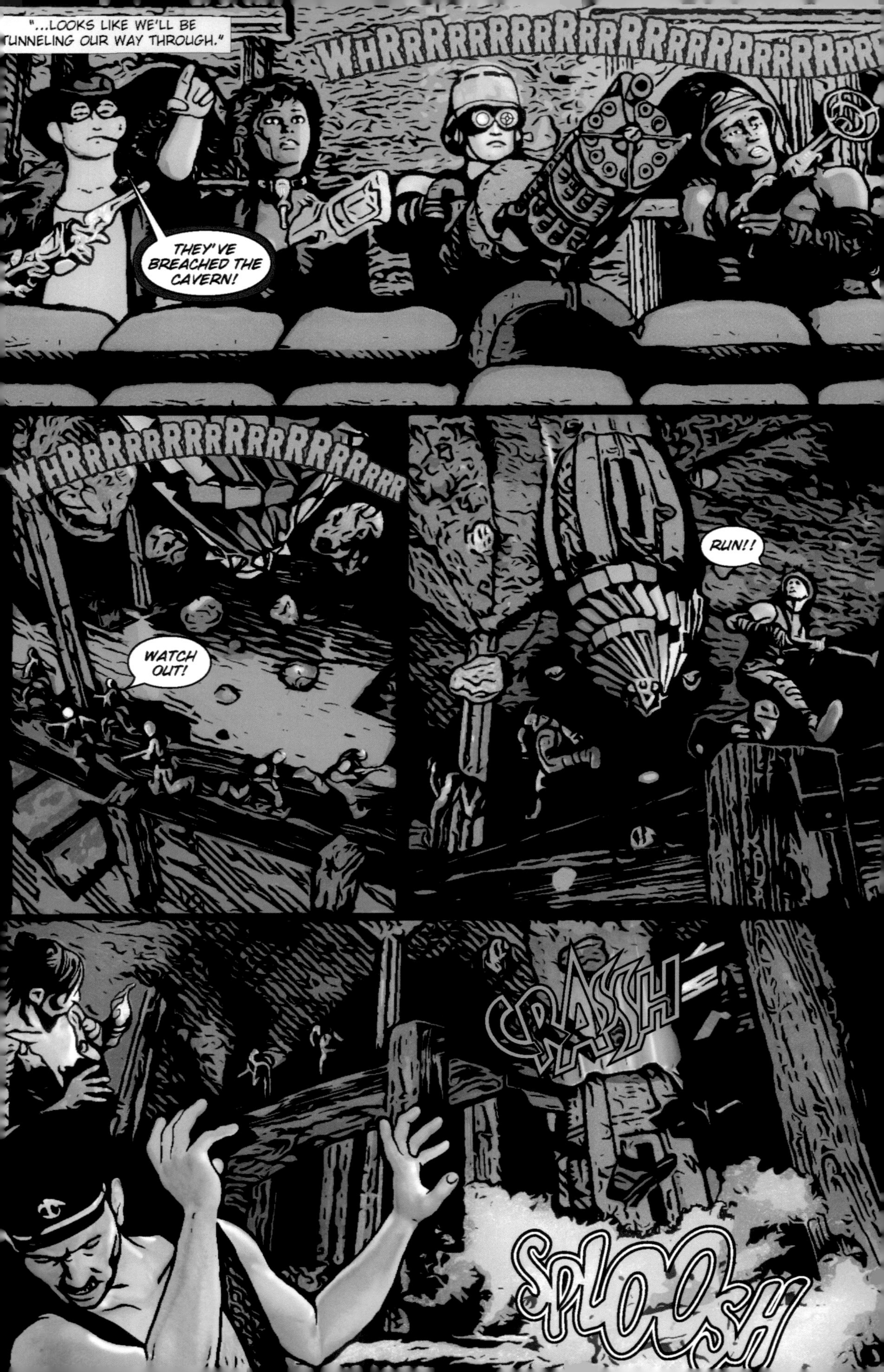
"...LOOKS LIKE WE'LL BE TUNNELING OUR WAY THROUGH."
WHRRRRRRRRRRRRRRRRRRRRRRRRRRR
THEY'VE BREACHED THE CAVERN!
WHRRRRRRRRRRRRRRRRRRRR
WATCH OUT!
RUN!!
CRASH
SPLOOSH

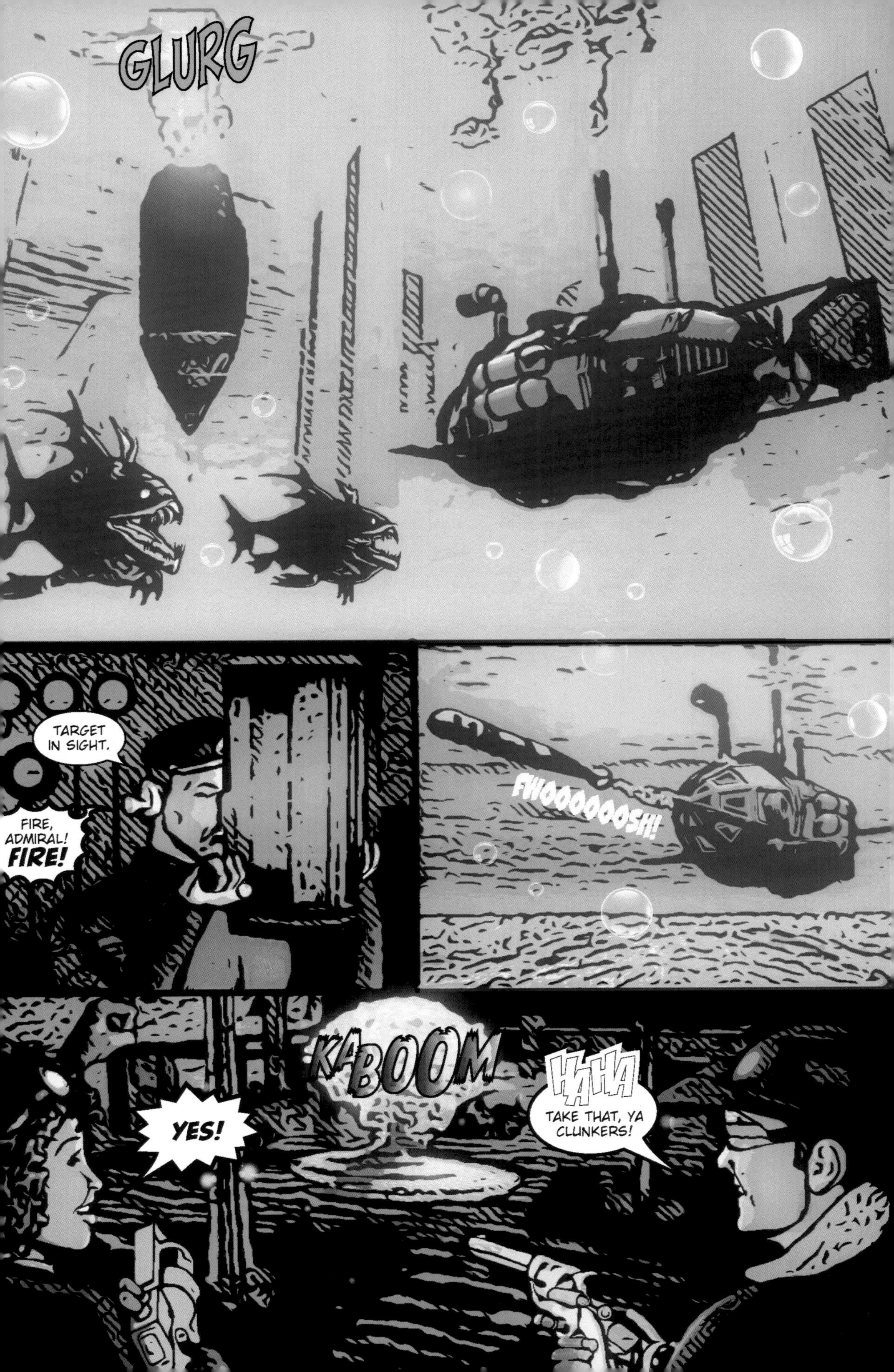
GLURG
TARGET IN SIGHT.
FIRE, ADMIRAL! FIRE!
FWOOOOOOSH!
KABOOM
YES!
HAHA
TAKE THAT, YA CLUNKERS!

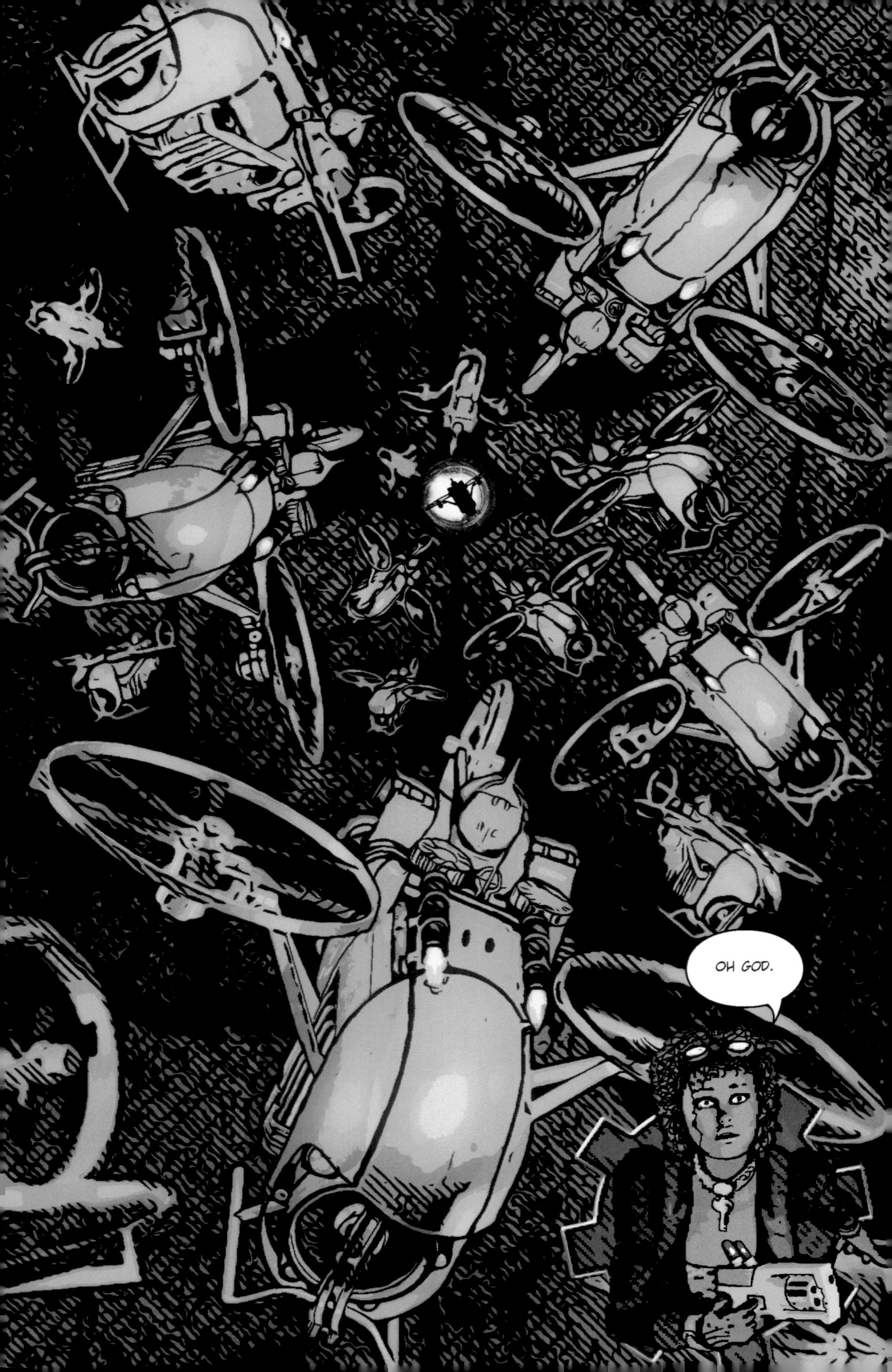
OH GOD.

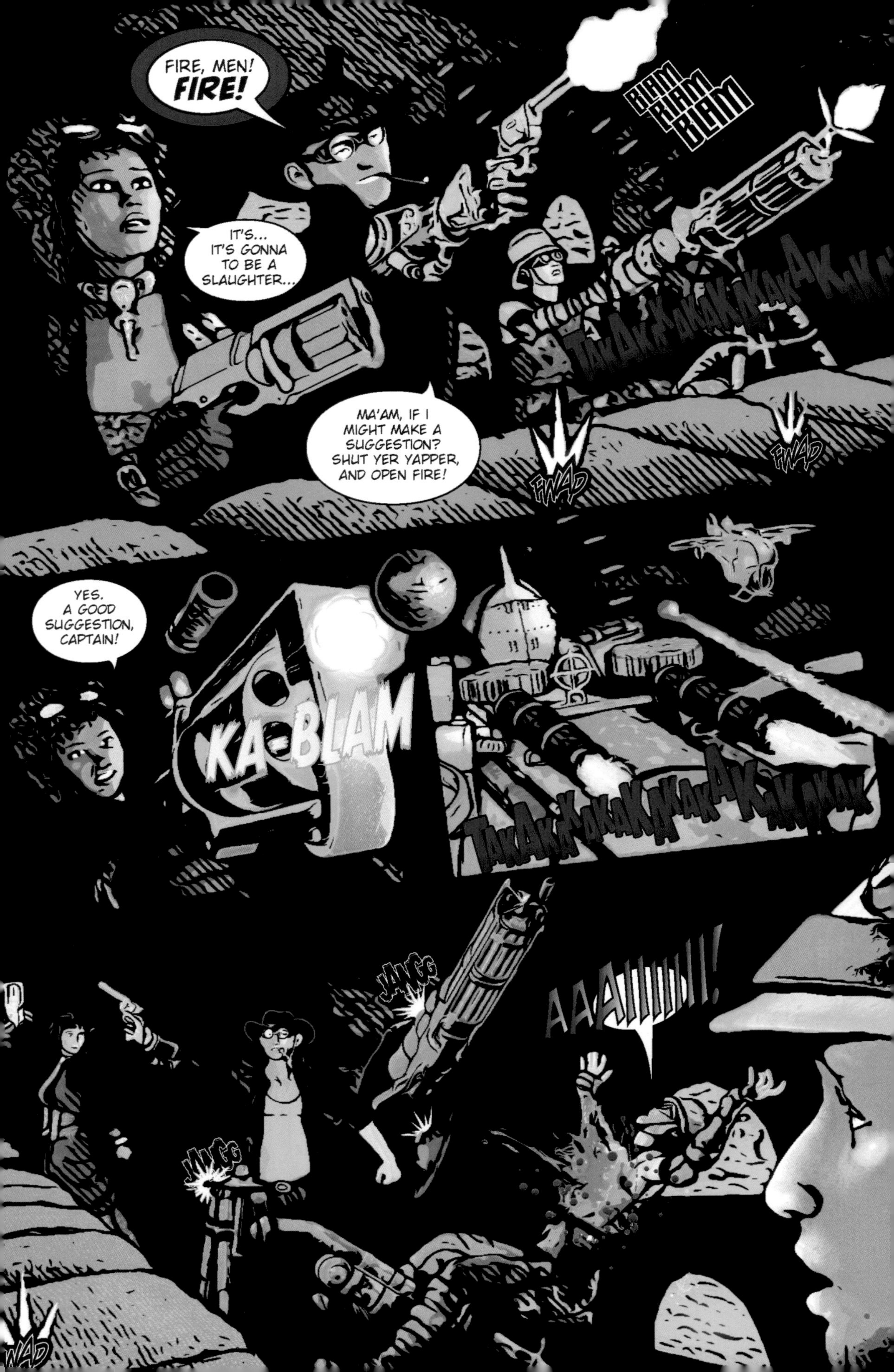
FIRE, MEN! FIRE!
BLAM BLAM BLAM
IT'S... IT'S GONNA TO BE A SLAUGHTER...
TAKAKAKAKAKAKAKAKAK
MA'AM, IF I MIGHT MAKE A SUGGESTION? SHUT YER YAPPER, AND OPEN FIRE!
FWAP
FWAP
YES. A GOOD SUGGESTION, CAPTAIN!
KA-BLAM
TAKAKAKAKAKAKAKAKAKAKAK
JANGG
AAAIIIIIII!
JANGG
WAD

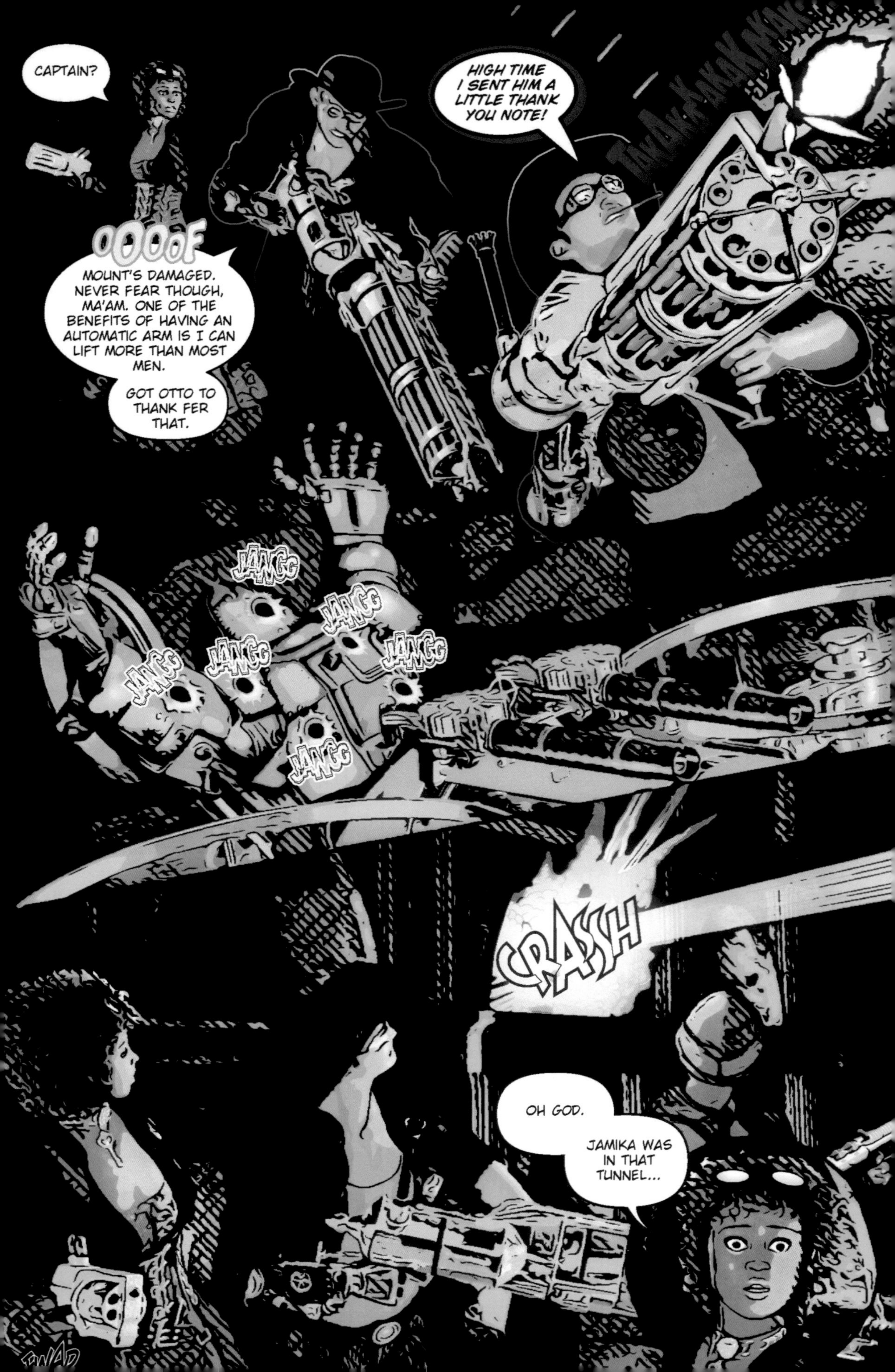
CAPTAIN?
HIGH TIME I SENT HIM A LITTLE THANK YOU NOTE!
TAKAKAKAKAKAK
OOOoF
MOUNT'S DAMAGED. NEVER FEAR THOUGH, MA'AM. ONE OF THE BENEFITS OF HAVING AN AUTOMATIC ARM IS I CAN LIFT MORE THAN MOST MEN.
GOT OTTO TO THANK FER THAT.
JANGG
JANGG
JANGG
JANGG
JANGG
JANGG
CRASH
OH GOD.
JAMIKA WAS IN THAT TUNNEL...

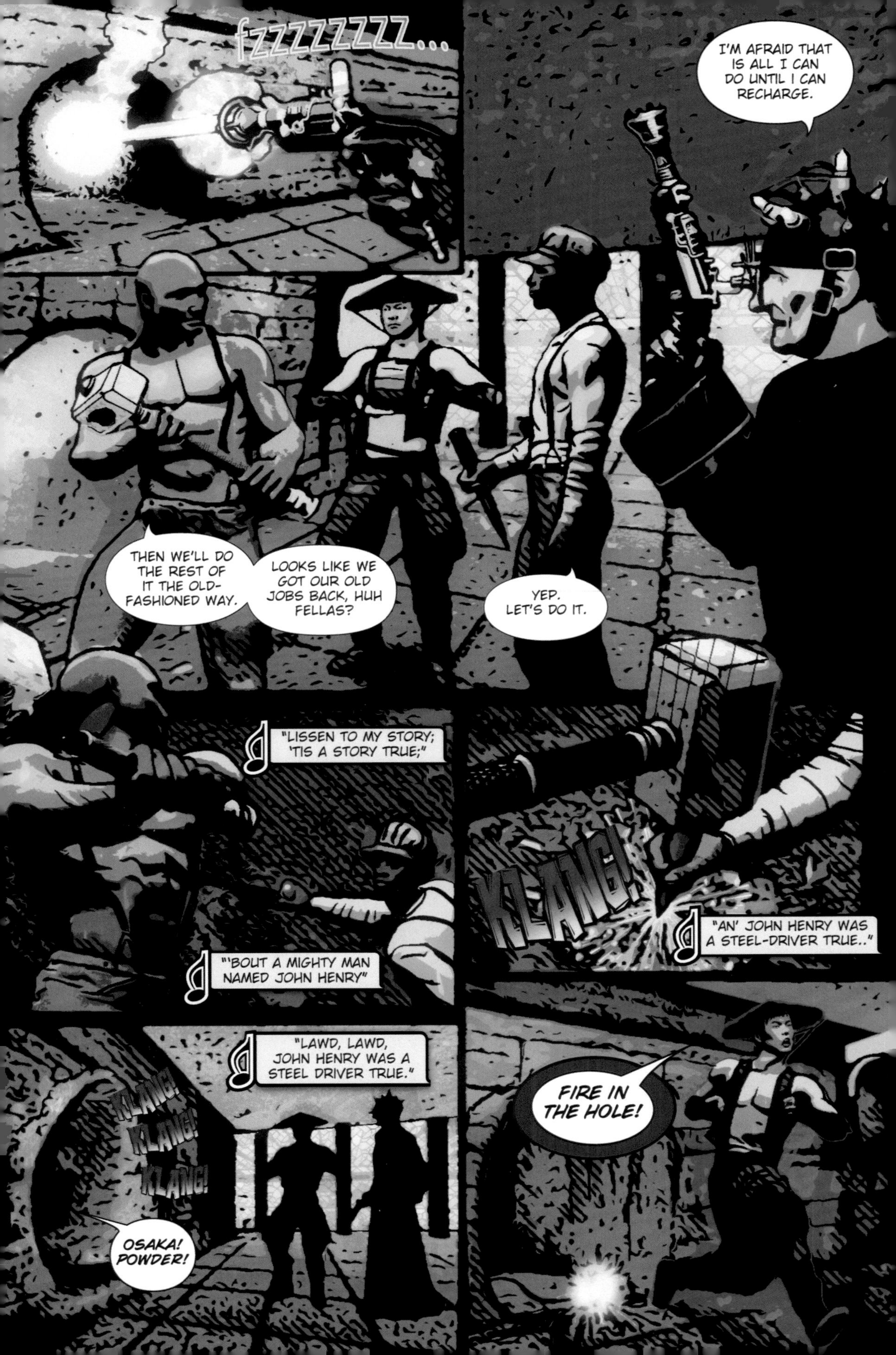

fzzzzzzzz...
I'M AFRAID THAT IS ALL I CAN DO UNTIL I CAN RECHARGE.
THEN WE'LL DO THE REST OF IT THE OLD-FASHIONED WAY.
LOOKS LIKE WE GOT OUR OLD JOBS BACK, HUH FELLAS?
YEP. LET'S DO IT.
"LISSEN TO MY STORY; 'TIS A STORY TRUE;"
"'BOUT A MIGHTY MAN NAMED JOHN HENRY"
KLANG!
"AN' JOHN HENRY WAS A STEEL-DRIVER TRUE.."
"LAWD, LAWD, JOHN HENRY WAS A STEEL DRIVER TRUE."
KLANG! KLANG! KLANG!
OSAKA! POWDER!
FIRE IN THE HOLE!

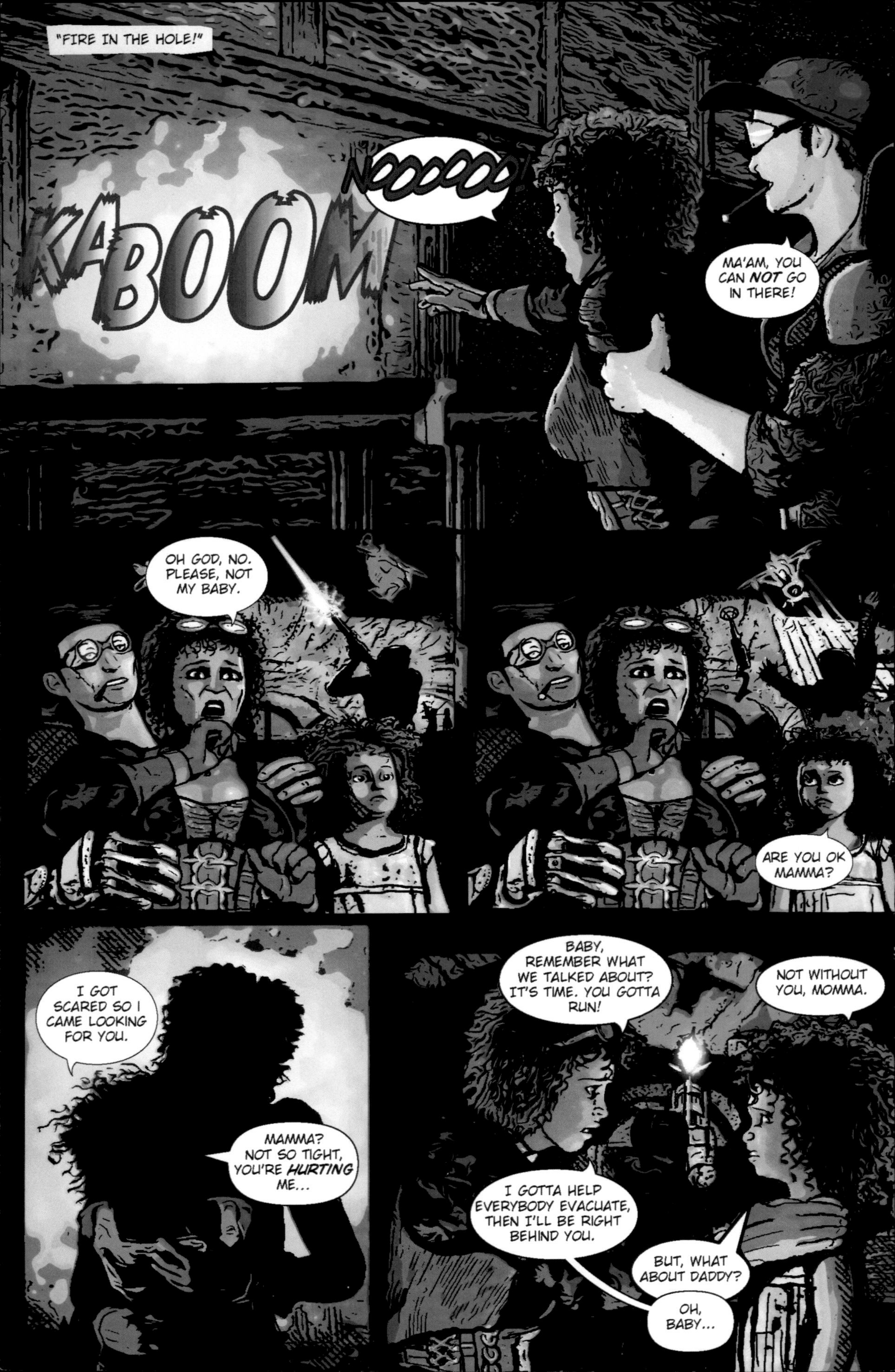
"FIRE IN THE HOLE!"
KABOOM
NOOOOOO!
MA'AM, YOU CAN NOT GO IN THERE!
OH GOD, NO. PLEASE, NOT MY BABY.
ARE YOU OK MAMMA?
I GOT SCARED SO I CAME LOOKING FOR YOU.
MAMMA? NOT SO TIGHT, YOU'RE HURTING ME...
BABY, REMEMBER WHAT WE TALKED ABOUT? IT'S TIME. YOU GOTTA RUN!
NOT WITHOUT YOU, MOMMA.
I GOTTA HELP EVERYBODY EVACUATE, THEN I'LL BE RIGHT BEHIND YOU.
BUT, WHAT ABOUT DADDY?
OH, BABY...

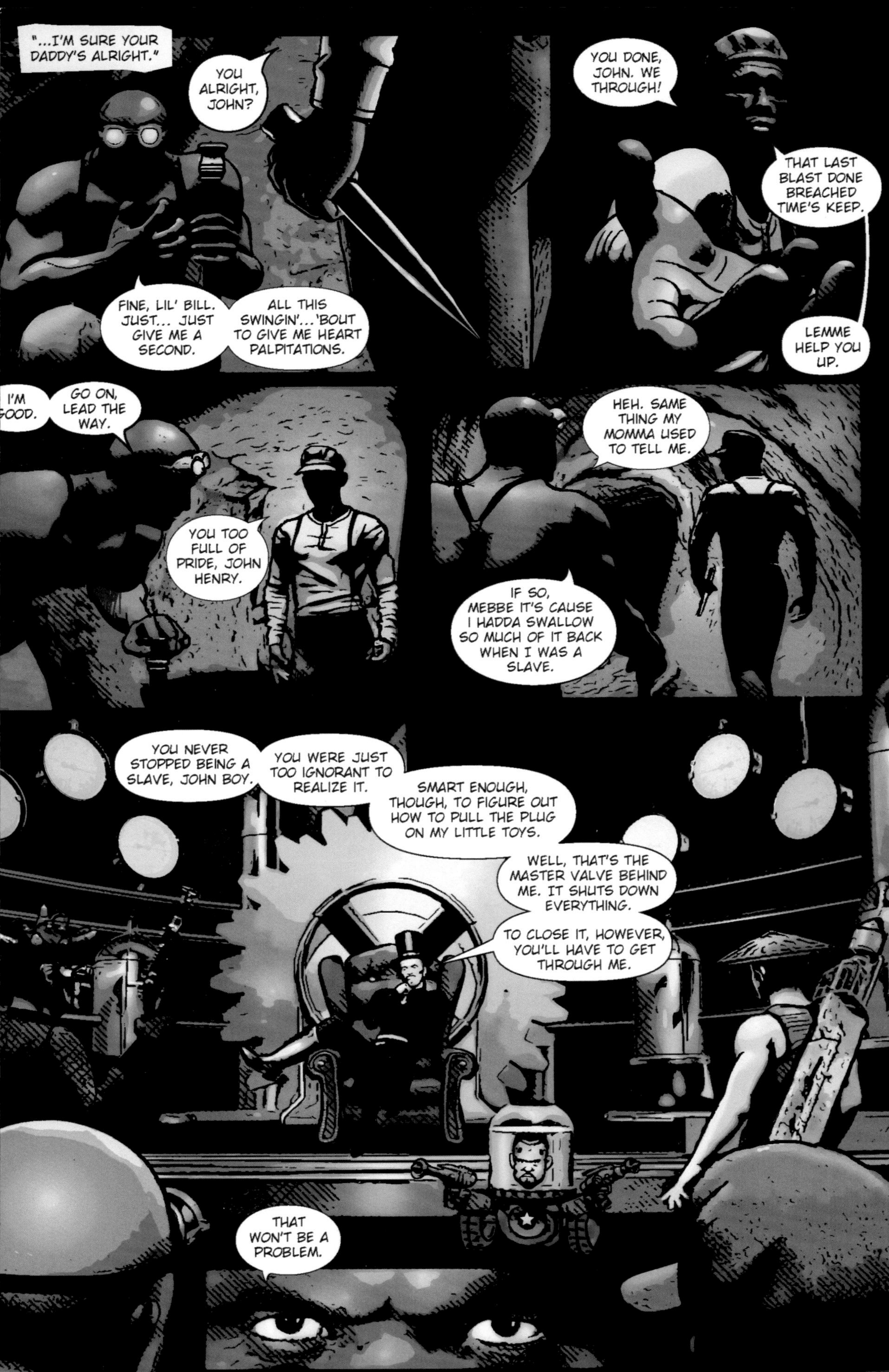
"...I'M SURE YOUR DADDY'S ALRIGHT."
YOU ALRIGHT, JOHN?
FINE, LIL' BILL. JUST... JUST GIVE ME A SECOND.
ALL THIS SWINGIN'...'BOUT TO GIVE ME HEART PALPITATIONS.
YOU DONE, JOHN. WE THROUGH!
THAT LAST BLAST DONE BREACHED TIME'S KEEP.
LEMME HELP YOU UP.
I'M GOOD.
GO ON, LEAD THE WAY.
YOU TOO FULL OF PRIDE, JOHN HENRY.
HEH. SAME THING MY MOMMA USED TO TELL ME.
IF SO, MEBBE IT'S CAUSE I HADDA SWALLOW SO MUCH OF IT BACK WHEN I WAS A SLAVE.
YOU NEVER STOPPED BEING A SLAVE, JOHN BOY.
YOU WERE JUST TOO IGNORANT TO REALIZE IT.
SMART ENOUGH, THOUGH, TO FIGURE OUT HOW TO PULL THE PLUG ON MY LITTLE TOYS.
WELL, THAT'S THE MASTER VALVE BEHIND ME. IT SHUTS DOWN EVERYTHING.
TO CLOSE IT, HOWEVER, YOU'LL HAVE TO GET THROUGH ME.
THAT WON'T BE A PROBLEM.

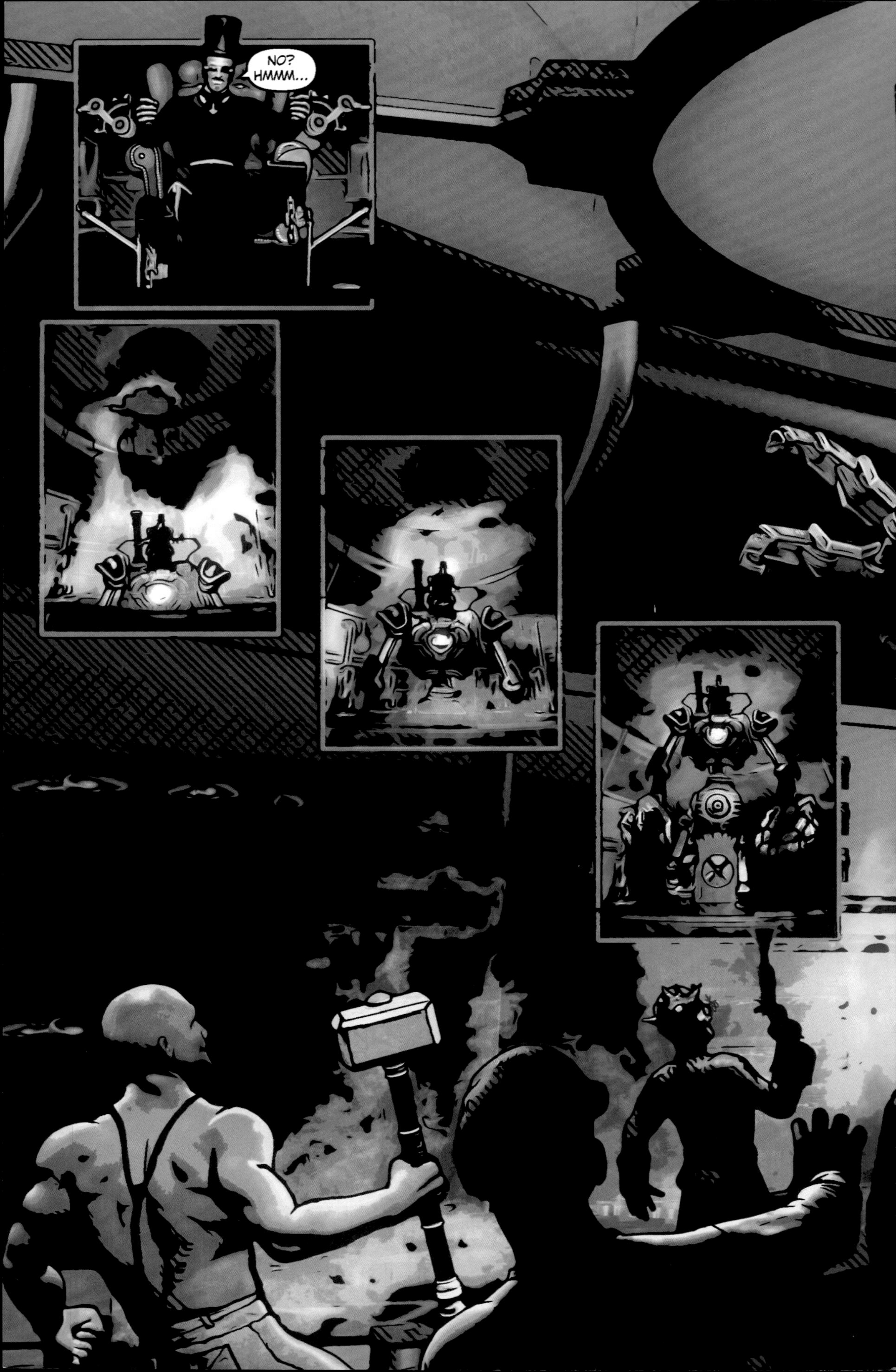
NO? HMMM...

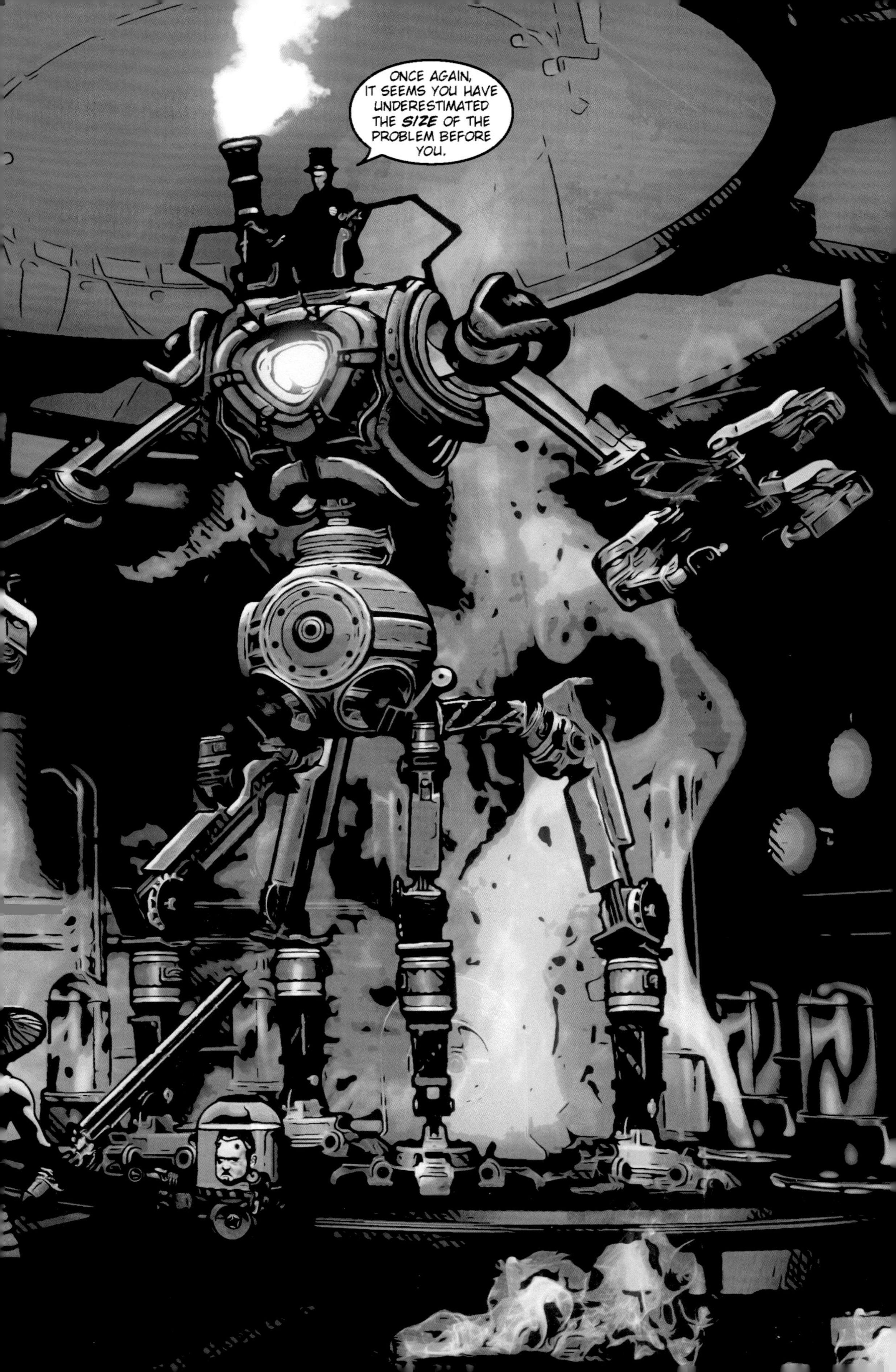
ONCE AGAIN, IT SEEMS YOU HAVE UNDERESTIMATED THE *SIZE* OF THE PROBLEM BEFORE YOU.

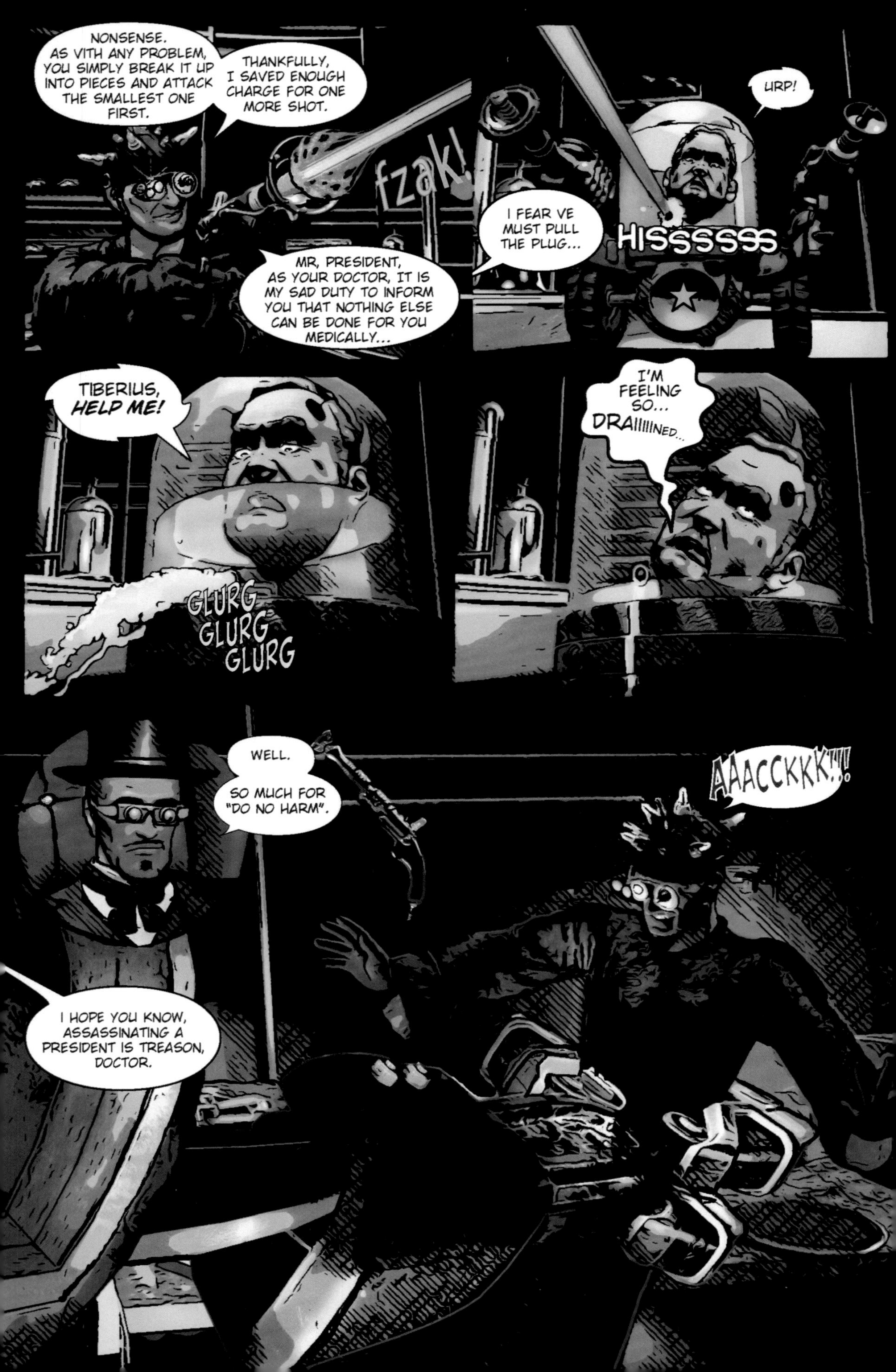
NONSENSE. AS VITH ANY PROBLEM, YOU SIMPLY BREAK IT UP INTO PIECES AND ATTACK THE SMALLEST ONE FIRST.
THANKFULLY, I SAVED ENOUGH CHARGE FOR ONE MORE SHOT.
fzak!
MR, PRESIDENT, AS YOUR DOCTOR, IT IS MY SAD DUTY TO INFORM YOU THAT NOTHING ELSE CAN BE DONE FOR YOU MEDICALLY...
I FEAR VE MUST PULL THE PLUG...
URP!
HISSSSSS
TIBERIUS, *HELP ME!*
GLURG GLURG GLURG
I'M FEELING SO... DRAIIIIINED...
WELL.
SO MUCH FOR "DO NO HARM".
AAACCKKK!!!
I HOPE YOU KNOW, ASSASSINATING A PRESIDENT IS TREASON, DOCTOR.

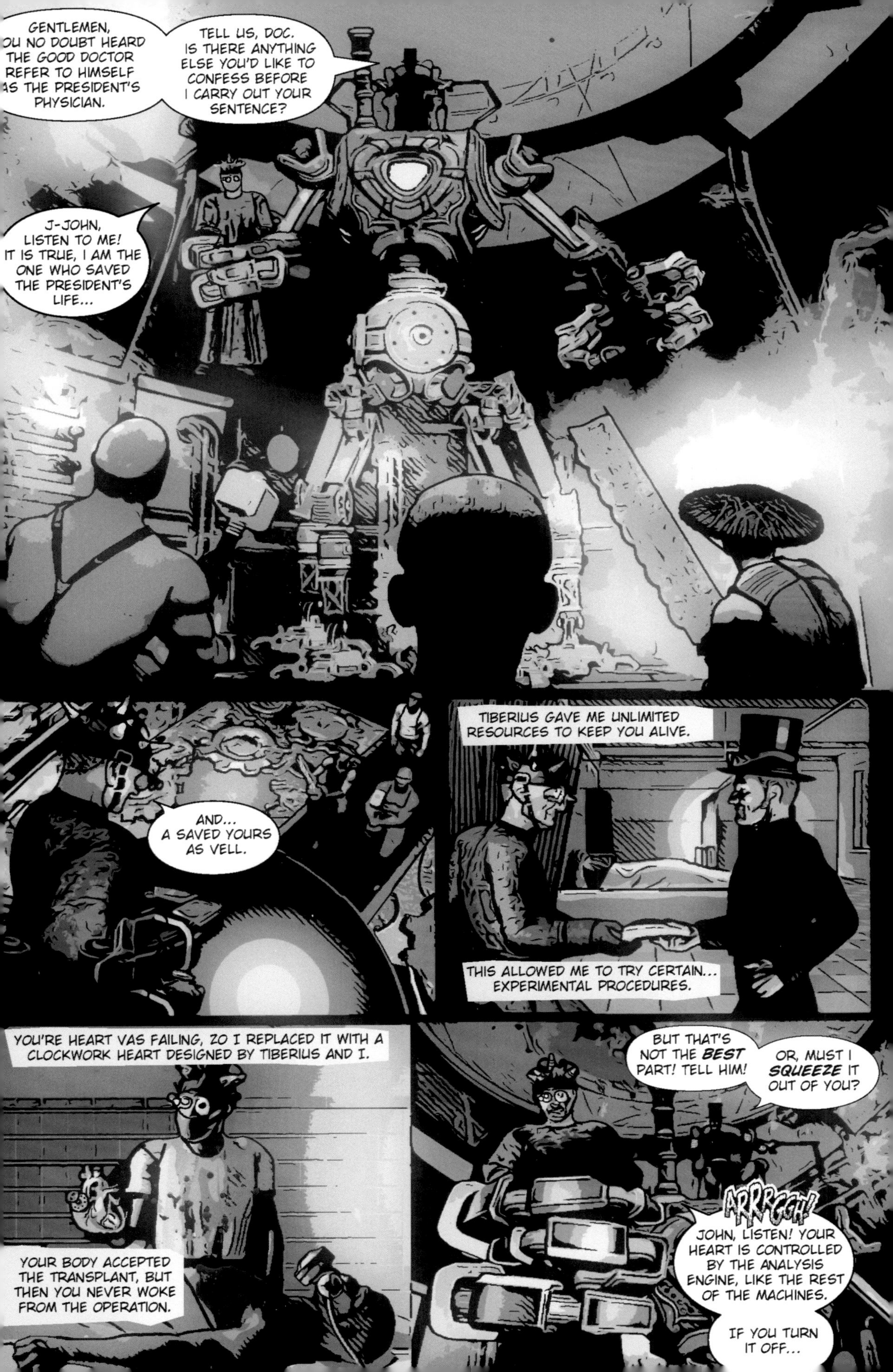
GENTLEMEN, YOU NO DOUBT HEARD THE GOOD DOCTOR REFER TO HIMSELF AS THE PRESIDENT'S PHYSICIAN.
TELL US, DOC. IS THERE ANYTHING ELSE YOU'D LIKE TO CONFESS BEFORE I CARRY OUT YOUR SENTENCE?
J-JOHN, LISTEN TO ME! IT IS TRUE, I AM THE ONE WHO SAVED THE PRESIDENT'S LIFE...
AND... A SAVED YOURS AS VELL.
TIBERIUS GAVE ME UNLIMITED RESOURCES TO KEEP YOU ALIVE.
THIS ALLOWED ME TO TRY CERTAIN... EXPERIMENTAL PROCEDURES.
YOU'RE HEART VAS FAILING, ZO I REPLACED IT WITH A CLOCKWORK HEART DESIGNED BY TIBERIUS AND I.
YOUR BODY ACCEPTED THE TRANSPLANT, BUT THEN YOU NEVER WOKE FROM THE OPERATION.
BUT THAT'S NOT THE **BEST** PART! TELL HIM!
OR, MUST I **SQUEEZE** IT OUT OF YOU?
ARRRGGH!
JOHN, LISTEN! YOUR HEART IS CONTROLLED BY THE ANALYSIS ENGINE, LIKE THE REST OF THE MACHINES.
IF YOU TURN IT OFF...

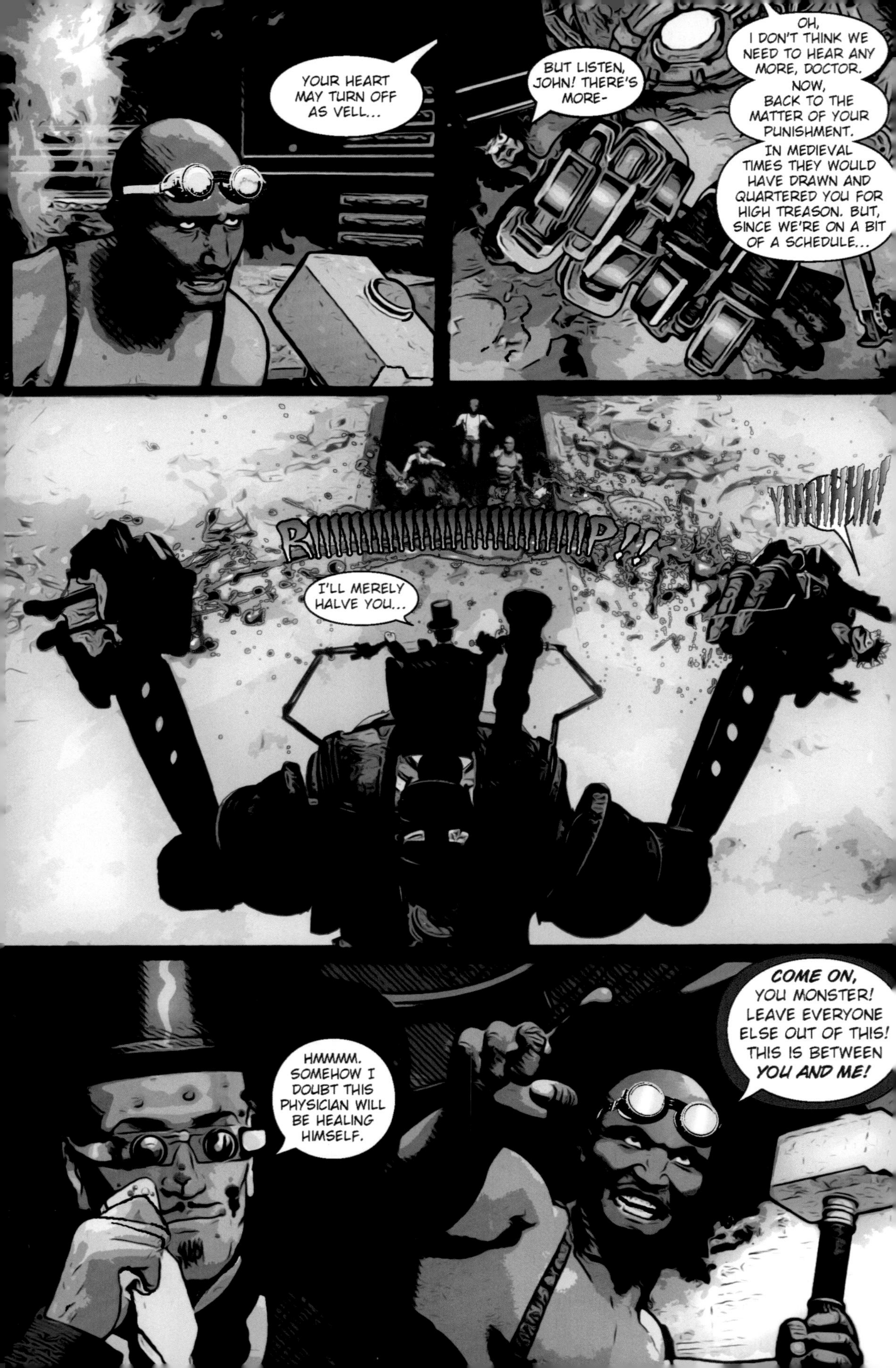
YOUR HEART MAY TURN OFF AS VELL...
BUT LISTEN, JOHN! THERE'S MORE-
OH, I DON'T THINK WE NEED TO HEAR ANY MORE, DOCTOR.
NOW, BACK TO THE MATTER OF YOUR PUNISHMENT.
IN MEDIEVAL TIMES THEY WOULD HAVE DRAWN AND QUARTERED YOU FOR HIGH TREASON. BUT, SINCE WE'RE ON A BIT OF A SCHEDULE...
RIIIIIIIIIIIIIIIIIIIIIIIIIIIP!!!
YAAAHHHHH!
I'LL MERELY HALVE YOU...
HMMMM. SOMEHOW I DOUBT THIS PHYSICIAN WILL BE HEALING HIMSELF.
COME ON, YOU MONSTER! LEAVE EVERYONE ELSE OUT OF THIS! THIS IS BETWEEN YOU AND ME!

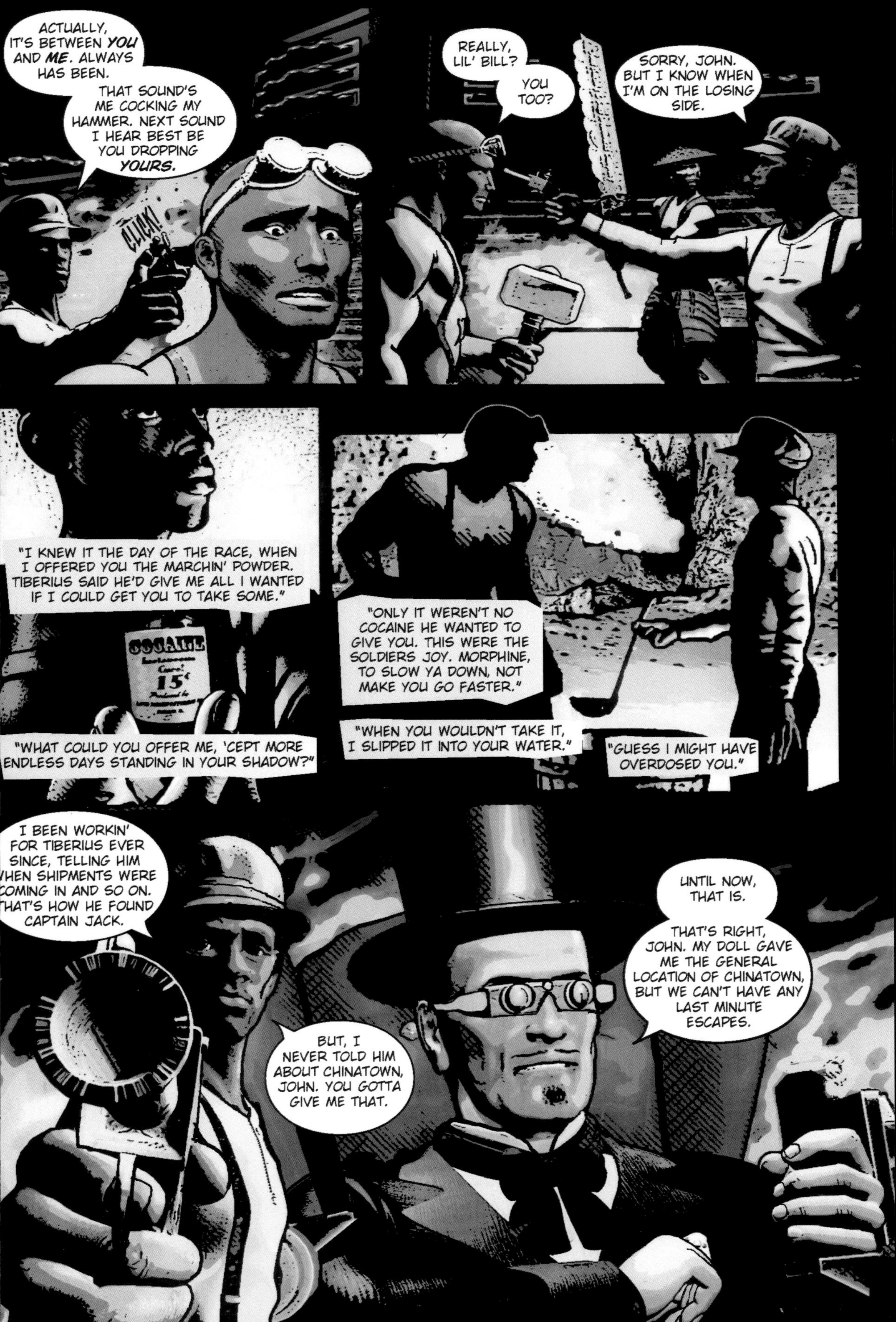
ACTUALLY, IT'S BETWEEN **YOU** AND **ME**. ALWAYS HAS BEEN.
THAT SOUND'S ME COCKING MY HAMMER. NEXT SOUND I HEAR BEST BE YOU DROPPING **YOURS**.
CLICK!
REALLY, LIL' BILL?
YOU TOO?
SORRY, JOHN. BUT I KNOW WHEN I'M ON THE LOSING SIDE.
"I KNEW IT THE DAY OF THE RACE, WHEN I OFFERED YOU THE MARCHIN' POWDER. TIBERIUS SAID HE'D GIVE ME ALL I WANTED IF I COULD GET YOU TO TAKE SOME."
"WHAT COULD YOU OFFER ME, 'CEPT MORE ENDLESS DAYS STANDING IN YOUR SHADOW?"
"ONLY IT WEREN'T NO COCAINE HE WANTED TO GIVE YOU. THIS WERE THE SOLDIERS JOY. MORPHINE, TO SLOW YA DOWN, NOT MAKE YOU GO FASTER."
"WHEN YOU WOULDN'T TAKE IT, I SLIPPED IT INTO YOUR WATER."
"GUESS I MIGHT HAVE OVERDOSED YOU."
I BEEN WORKIN' FOR TIBERIUS EVER SINCE, TELLING HIM WHEN SHIPMENTS WERE COMING IN AND SO ON. THAT'S HOW HE FOUND CAPTAIN JACK.
BUT, I NEVER TOLD HIM ABOUT CHINATOWN, JOHN. YOU GOTTA GIVE ME THAT.
UNTIL NOW, THAT IS.
THAT'S RIGHT, JOHN. MY DOLL GAVE ME THE GENERAL LOCATION OF CHINATOWN, BUT WE CAN'T HAVE ANY LAST MINUTE ESCAPES.

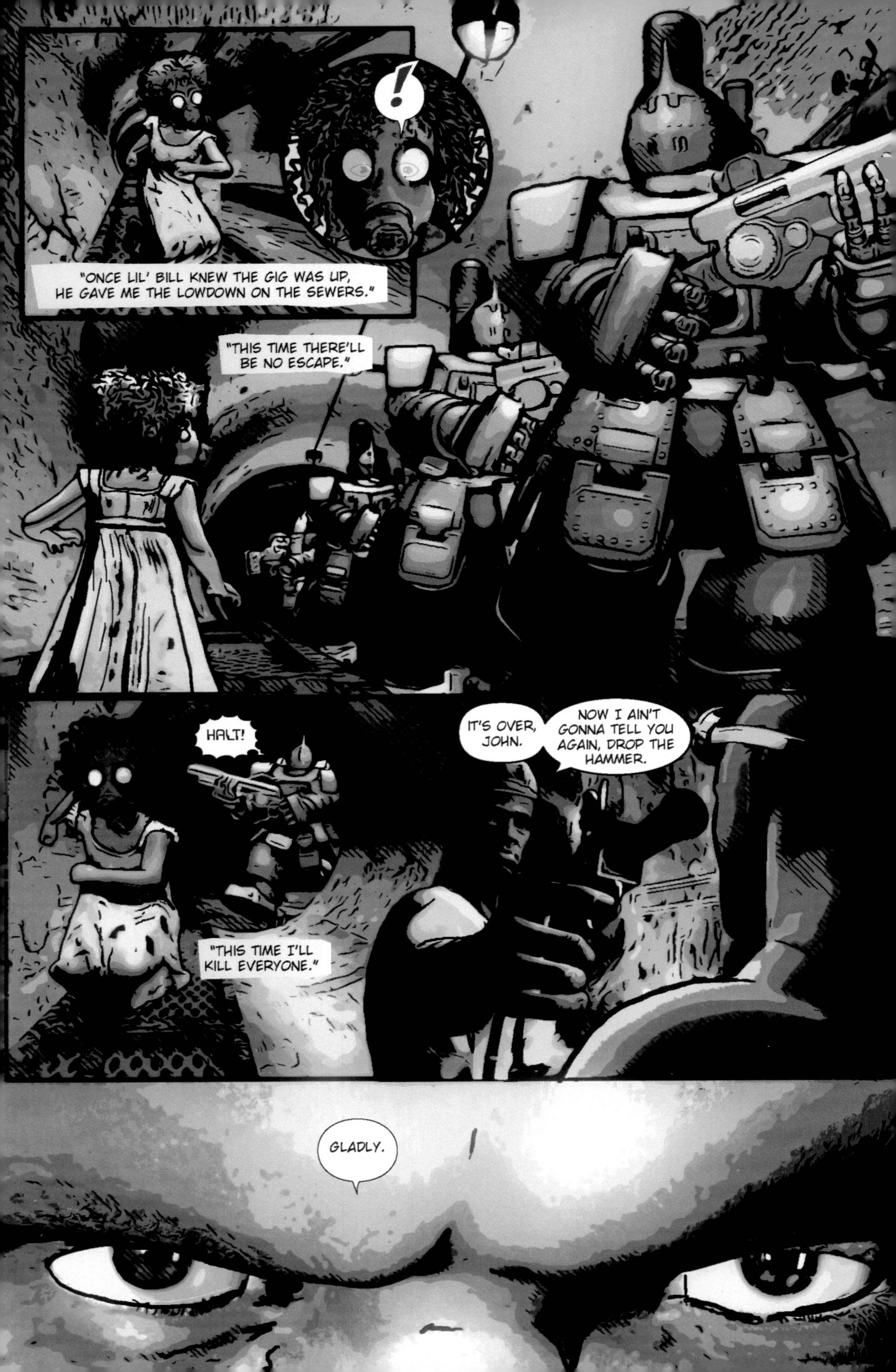
!
"ONCE LIL' BILL KNEW THE GIG WAS UP, HE GAVE ME THE LOWDOWN ON THE SEWERS."
"THIS TIME THERE'LL BE NO ESCAPE."
HALT!
IT'S OVER, JOHN.
NOW I AIN'T GONNA TELL YOU AGAIN, DROP THE HAMMER.
"THIS TIME I'LL KILL EVERYONE."
GLADLY.

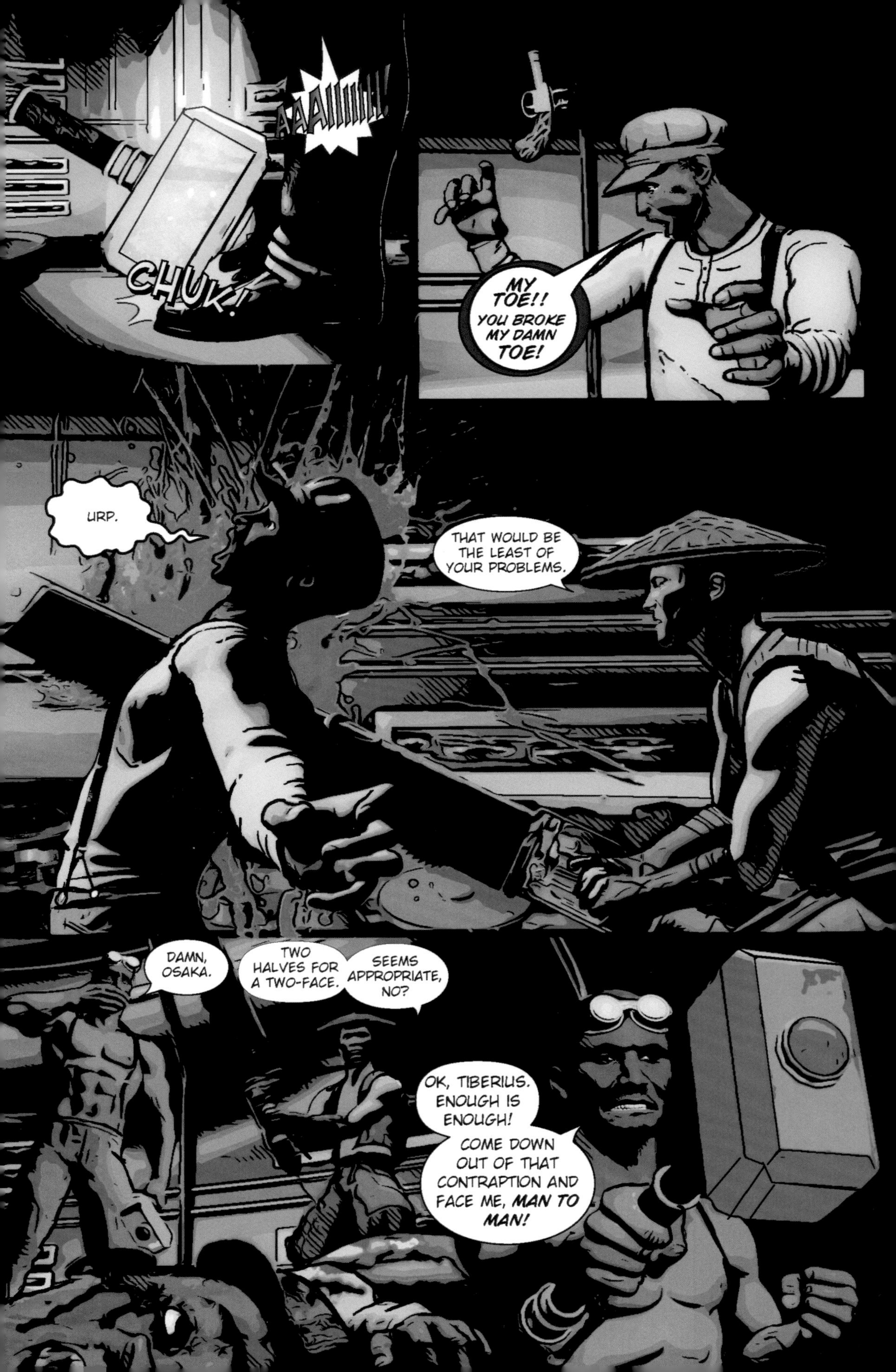
AAAIIIIIII!!
CHUK!
MY TOE!! YOU BROKE MY DAMN TOE!
URP.
THAT WOULD BE THE LEAST OF YOUR PROBLEMS.
DAMN, OSAKA.
TWO HALVES FOR A TWO-FACE.
SEEMS APPROPRIATE, NO?
OK, TIBERIUS. ENOUGH IS ENOUGH!
COME DOWN OUT OF THAT CONTRAPTION AND FACE ME, *MAN TO MAN!*

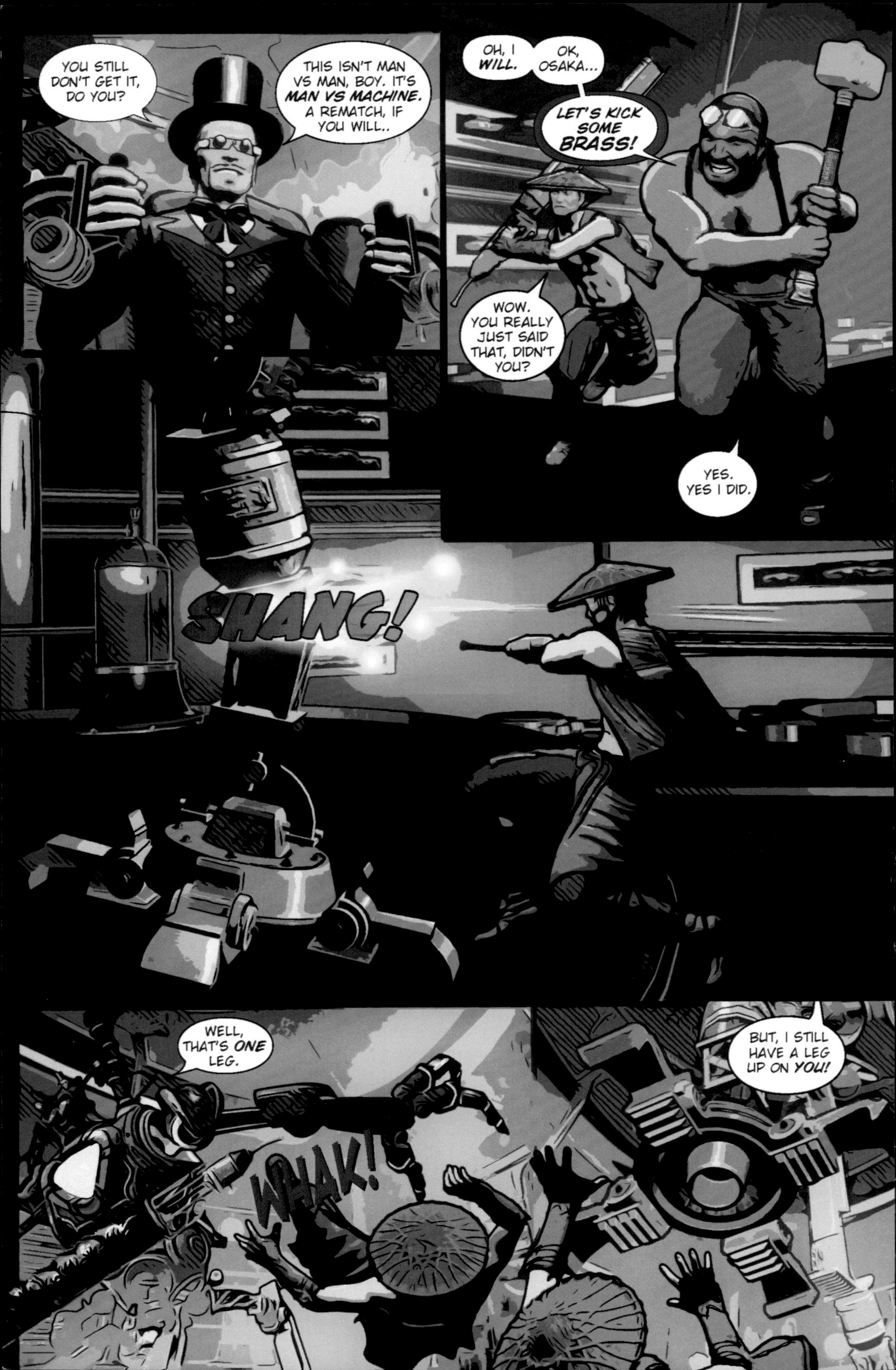
YOU STILL DON'T GET IT, DO YOU?
THIS ISN'T MAN VS MAN, BOY. IT'S MAN VS MACHINE. A REMATCH, IF YOU WILL..
OH, I WILL.
OK, OSAKA...
LET'S KICK SOME BRASS!
WOW. YOU REALLY JUST SAID THAT, DIDN'T YOU?
YES. YES I DID.
SHANG!
WELL, THAT'S ONE LEG.
BUT, I STILL HAVE A LEG UP ON YOU!
WHAK!

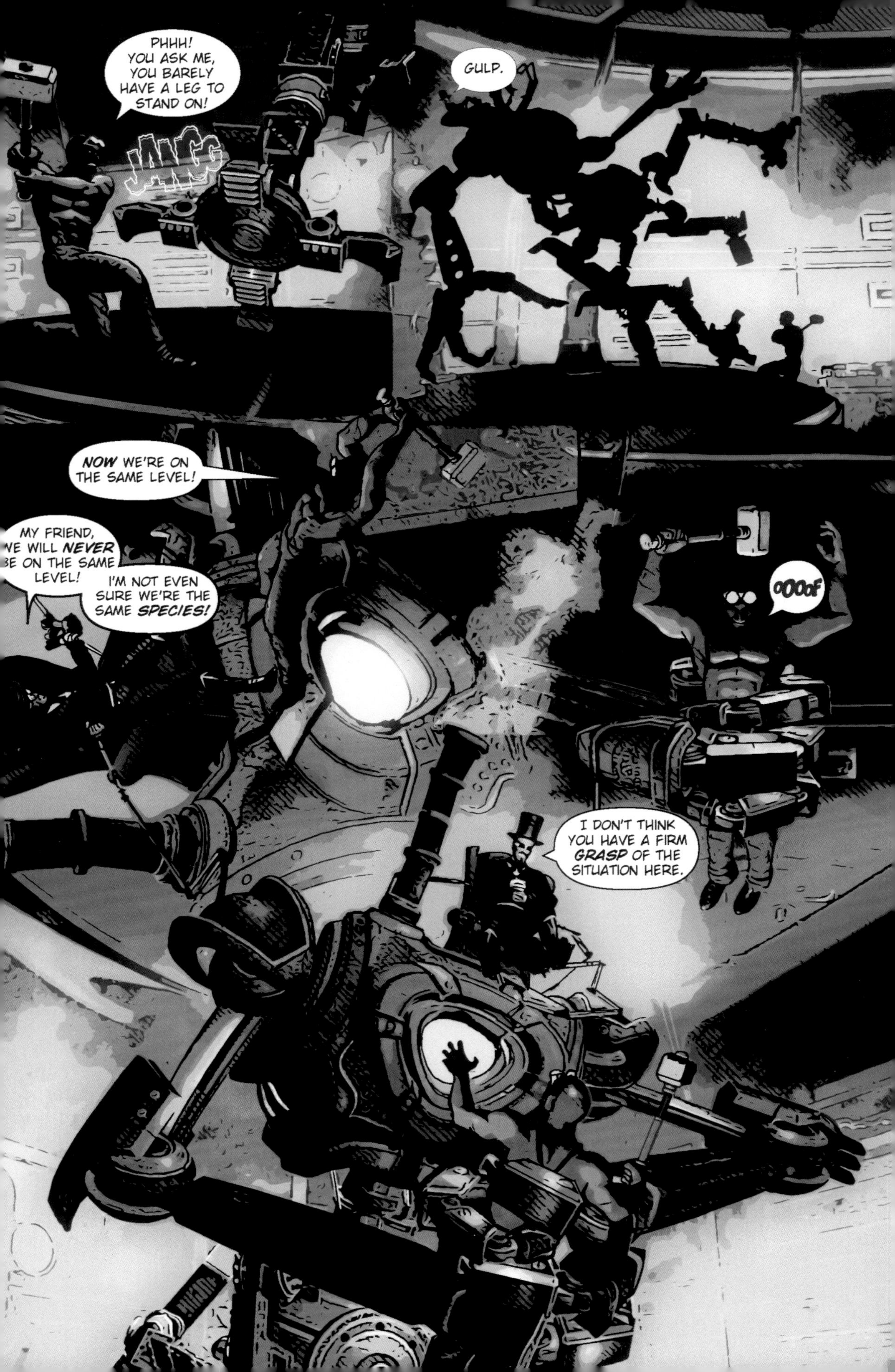
PHHH! YOU ASK ME, YOU BARELY HAVE A LEG TO STAND ON!
JANG
GULP.
NOW WE'RE ON THE SAME LEVEL!
MY FRIEND, WE WILL NEVER BE ON THE SAME LEVEL!
I'M NOT EVEN SURE WE'RE THE SAME SPECIES!
OOOOF
I DON'T THINK YOU HAVE A FIRM GRASP OF THE SITUATION HERE.

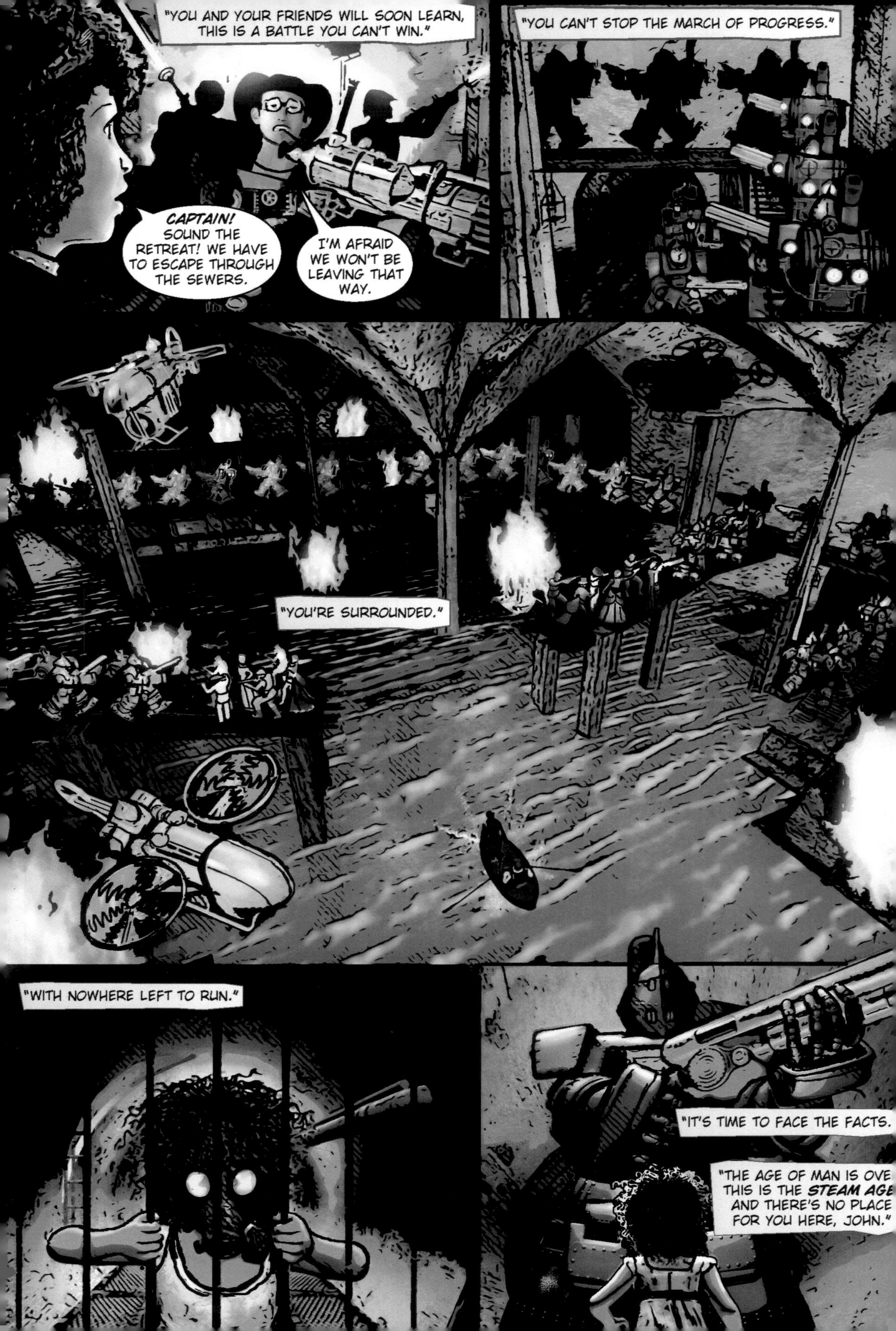
"YOU AND YOUR FRIENDS WILL SOON LEARN, THIS IS A BATTLE YOU CAN'T WIN."
CAPTAIN! SOUND THE RETREAT! WE HAVE TO ESCAPE THROUGH THE SEWERS.
I'M AFRAID WE WON'T BE LEAVING THAT WAY.
"YOU CAN'T STOP THE MARCH OF PROGRESS."
"YOU'RE SURROUNDED."
"WITH NOWHERE LEFT TO RUN."
"IT'S TIME TO FACE THE FACTS.
"THE AGE OF MAN IS OVE
THIS IS THE STEAM AGE
AND THERE'S NO PLACE
FOR YOU HERE, JOHN."

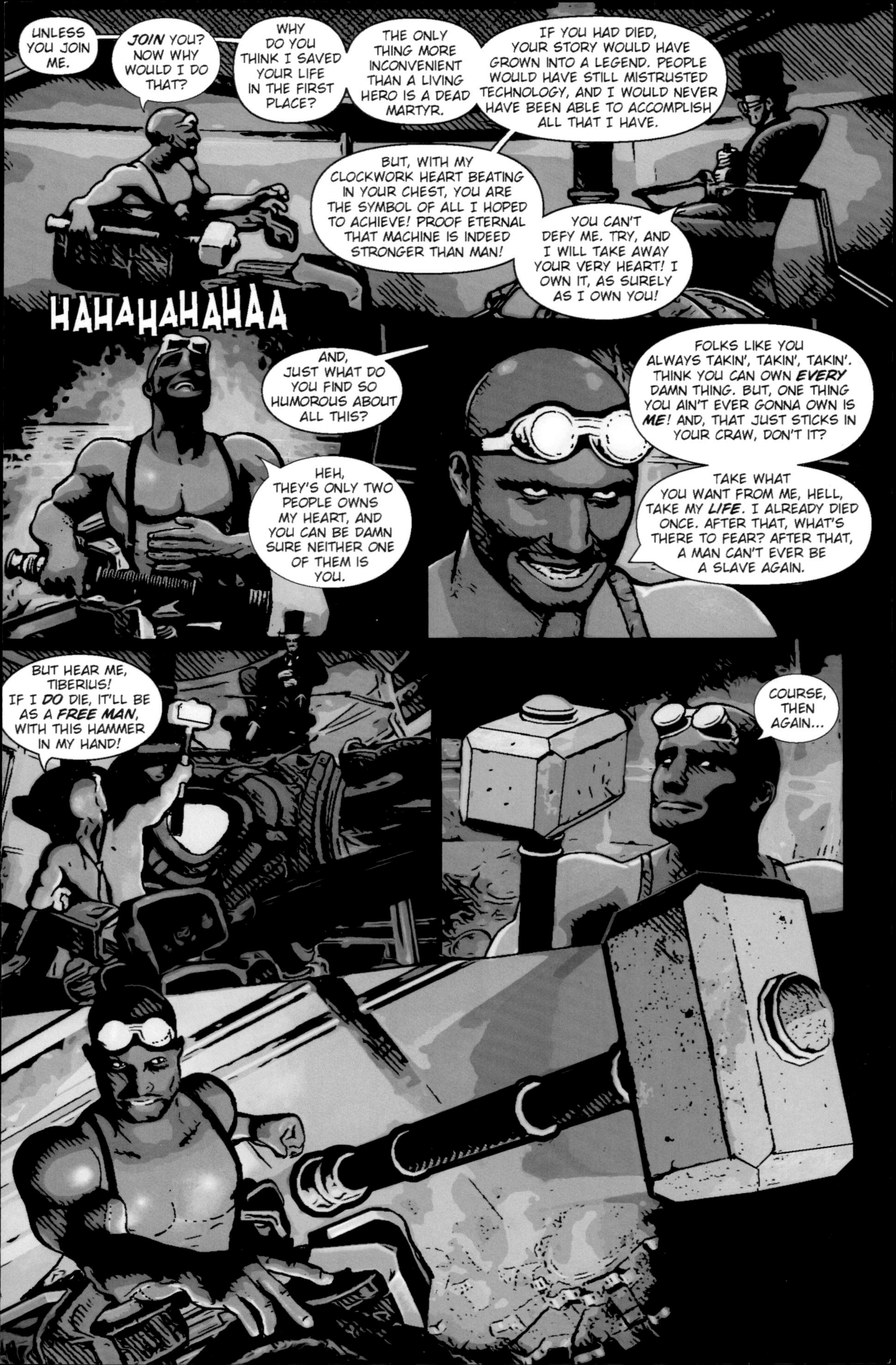

UNLESS YOU JOIN ME.
JOIN YOU? NOW WHY WOULD I DO THAT?
WHY DO YOU THINK I SAVED YOUR LIFE IN THE FIRST PLACE?
THE ONLY THING MORE INCONVENIENT THAN A LIVING HERO IS A DEAD MARTYR.
IF YOU HAD DIED, YOUR STORY WOULD HAVE GROWN INTO A LEGEND. PEOPLE WOULD HAVE STILL MISTRUSTED TECHNOLOGY, AND I WOULD NEVER HAVE BEEN ABLE TO ACCOMPLISH ALL THAT I HAVE.
BUT, WITH MY CLOCKWORK HEART BEATING IN YOUR CHEST, YOU ARE THE SYMBOL OF ALL I HOPED TO ACHIEVE! PROOF ETERNAL THAT MACHINE IS INDEED STRONGER THAN MAN!
YOU CAN'T DEFY ME. TRY, AND I WILL TAKE AWAY YOUR VERY HEART! I OWN IT, AS SURELY AS I OWN YOU!
HAHAHAHAHAA
AND, JUST WHAT DO YOU FIND SO HUMOROUS ABOUT ALL THIS?
HEH, THEY'S ONLY TWO PEOPLE OWNS MY HEART, AND YOU CAN BE DAMN SURE NEITHER ONE OF THEM IS YOU.
FOLKS LIKE YOU ALWAYS TAKIN', TAKIN', TAKIN'. THINK YOU CAN OWN *EVERY* DAMN THING. BUT, ONE THING YOU AIN'T EVER GONNA OWN IS *ME!* AND, THAT JUST STICKS IN YOUR CRAW, DON'T IT?
TAKE WHAT YOU WANT FROM ME, HELL, TAKE MY *LIFE*. I ALREADY DIED ONCE. AFTER THAT, WHAT'S THERE TO FEAR? AFTER THAT, A MAN CAN'T EVER BE A SLAVE AGAIN.
BUT HEAR ME, TIBERIUS! IF I *DO* DIE, IT'LL BE AS A *FREE MAN*, WITH THIS HAMMER IN MY HAND!
COURSE, THEN AGAIN...

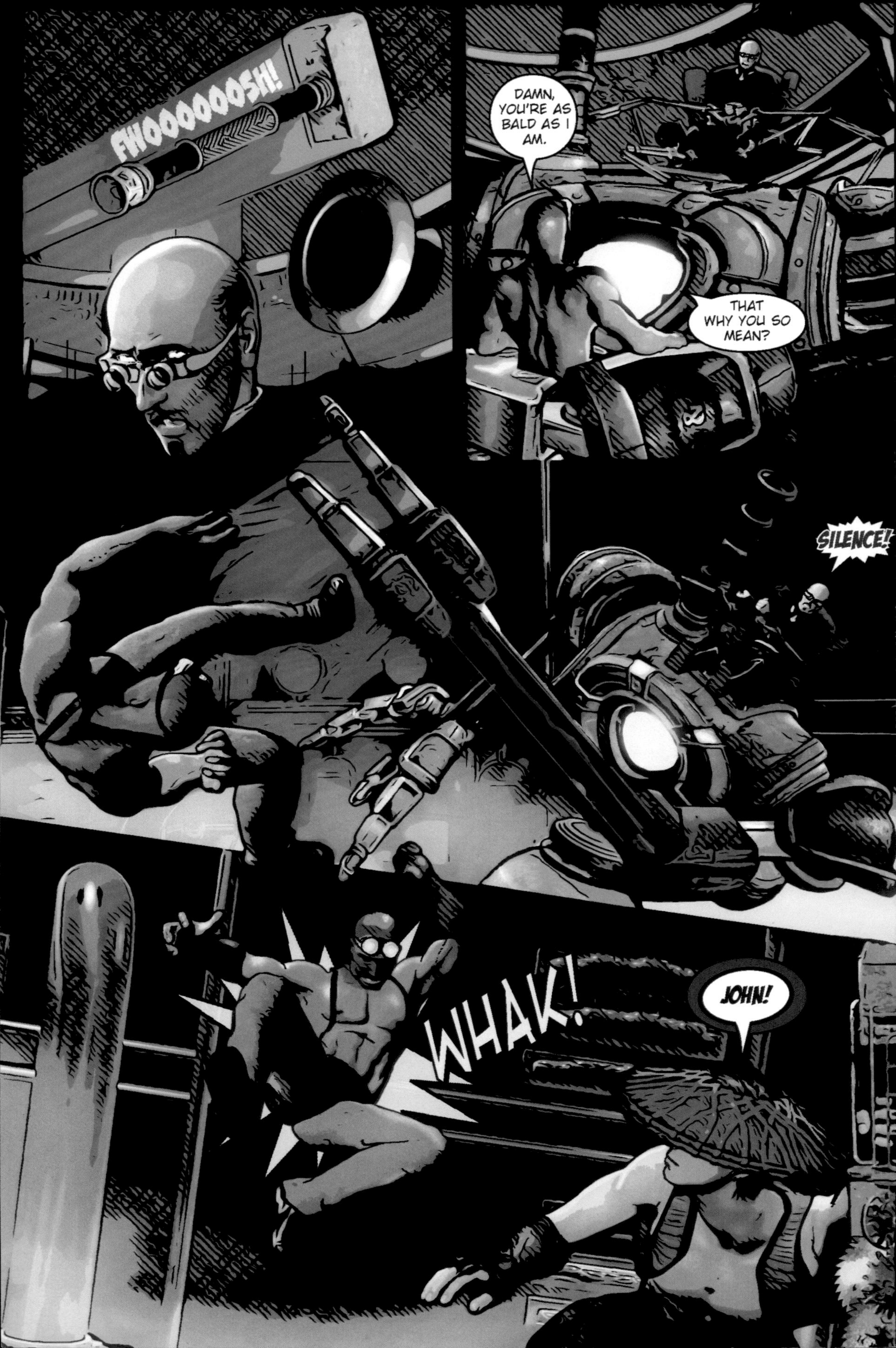
FWOOOOOOSH!
DAMN, YOU'RE AS BALD AS I AM.
THAT WHY YOU SO MEAN?
SILENCE!
WHAK!
JOHN!

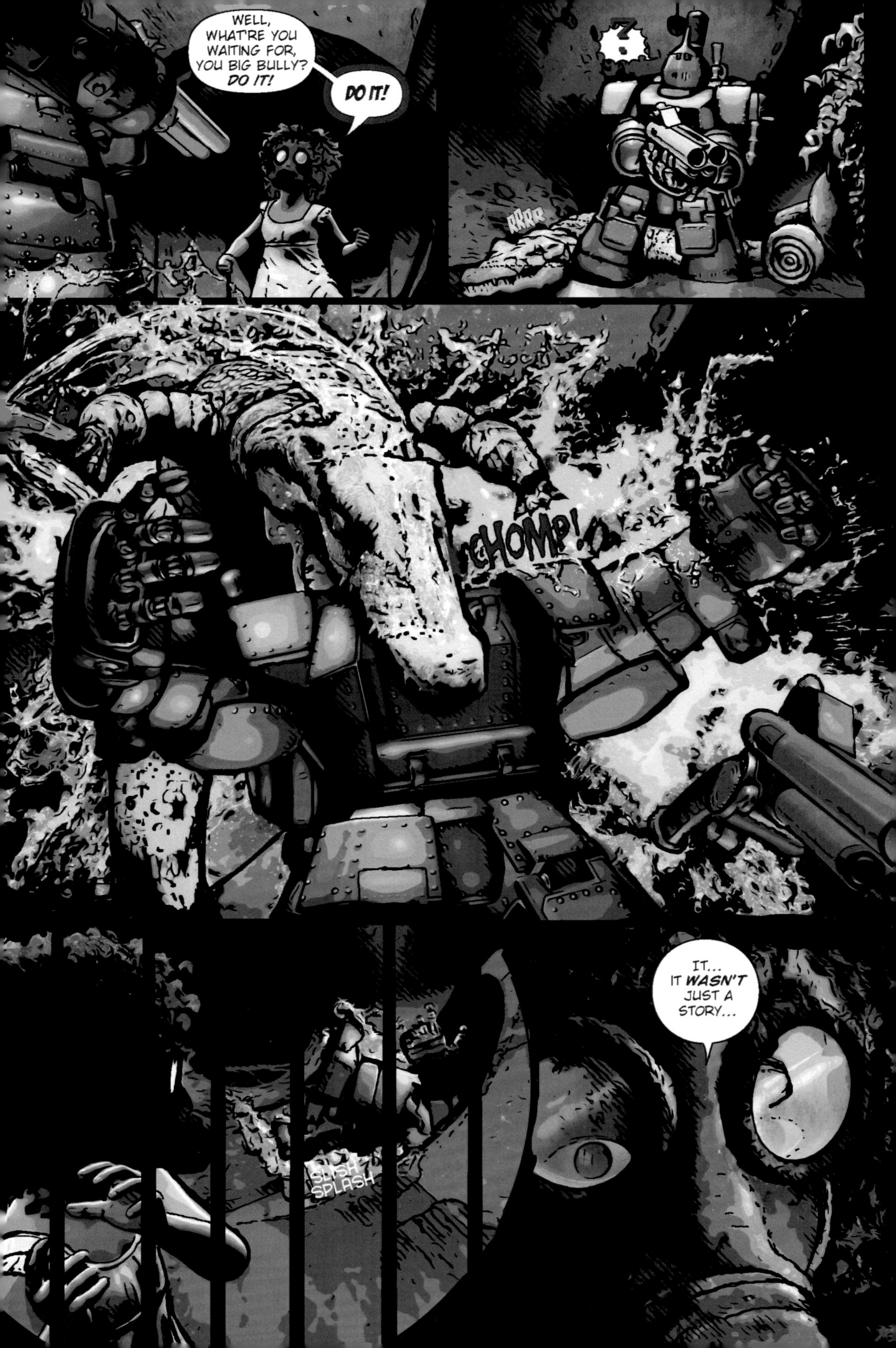
WELL, WHAT'RE YOU WAITING FOR, YOU BIG BULLY? DO IT!
DO IT!
?
RRRR
CHOMP!
SLISH SPLASH
IT... IT WASN'T JUST A STORY...

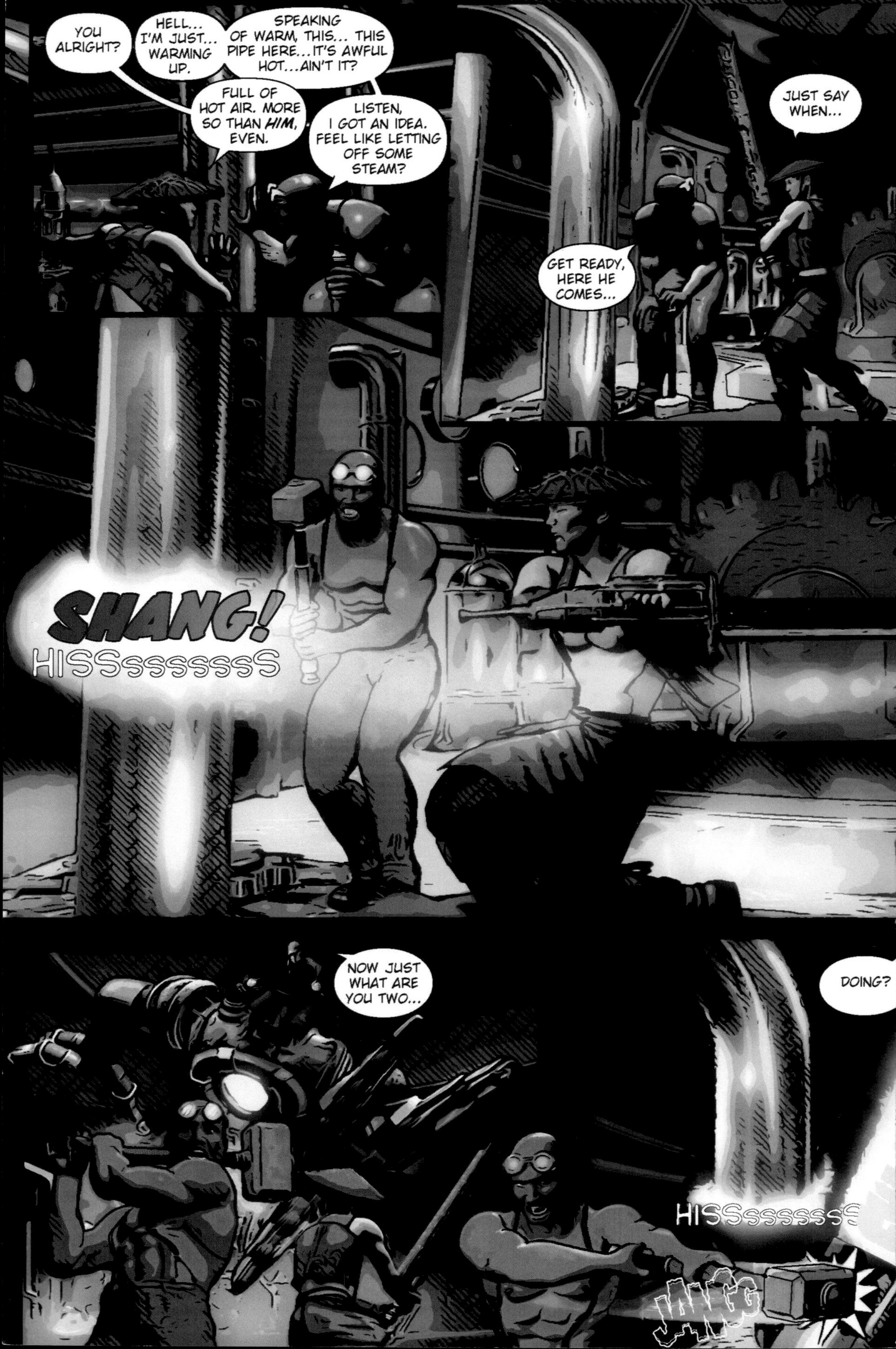
YOU ALRIGHT?
HELL... I'M JUST... WARMING UP.
SPEAKING OF WARM, THIS... THIS PIPE HERE... IT'S AWFUL HOT... AIN'T IT?
FULL OF HOT AIR. MORE SO THAN *HIM*, EVEN.
LISTEN, I GOT AN IDEA. FEEL LIKE LETTING OFF SOME STEAM?
JUST SAY WHEN...
GET READY, HERE HE COMES...
SHANG!
HISSsssssssS
NOW JUST WHAT ARE YOU TWO...
DOING?
HISSsssssssS
JANG

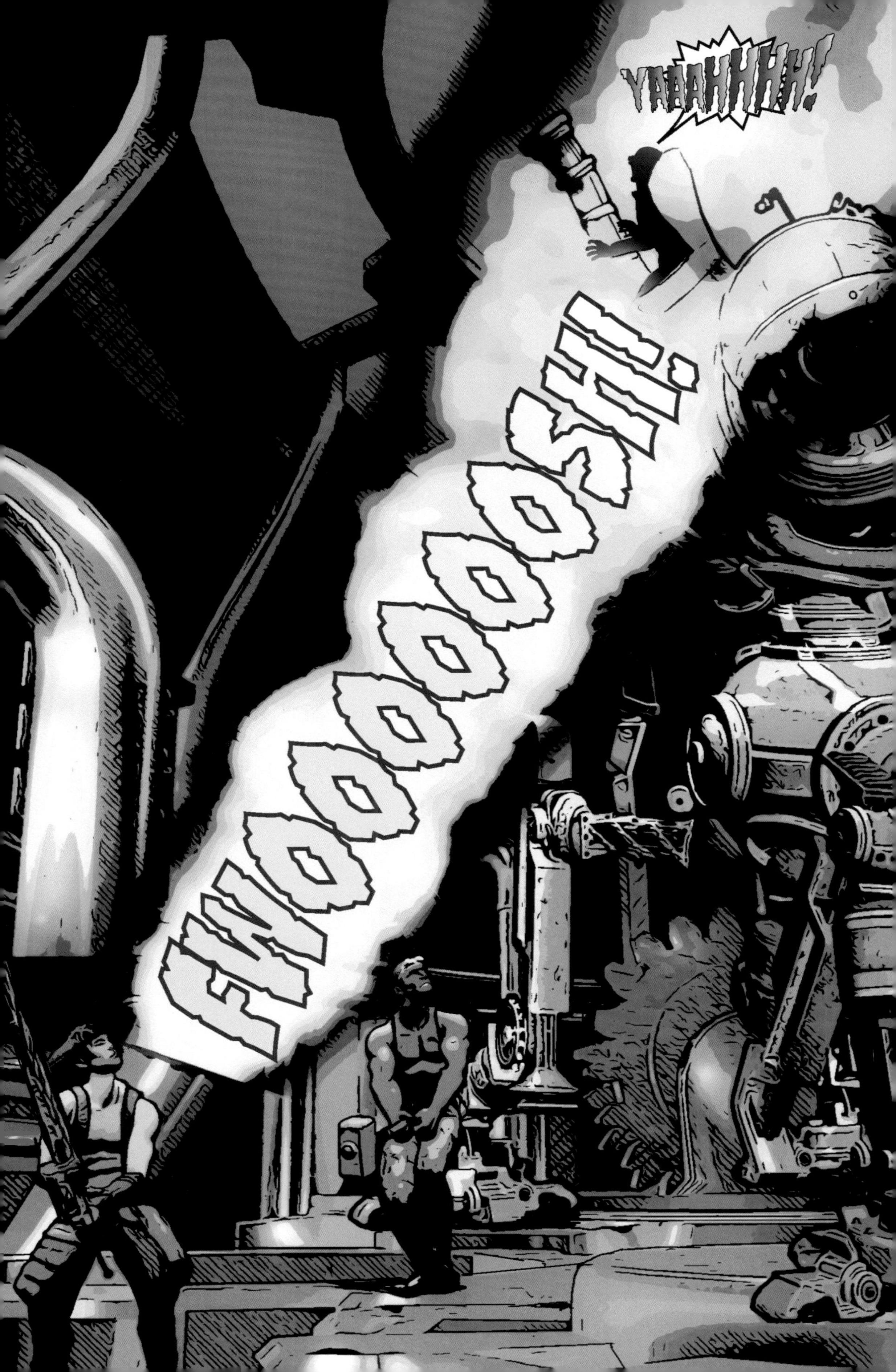
YAAAHHHH!
FWOOOOOOSH!!

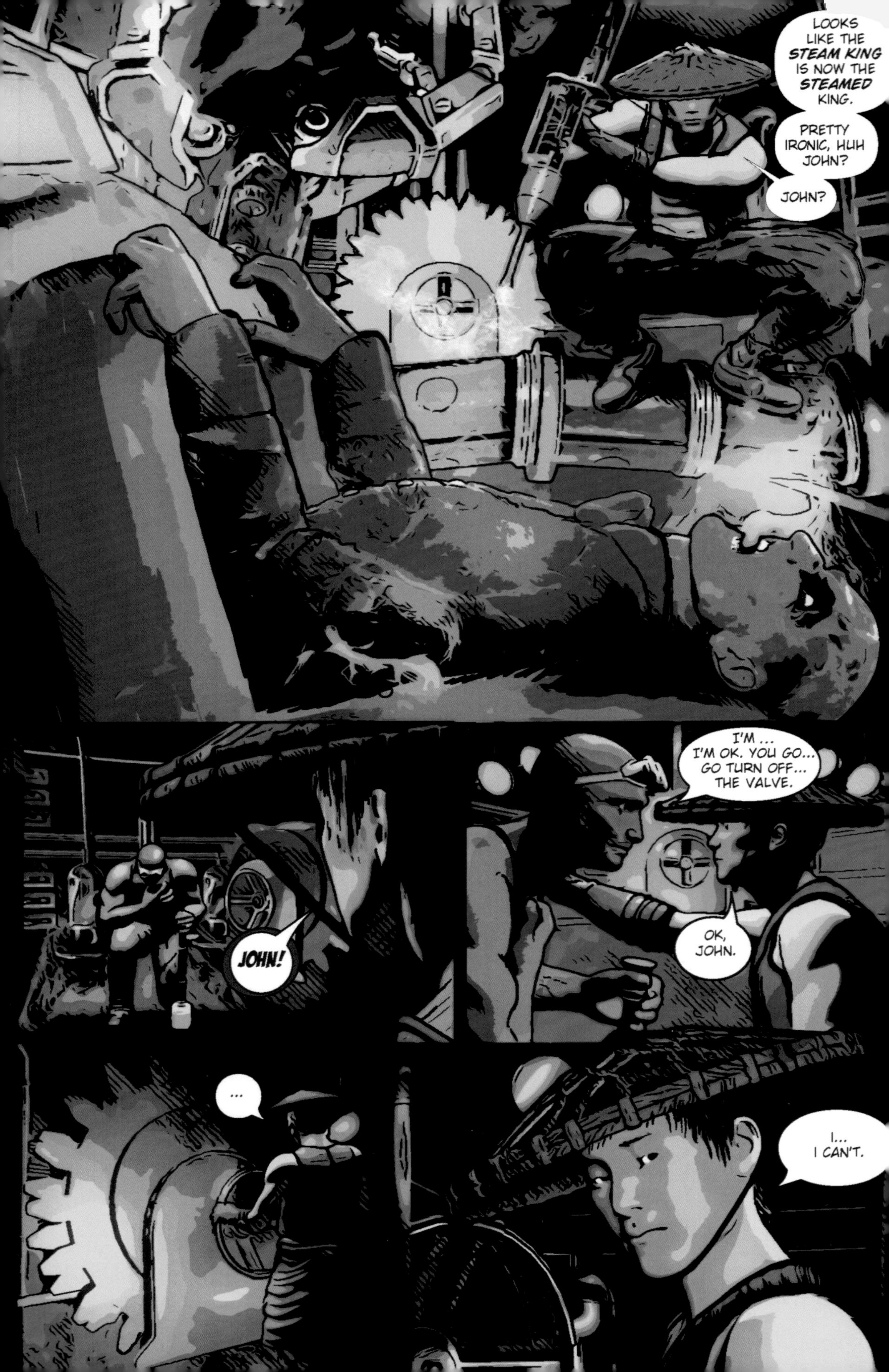
LOOKS LIKE THE STEAM KING IS NOW THE STEAMED KING.
PRETTY IRONIC, HUH JOHN?
JOHN?
JOHN!
I'M ... I'M OK. YOU GO... GO TURN OFF... THE VALVE.
OK, JOHN.
...
I... I CAN'T.

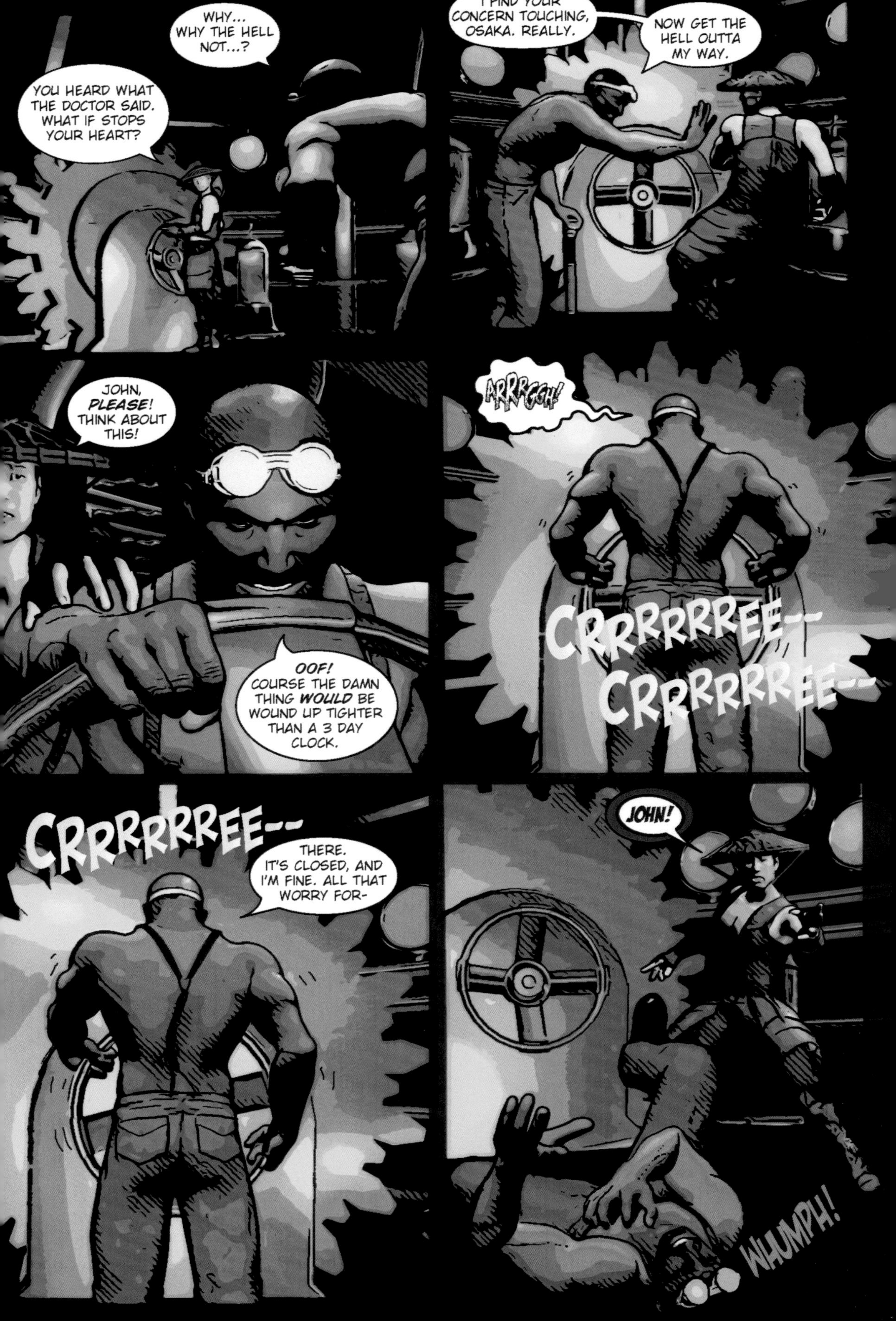
WHY... WHY THE HELL NOT...?
YOU HEARD WHAT THE DOCTOR SAID. WHAT IF STOPS YOUR HEART?
I FIND YOUR CONCERN TOUCHING, OSAKA. REALLY.
NOW GET THE HELL OUTTA MY WAY.
JOHN, PLEASE! THINK ABOUT THIS!
OOF! COURSE THE DAMN THING WOULD BE WOUND UP TIGHTER THAN A 3 DAY CLOCK.
ARRRGGH!
CRRRRRREE--
CRRRRRREE--
CRRRRRREE--
THERE. IT'S CLOSED, AND I'M FINE. ALL THAT WORRY FOR-
JOHN!
WHUMPH!

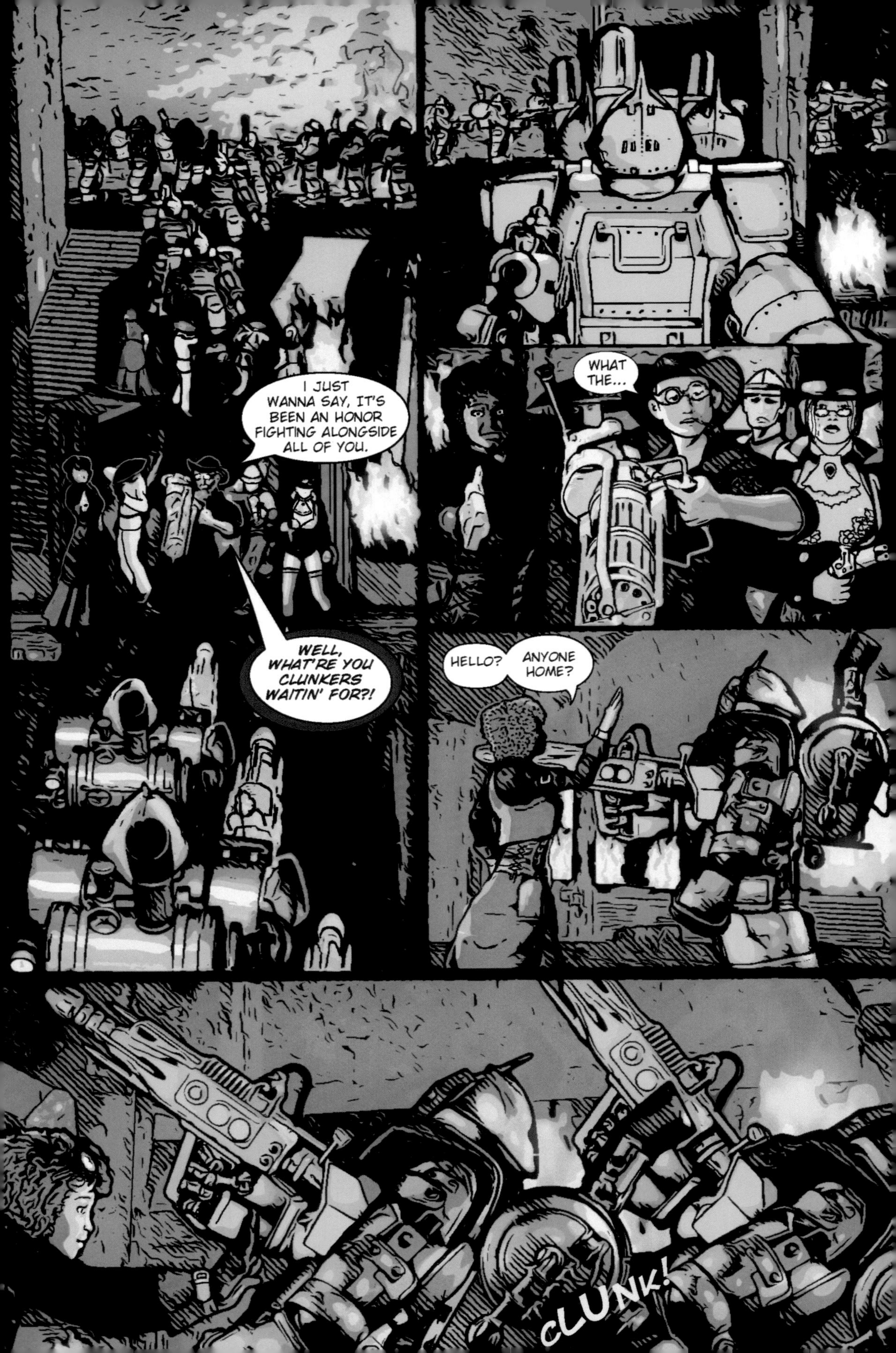
I JUST WANNA SAY, IT'S BEEN AN HONOR FIGHTING ALONGSIDE ALL OF YOU.
WELL, WHAT'RE YOU CLUNKERS WAITIN' FOR?!
WHAT THE...
HELLO?
ANYONE HOME?
CLUNK!

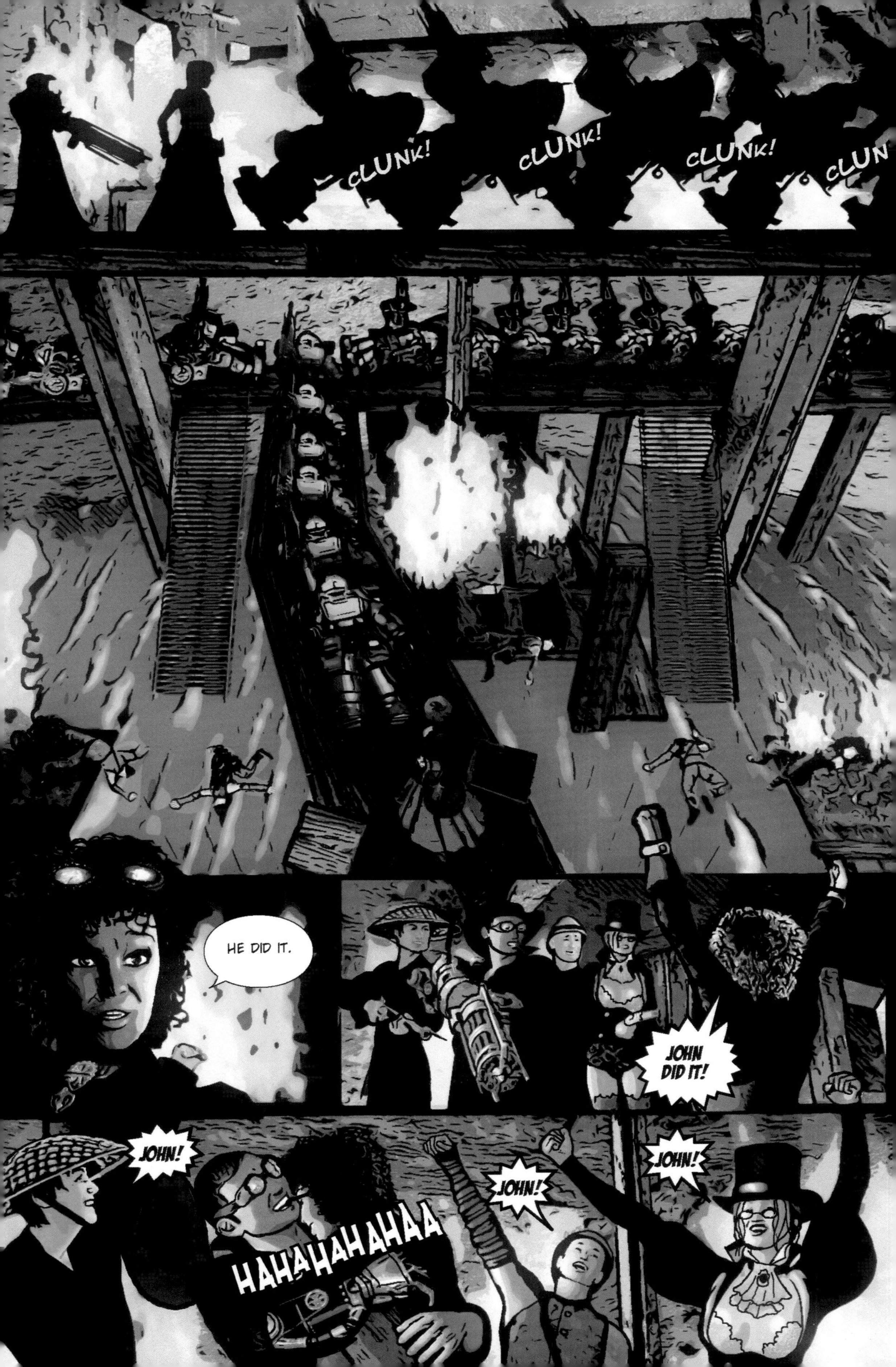
CLUNK!
CLUNK!
CLUNK!
CLUN
HE DID IT.
JOHN DID IT!
JOHN!
HAHAHAHAHAA
JOHN!
JOHN!

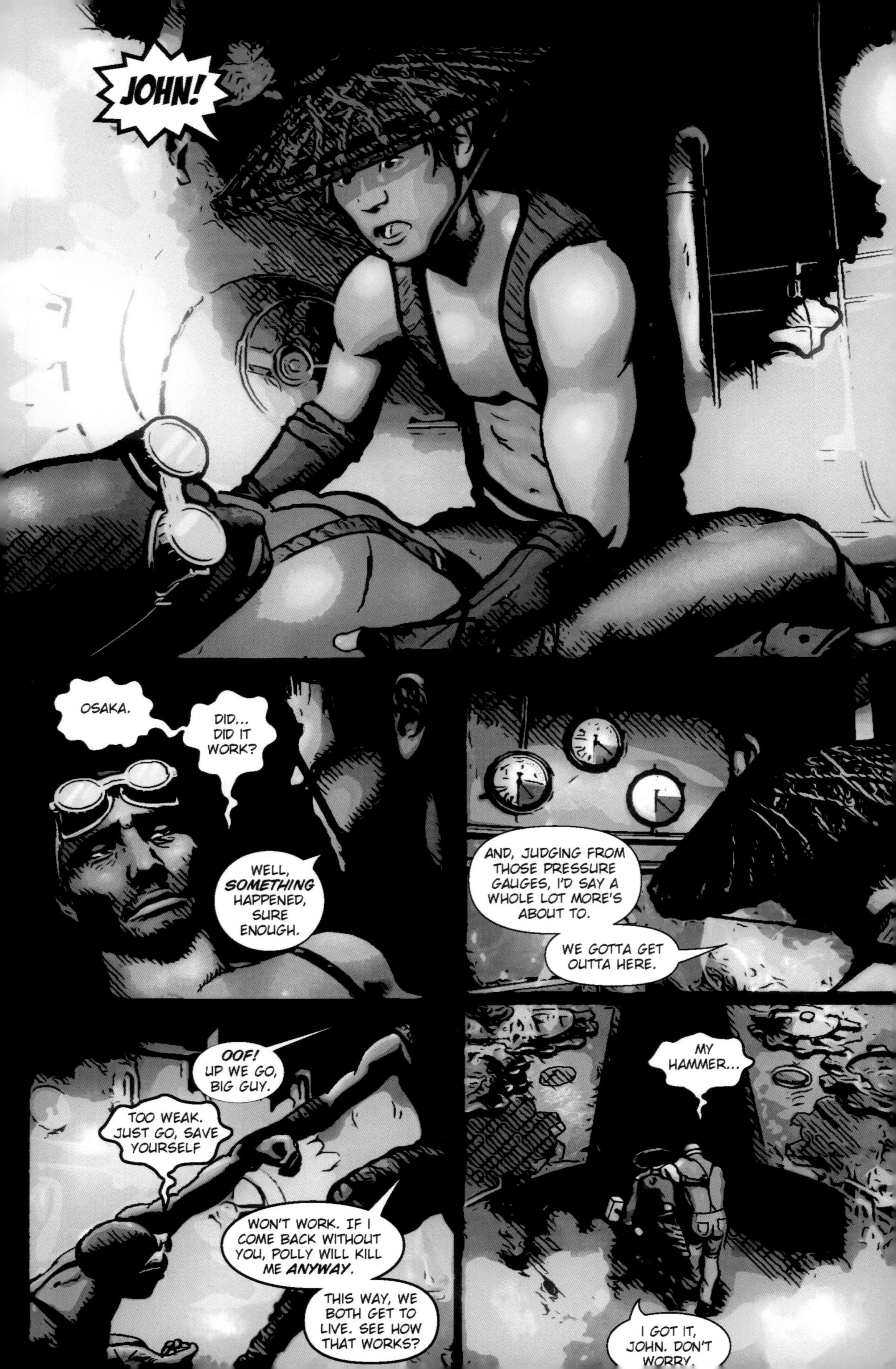
JOHN!
OSAKA.
DID... DID IT WORK?
WELL, SOMETHING HAPPENED, SURE ENOUGH.
AND, JUDGING FROM THOSE PRESSURE GAUGES, I'D SAY A WHOLE LOT MORE'S ABOUT TO.
WE GOTTA GET OUTTA HERE.
OOF! UP WE GO, BIG GUY.
TOO WEAK. JUST GO, SAVE YOURSELF
WON'T WORK. IF I COME BACK WITHOUT YOU, POLLY WILL KILL ME ANYWAY.
THIS WAY, WE BOTH GET TO LIVE. SEE HOW THAT WORKS?
MY HAMMER...
I GOT IT, JOHN. DON'T WORRY.

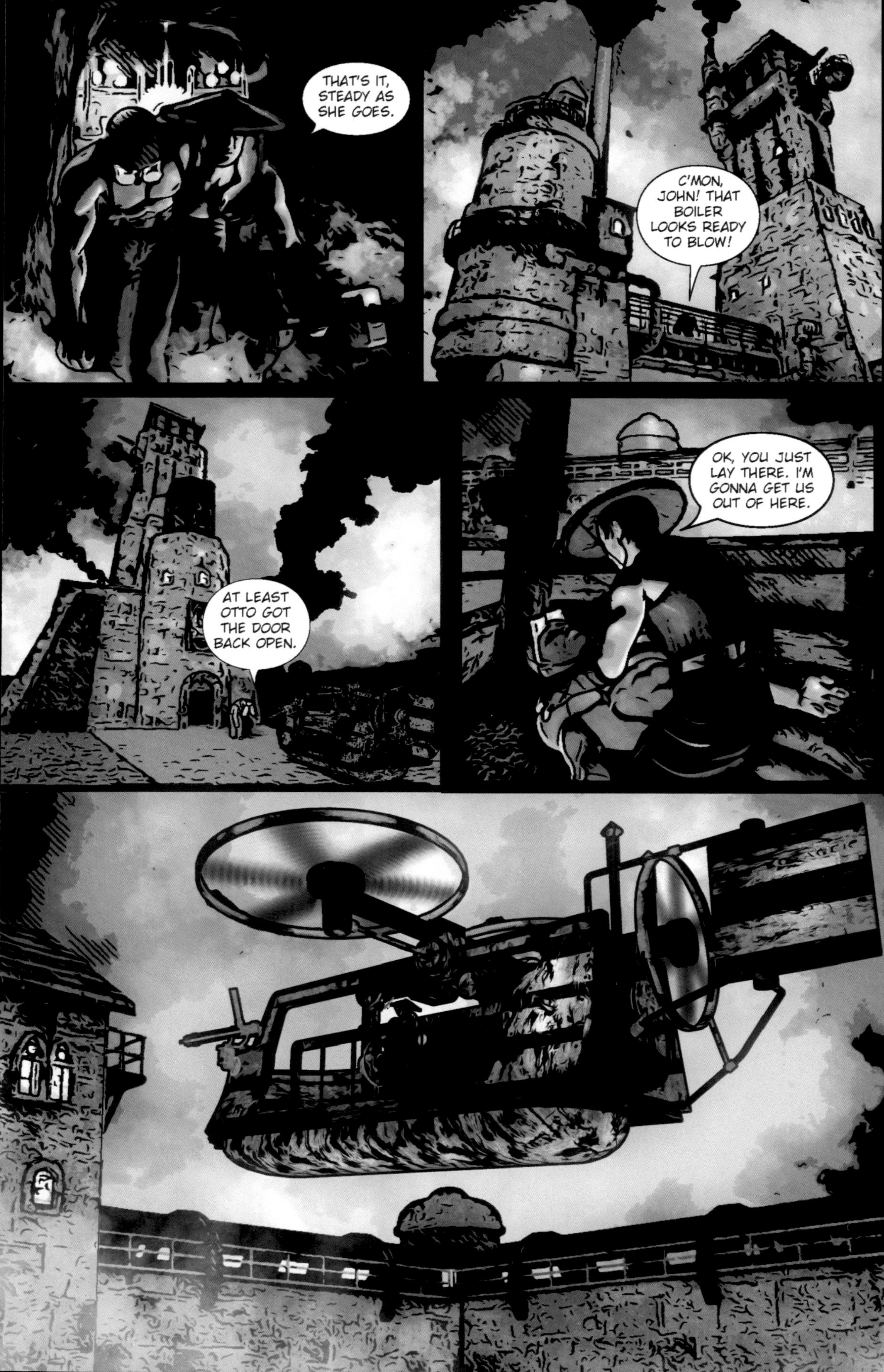
THAT'S IT, STEADY AS SHE GOES.
C'MON, JOHN! THAT BOILER LOOKS READY TO BLOW!
AT LEAST OTTO GOT THE DOOR BACK OPEN.
OK, YOU JUST LAY THERE. I'M GONNA GET US OUT OF HERE.

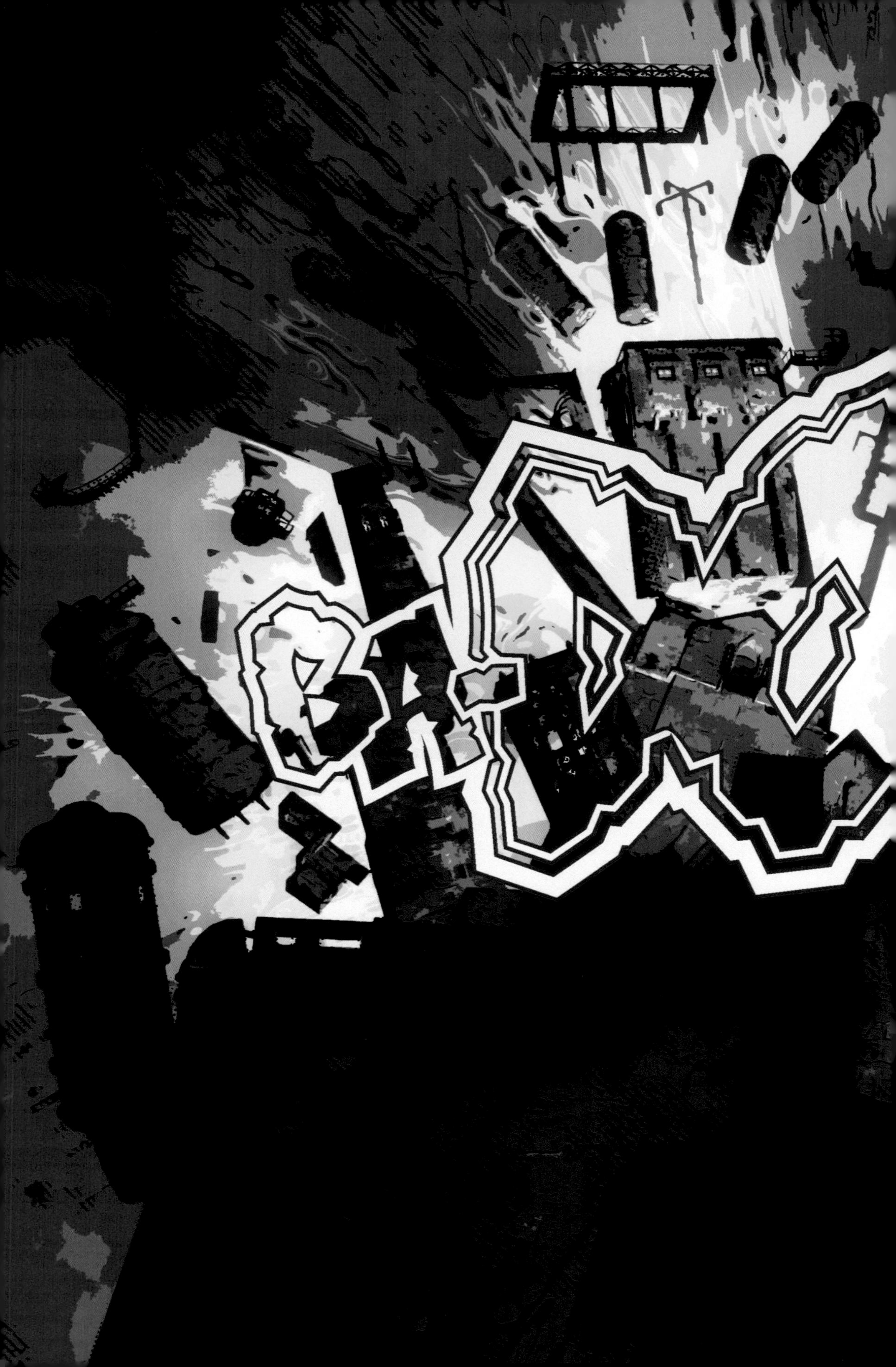

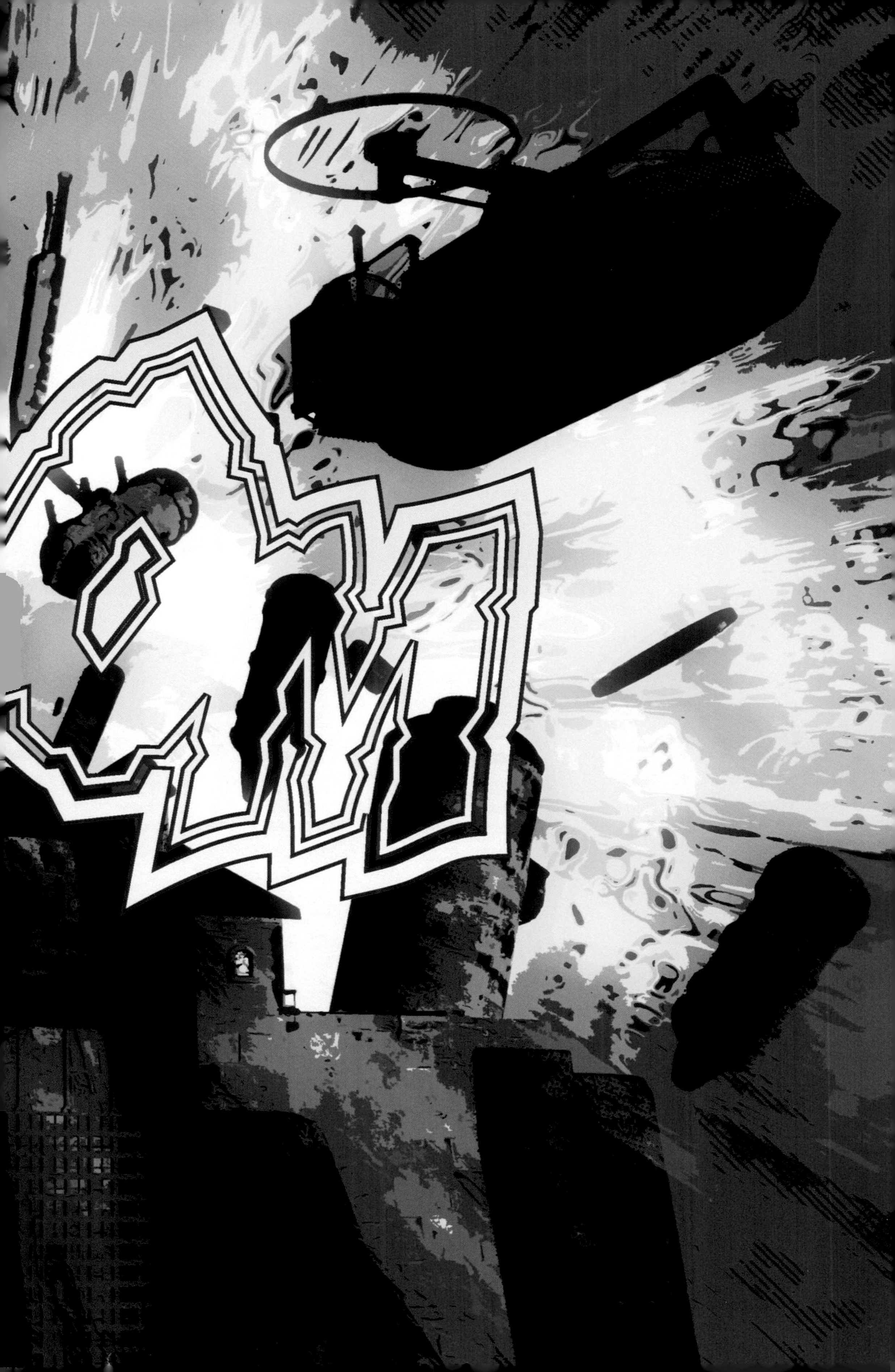

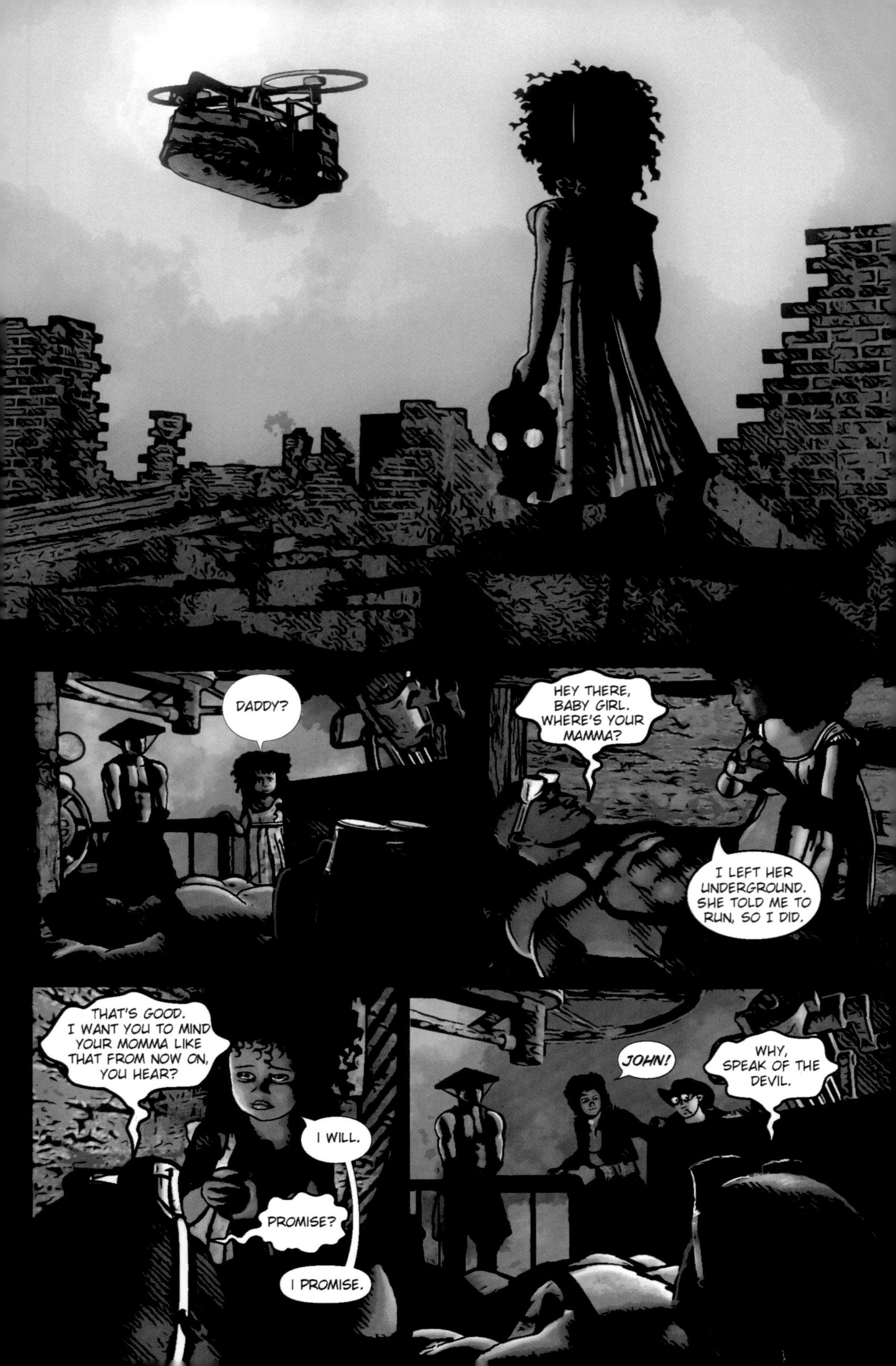
DADDY?
HEY THERE, BABY GIRL. WHERE'S YOUR MAMMA?
I LEFT HER UNDERGROUND. SHE TOLD ME TO RUN, SO I DID.
THAT'S GOOD. I WANT YOU TO MIND YOUR MOMMA LIKE THAT FROM NOW ON, YOU HEAR?
I WILL.
PROMISE?
I PROMISE.
JOHN!
WHY, SPEAK OF THE DEVIL.

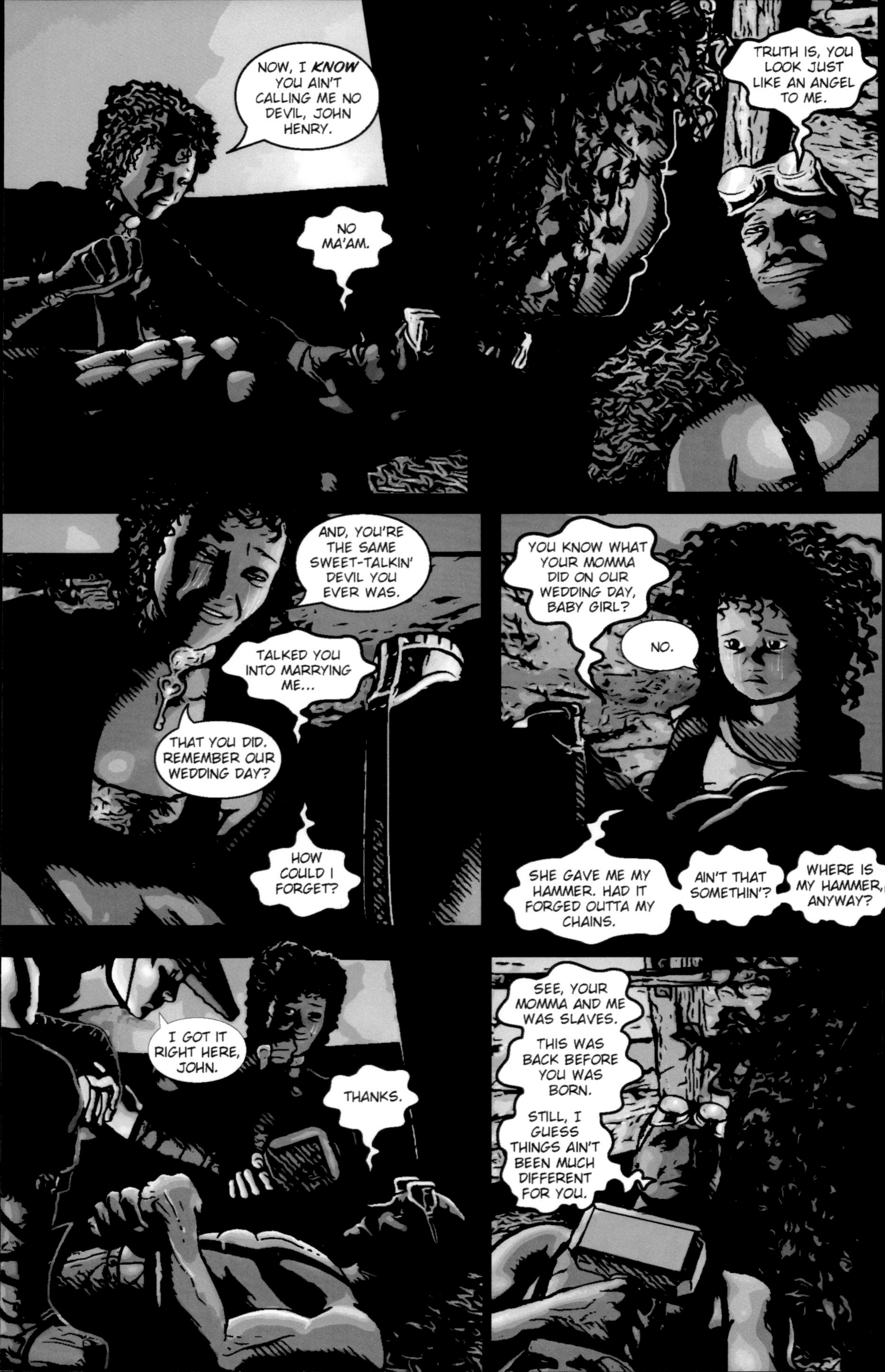
NOW, I *KNOW* YOU AIN'T CALLING ME NO DEVIL, JOHN HENRY.
NO MA'AM.
TRUTH IS, YOU LOOK JUST LIKE AN ANGEL TO ME.
AND, YOU'RE THE SAME SWEET-TALKIN' DEVIL YOU EVER WAS.
TALKED YOU INTO MARRYING ME...
THAT YOU DID. REMEMBER OUR WEDDING DAY?
HOW COULD I FORGET?
YOU KNOW WHAT YOUR MOMMA DID ON OUR WEDDING DAY, BABY GIRL?
NO.
SHE GAVE ME MY HAMMER. HAD IT FORGED OUTTA MY CHAINS.
AIN'T THAT SOMETHIN'?
WHERE IS MY HAMMER, ANYWAY?
I GOT IT RIGHT HERE, JOHN.
THANKS.
SEE, YOUR MOMMA AND ME WAS SLAVES.
THIS WAS BACK BEFORE YOU WAS BORN.
STILL, I GUESS THINGS AIN'T BEEN MUCH DIFFERENT FOR YOU.

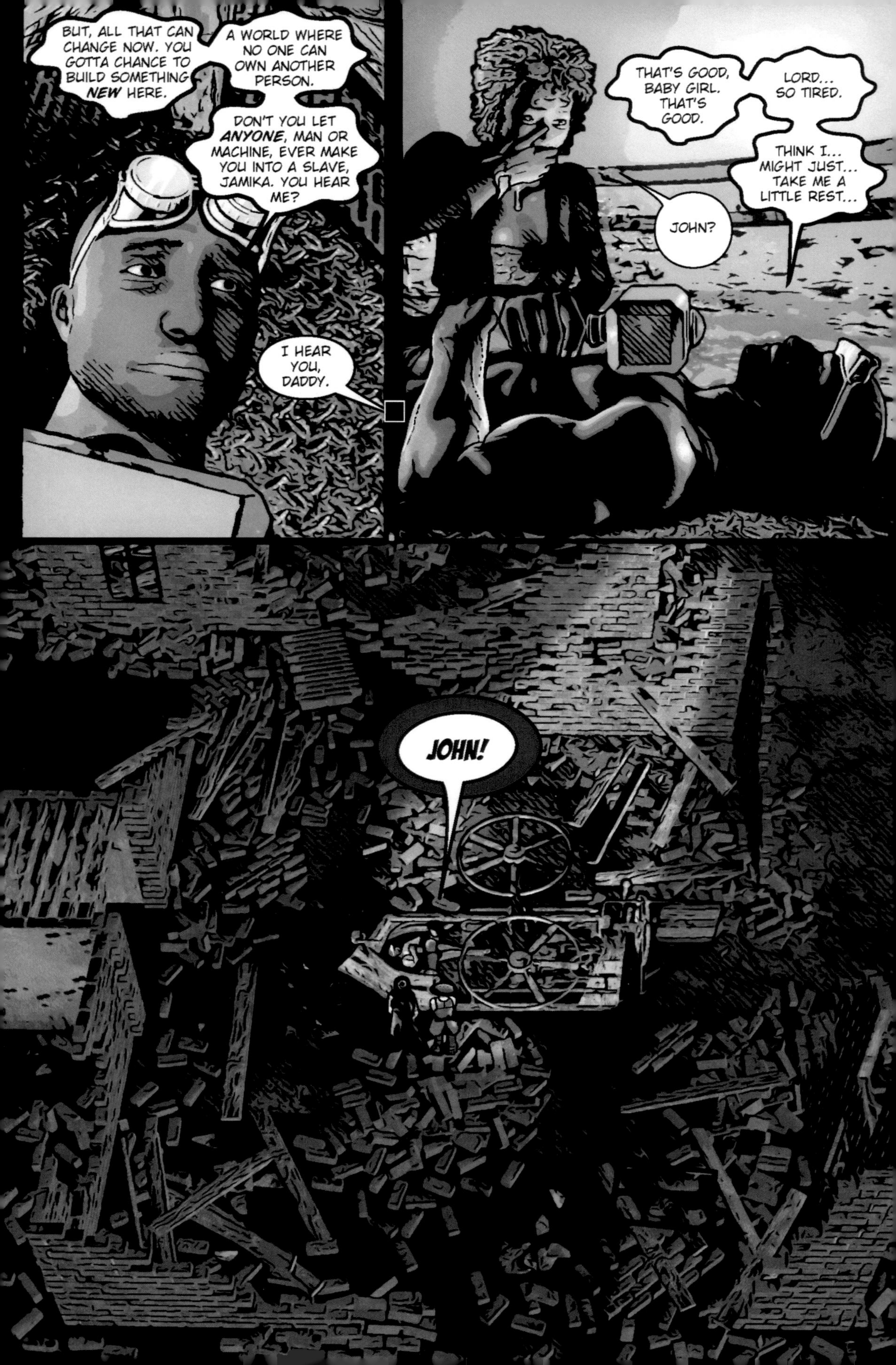
BUT, ALL THAT CAN CHANGE NOW. YOU GOTTA CHANCE TO BUILD SOMETHING NEW HERE.
A WORLD WHERE NO ONE CAN OWN ANOTHER PERSON.
DON'T YOU LET ANYONE, MAN OR MACHINE, EVER MAKE YOU INTO A SLAVE, JAMIKA. YOU HEAR ME?
I HEAR YOU, DADDY.
THAT'S GOOD, BABY GIRL. THAT'S GOOD.
LORD... SO TIRED.
THINK I... MIGHT JUST... TAKE ME A LITTLE REST...
JOHN?
JOHN!

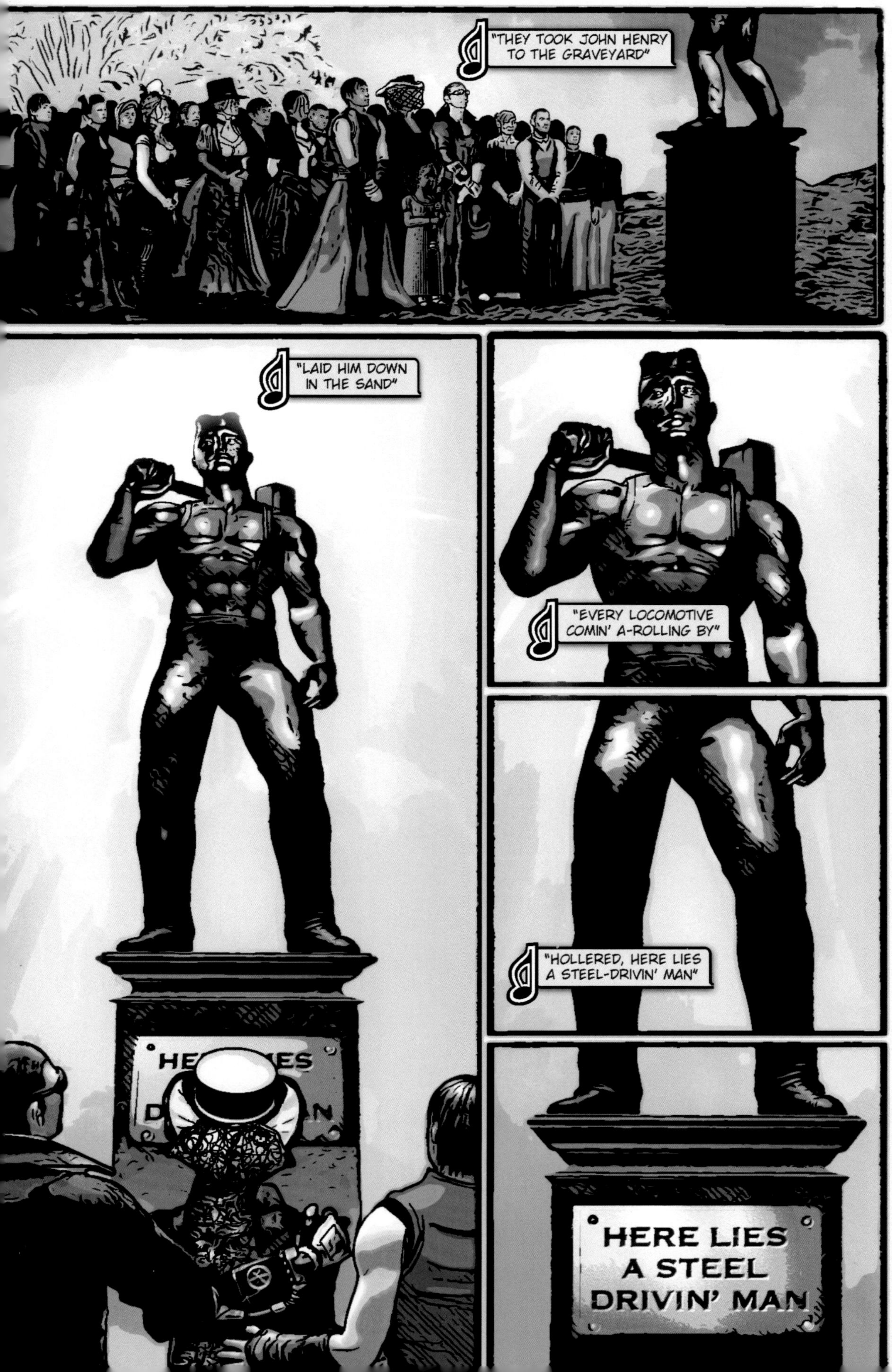
"THEY TOOK JOHN HENRY TO THE GRAVEYARD"
"LAID HIM DOWN IN THE SAND"
"EVERY LOCOMOTIVE COMIN' A-ROLLING BY"
"HOLLERED, HERE LIES A STEEL-DRIVIN' MAN"
HERE LIES A STEEL DRIVIN' MAN

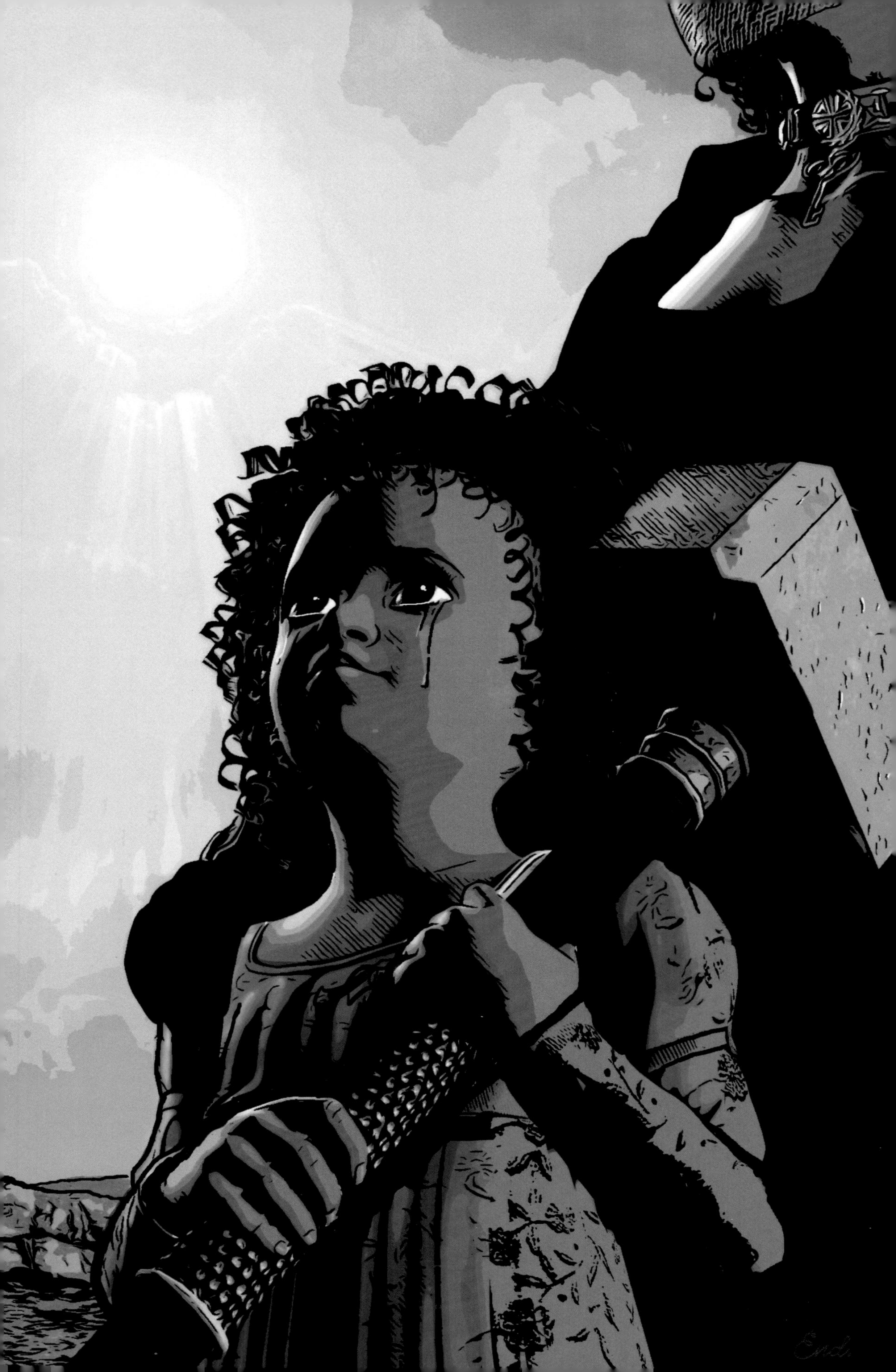
End

JOHN HENRY
STEEL DRIVING MAN OF STEEL

Why a John Henry comic, you ask? To which I would answer, why not? Moreover, why hasn't one happened before now? (Not counting, of course, the DC character John Henry Irons, who was technically named *after* the famous folk hero.) Moreover, I would argue that John Henry was the very first superhero. But you might ask, doesn't that title belong to Superman? Well, yes and no.

I believe that superheroes fill a cultural need. During the Great Depression of the 30s, there was a need for an everyman, working-class hero, a champion to stand up for the little guy. Before he was battling intergalactic menaces like Braniac and Doomsday, the early Superman was this very hero. As first envisioned by Jerry Siegel and Joe Schubert in Action Comics #1 in 1937, Superman tackled corrupt businessmen and slum lords.

Long before the Great Depression and Superman, however, there was the Depression of 1873, a time marked by turmoil and uncertainly as the end of reconstruction collided with the peak of the industrial revolution. Many freed slaves, now working as laborers, found their livelihoods threatened by mechanization. Thus, much as the legend of Superman rose from the uncertainty of the depression, the legend of John Henry came from an earlier economic turmoil. Is it any wonder the aforementioned John Henry of DC Comics found himself standing in for Superman after DC staged the Man of Steel's death in 1993?

The legend of John Henry has been passed down to us through the tradition of "hammer songs", folk songs that railroad workers sang to keep time and pace themselves during the long, backbreaking hours spent swinging a pick or hammer. Although there is some evidence that a real John Henry *did* exist, it was through these songs that his myth grew to heroic proportions. Soon he was truly a "superman" in his own right, a towering figure who could hammer his way through rock faster than a steam drill. These songs would later strike a chord, so to speak, with radical union folk singers and organizers in the 30s. They saw John Henry as a proletarian hero; an icon of the working class that they used as a symbol to rally workers.

Artists of this time depicted John Henry as massive, with ballooning muscles about to burst from form-fitting, worker's clothing. As Scott Reynolds Nelson notes in his book "Steel Drivin' Man", one art deco artist, Hugo Gellert, was particularly influential in establishing this muscle-bound archetype of the working man in the Union posters, magazines, and newspapers of the day. Early comic creators such as Jack Kirby, Jerry Siegel and Joe Schubert grew up surrounded by Gellert's work, and were no doubt

Statue of John Henry above the Big Bend tunnel on the C&O railroad, where many believe the Man vs. Machine competition originally took place.

influenced by it. The rounded, hairless, muscular strongman soon became a part of the cartoonists' visual vocabulary. While the early superheroes' skin grew lighter and their clothes transformed into the tights of the "circus strong man", their cause remained rooted firmly in the corner of the little guy. Thus, the "Steel Driving Man" became "The Man of Steel." Small wonder Grant Morrison, in his "New 52" reboot of Action Comics, decided to take Superman back to his roots by dressing him in patched jeans, t-shirt and work boots.

Although my story takes place in an alternate Victorian universe, I've tried to imagine a world in which capitalism has been allowed to run unchecked, a truly laissez-faire universe. In this world one man, an archetypical robber baron, has completely replaced the working class with automatons, all to maximize his own profit and power. Thus, John Henry's worst nightmare, a world in which there's no place for the common man (in fact no place for man, period) is realized. Just as in our own history, during the Reconstruction and the Depression, in the alternate history of "The Steam Age", the steel-driving man stands defiant.

So, why a John Henry comic? Because, as America once again finds itself in a time of economic turmoil, I think the time is ripe for John Henry to take his rightful place among all the other comic book characters he helped inspire. To stand, once again, as a true hero for our times.

Thanks for coming aboard! John Henry laid the tracks, I hope you enjoyed the ride...

Dwayne Harris

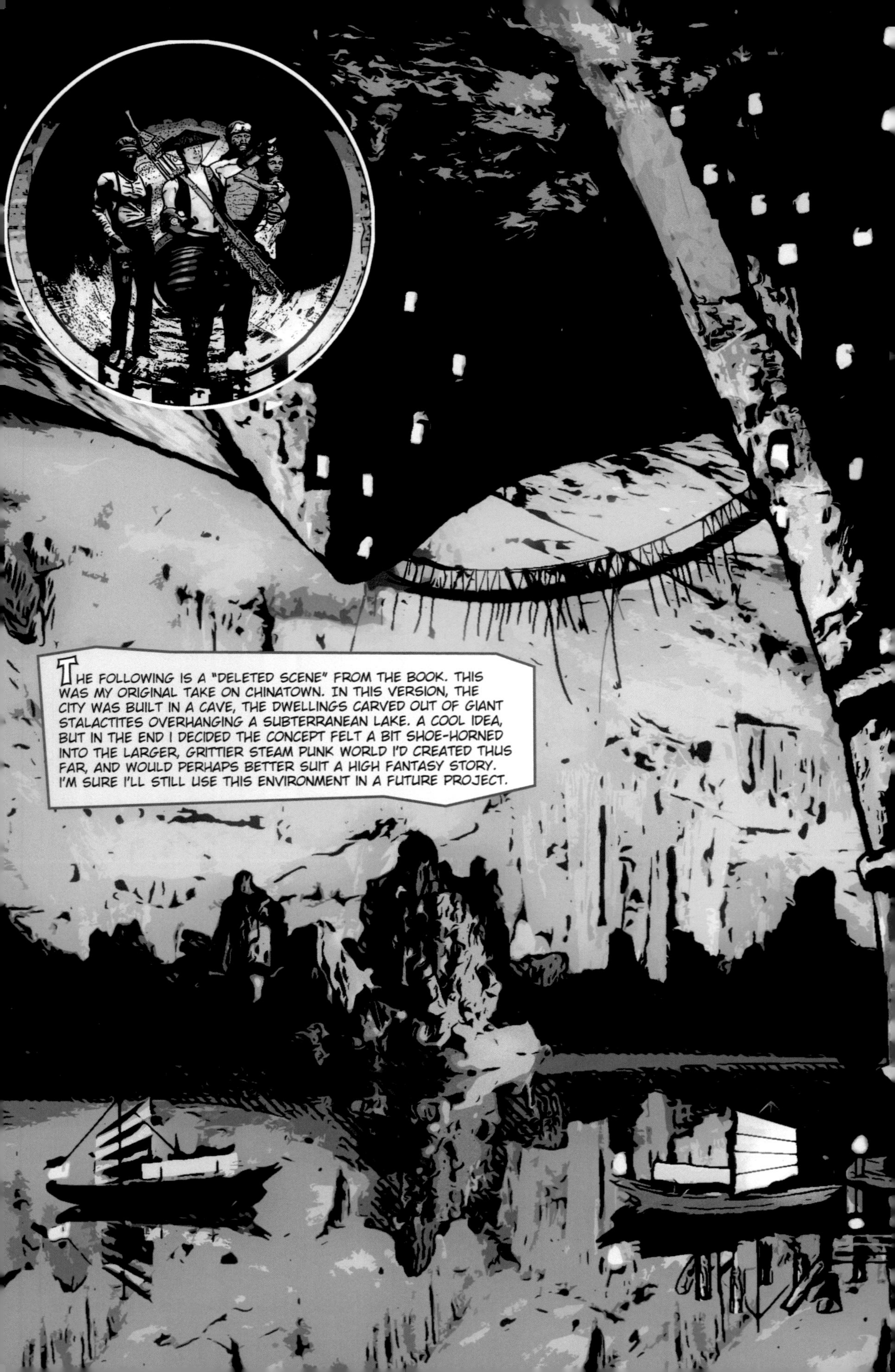
THE FOLLOWING IS A "DELETED SCENE" FROM THE BOOK. THIS WAS MY ORIGINAL TAKE ON CHINATOWN. IN THIS VERSION, THE CITY WAS BUILT IN A CAVE, THE DWELLINGS CARVED OUT OF GIANT STALACTITES OVERHANGING A SUBTERRANEAN LAKE. A COOL IDEA, BUT IN THE END I DECIDED THE CONCEPT FELT A BIT SHOE-HORNED INTO THE LARGER, GRITTIER STEAM PUNK WORLD I'D CREATED THUS FAR, AND WOULD PERHAPS BETTER SUIT A HIGH FANTASY STORY. I'M SURE I'LL STILL USE THIS ENVIRONMENT IN A FUTURE PROJECT.

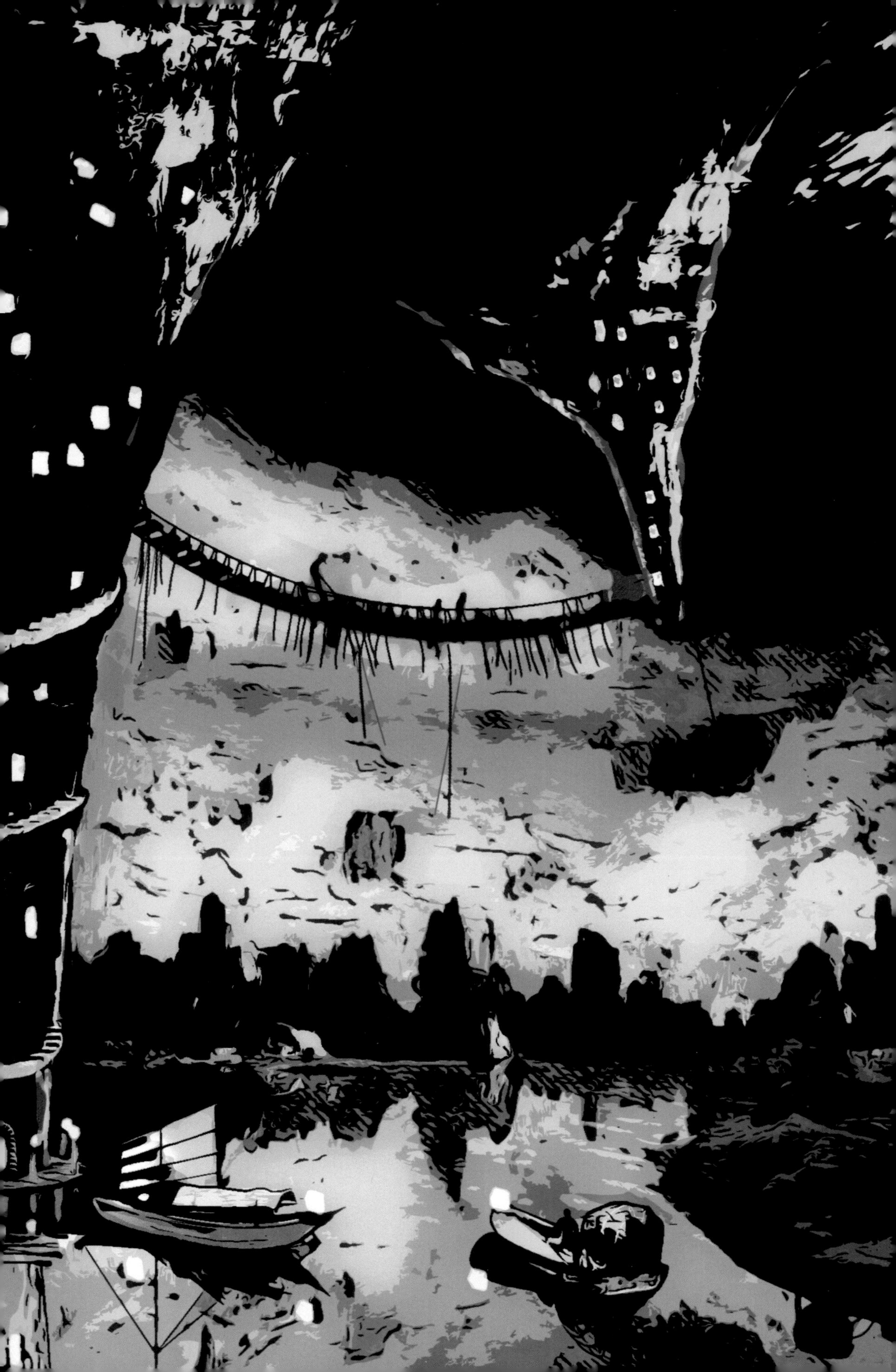

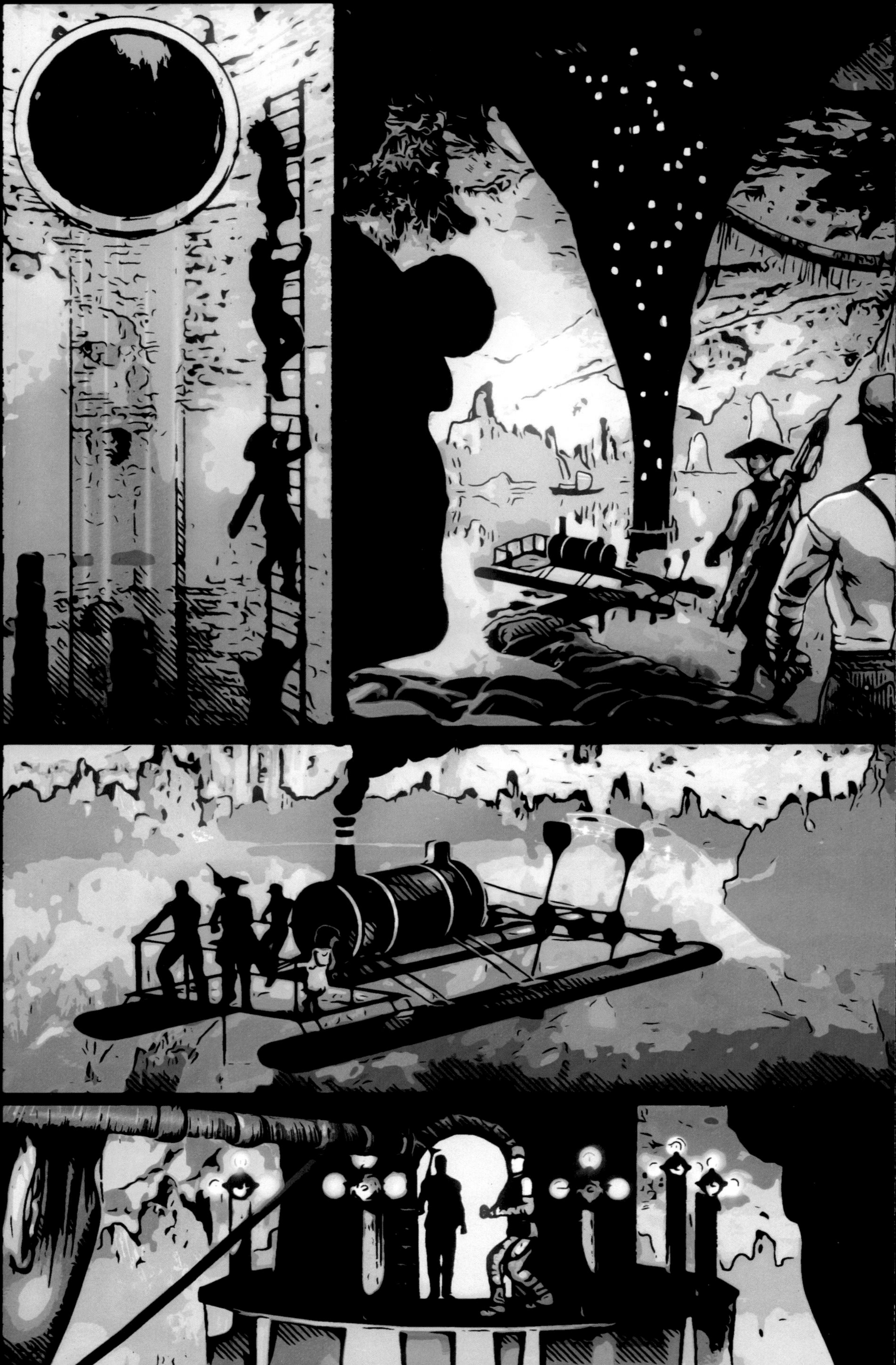